Healing
~~*Heeling*~~ *with Dolly Lama:*
Finding God in Dog

Dedicated to all the dogs I've loved before.
They each have a piece of my heart.

And to all the angels – celestial, human, and canine –
who guide my journey toward divine completeness.

Healing
~~Heeling~~ with Dolly Lama:
Finding God in Dog

Patricia A. Nugent

Healing with Dolly Lama: Finding God in Dog
Copyright © 2021 by Patricia A. Nugent

Printed in the United States of America.

Journal Arts Press • Hadley, New York

ISBN: 978-0-578-25348-0

The Lessons

Prologue: Fall from Grace

She lies motionless at the bottom of the steps. I only know she's alive because I hear faint whimpering.

I run to her, fall to my knees and lift her gently into my arms, causing her to cry out in pain. I cry out as well, my face turned upward. "Please! Don't take her from me. Please. I'll do anything if you save her. An-y-thing."

Minutes before, my puppy had been standing on the deck, her round brown eyes watching me descend the steps. Her brow furrowed. Like mine.

"Come, Dolly. Let's go potty," I'd said.

Dolly didn't budge; she never has come when called. Instead, she usually takes off in the opposite direction. Plus, she much prefers toileting on my new carpets than in the natural world.

As the sun made way for the moon that hot August evening, I called again.

"C'mon, Dolly. Time for potty."

She was frozen in place. "Damn it, Dolly! It's getting dark. Hurry up!"

Not a muscle twitched. Except in my own tight jaw.

In the weeks since arriving together at my newly-constructed home, we'd not taken this route off the deck before. So I climbed back up the steps to toss down her favorite toy as an incentive, bemoaning my obligation to this golden retriever furball. While continuing to call her, I headed toward the lake. Suddenly I heard a *thump* and an *oomph*, and turned around to see Dolly on the compacted barren ground, her stubby legs splayed out to her sides. Because I'd forgotten puppies can't navigate steps.

To avoid the steps, she'd wiggled on her belly under the deck railing, landing hard, ten feet below. For once, she'd attempted to come when called.

* * *

Friends who know how this puppy came into my life might underestimate my despair over her fall. After all, I'd been trying to give her away for weeks, even as I complained about receiving her as a gift myself. Crawling into bed exhausted, I'd mentally make lists of friends I could give her to. But I didn't want to burden them the way I'd been burdened. And I couldn't give her to a stranger.

The Law of Attraction would assert that I summoned Dolly to my life. Popularized in Rhonda Byrne's *The Secret*, this natural law of the Universe can be summed up as *You attract what you focus on*, which Norman Vincent Peale termed *the power of positive thinking* in the 1950s. For months prior to my retirement, the Universe had heard me announce to all who'd listen, "I'm going to get a golden retriever and write the Great American Novel when I retire."

My declaration should have been more specific. My intended golden was to be a fully-grown, rescued, male: housebroken, neutered, calm, and content to lie at my feet while I blithely tap away on my keyboard.

In other words, my next dog was going to be everything Dolly is not.

Perhaps I attracted this accident because I didn't want her in my life: *Negative thoughts attract negative events.*

Two compounded, unintended consequences: an unwanted puppy followed by an unwanted incident. And now, holding Dolly to my chest, listening to her labored breathing as my tears drop onto her soft fur, I realize I'd never wanted or needed anything as much as this puppy. She filled an emotional void I didn't know existed.

Please don't let this be one of those lessons learned too late. I'll do anything.

Anything.

Part I: *Intercessions*

The Gift

If the gods bring to you a strange and frightening creature, accept the gift as if it were one you had chosen.

- Jane Hirschfield

I'd been dog-free for more than four years, having relinquished custody of my last golden retriever to my husband when we separated. I enjoyed the freedom of not having a dog. Appreciated not having dog hair in my mouth. On my clothes. In my car. But once you've had a dog, it's hard to live without.

Those who've known the love of a dog can't help smile at all-things-dog: photos, jokes, commercials, stories, movies. Dogs sell because the unconditional love they offer makes them irresistible. Dog addictions are hard to break – recidivism in rehab would near one-hundred percent. My first dog, Punkin, opened up a whole new species for me to love, to connect with on a different level. I'd spent thirty years prior afraid of dogs. Then became one of those people who couldn't imagine anyone not loving my dog, as annoying as that can be, even to fellow dog lovers.

That's why I knew I'd get another dog...someday. But when I moved from an 18-room house with my husband to a five-room townhouse alone, with no appreciable yard, it was easier to not have a four-legged roommate. My ten-hour workdays as a school district administrator wouldn't have been fair to such a social being.

Yes, I'd wanted another dog – longed for the companionship. But the timing had to be right. Retirement and a new home on a mountain lake had set the stage for a golden retriever of my choosing in the near future. *What would the lucky dog be like?* I wondered. Instead, my selection of my dream dog had been preempted, and there I was on the deck with a 14-week-old golden retriever puppy gnawing on my shoe while I ate cold chicken lo mein. Despite the resplendent orange and pink sunset, I felt trapped and pathetic. And alone.

Come, Dolly. Let's go potty.

Doesn't everyone know it's never a good idea to gift a puppy? There's a chemistry to the canine-human match, a soul connection that tells you *this is right – we belong together.*

This hadn't felt like that.

No, this was the worst possible gift for a new retiree. How did I end up with this puppy?

* * *

I first saw her furry little face in a photo sent to my work email. "Your New Pup" the subject line read. The photo boasted a little orange puppy, asleep on the floor of the transportation director's office.

I wasn't alarmed at first, humored in fact, playfully writing back, "Whose new pup?"

"YOUR new pup," the cryptic reply. My stomach turned over as I began to realize what was happening. Returning from the bathroom, I called the transportation director to be told, "We brought her over to your office, but you were in a meeting. She's here now whenever you want to pick her up."

Pick who up?

My heart beat faster as I peppered him with questions. He told me Dave, a bus driver, secured this puppy for me following a casual conversation we'd had about a local farmer giving away golden retriever puppies. Since there was only one left, Dave thought it best to snag her for me.

A gift.

The last of the litter, the puppy others left behind. Eight weeks old. Waiting for me to pick her up.

When Dave returned my call, I started right in: "Dave, there must be a misunderstanding. I was curious about why this farmer-guy would give away golden puppies when they sell for thousands of dollars but never intended for you to get one for me. I'm sorry you went to all that trouble but...."

"I can't take her back," he interrupted, silencing my high-pitched, panicky voice. "The guy was clear about that. He was glad to finally have them all placed."

I bet.

Taking a deep breath, I rattled off numerous reasons why I couldn't accept her: "Dave, this was most kind of you. Thank you from the bottom of my heart. But I don't have a fenced yard, and I have plans to travel, and I don't have any doggie supplies and...and..."

"At least meet her. Then decide if you want her or not. Stop over after work. She can stay at my house tonight."

Smart guy.

I forwarded her photo to several friends, lamenting my dilemma. One wrote back, "What a disaster!" Another wrote, "This sounds like a nightmare!" The last responded, "Get two puppies. It'll be easier."

Only my neighbor Doris responded, "I think she'll be good for you."

* * *

From my car window, I spotted an orange furball waddling through the grass, which was as high as her belly. Although I considered simply waving as I drove by the suburban ranch, I parked the car and introduced myself to Dave's wife, Kathy, and daughter, Christine, who were watching the puppy with delight. Every few seconds, the puppy would doze and then tear off again with a burst of energy. Kathy and Christine closely watched my face to gauge my reaction and, no doubt, to determine if I were worthy.

I wasn't.

Dave yanked me out of earshot: "You have to take her soon because they're getting attached; they've already named her!" *That's a good thing,* I thought, *because, cute as she is, I don't want an untrained, needy puppy when I'm soon to be free of obligations and schedules. My retirement plans don't include this puppy. I wanted a dog, not a puppy. A dog! There's a big difference. And certainly, no puppy right now.*

DAMN IT! How did I get into this mess?

Despite my protestations, I got down on my panty-hosed knees in my business suit and scooped up the squirming critter. We both have brown eyes, I noted, and heard myself whisper, "You're such a little dolly," while snuggling her close. She smelled like a graham cracker, with a shiny black nose and blonde eyelashes. I kissed the top of her soft head.

My reasoning powers were quickly restored, snatched from the jaws of the furry little temptress, and I declared, "I have to make sure she's healthy before I can commit. I'd like to have a veterinarian examine her." With embarrassment, I realized I wasn't graciously accepting this gift, but I felt cornered and needed to buy time.

"Sure, okay," Kathy responded, bringing me a phone book. The nearby clinic happened to have an immediate opening. (The Universe was conspiring.) Two hundred dollars later, the vet declared her good-to-go. And "such-a-little-dolly" became my Dolly.

Naming is the first step toward attachment. I named her the endearment my mother had called me, and her Polish mother had called her.

But I couldn't yet take possession. I had one more week left in my career and a subsequent week-long vacation planned before I could begin my new job as this puppy's nanny. Over Dave's objections, Kathy and Christine offered to watch Dolly for two weeks while I finished the school year and went on what-would-be my last unencumbered trip for a while – what I'd once hoped would be the first of many.

The next day, Dave's co-workers presented me with a $100 gift card from a pet store to make sure I didn't back out. Yet during my last two weeks of freedom, I didn't once stop to see my pup.

* * *

At the Jersey Shore, I left the sandy beach and ocean air to scour pet stores for what a puppy might need. Another $200 later, I felt somewhat prepared for Dolly's physical care. But emotionally, I wasn't ready.

My parents had died a few years earlier, ten months apart. While continuing to work full time, I'd spent 18 months as their caregiver. In many ways, I was still grieving; flashbacks were all-too-common. A hospice counselor had diagnosed it as post-traumatic stress disorder (PTSD), somewhat akin to what veterans suffer. Caregivers are often at war: fighting the disease, fighting doctors, fighting other family members, fighting their own guilt, fighting insurance companies, sometimes even fighting the patient. They are at increased risk for significant health problems, the result of long-term stress and lack of self-care. More than half of all caregivers show signs of clinical depression; I sure did. My mental and physical health, even my marriage, had suffered as a result of that tour of duty.

When offered this puppy, I feared I didn't have the emotional or physical reserves to take care of another living thing. A puppy would depend on me for her life. Like my infirm parents who wouldn't eat unless I was by their sides.

Returning from vacation, I dutifully, albeit reluctantly, showed up to claim my gift. "We weren't sure you'd come back," Kathy joked, perhaps hoping I wouldn't. Christine was red-eyed and sniffling, as she handed over Now-My-Puppy.

"*Hello, Dolly. Well, hello, Dolly,*" I sang, masking my apprehension. They laughed, breaking the tension, while Dolly lunged at my face, baring her pointy little teeth and snapping. "Oh, she does that," they told me continuing to laugh. I'd stopped laughing.

As we started out for my new home in the Adirondack Mountains of New York State, Dolly rode in the passenger seat, nestled in a little cardboard box labeled *Pepperoni*. I was relieved she didn't wake during the hour ride; I had no plan for managing a moving furball in the car should she climb out of the makeshift cage.

In truth, I had no plan for managing her at all. I didn't yet realize this puppy – this unwanted gift – had arrived to manage me.

Damn-It-Dolly

> *The health benefits of swearing include increased
> circulation, elevated endorphins, and an overall sense
> of calm, control, and well-being. The key is to do
> it sparingly and not to get angry at the same time,
> which would be very bad for you.*
>
> — Neel Burton, MD

Our first few weeks together had not gone smoothly. That's an understated understatement.

During those weeks with Dave's family, the wild thing had been blissfully unencumbered by collar or leash. Naked. Her seeming-ability to turn her head 360 degrees while rapidly snapping her jaw, loaded with needle-teeth, rivaled any possessed demon, making it a challenge to buckle a collar around her furry orange neck. My neighbor Doris held down ten squirming and nipping pounds, akin to roping a calf, so I could adorn my puppy with a way-too-big royal blue collar, signaling my eagerness for her to grow up fast.

The next step was to attach a leash. That's when Dolly played possum. Down she'd go, refusing to budge, no matter how much I tugged. As she lay motionless on her side in my driveway one afternoon, the letter carrier assumed she was near death. He jumped out of his official U.S. Post Office vehicle shouting, "Should I call a vet?"

I flashed him a reassuring smile through clenched teeth. "No, she's okay. Just doesn't like the leash." The royal blue leash that matched the unwelcomed collar. He stared at Dolly's lifeless body for a full minute before getting back in his truck and driving away. I wondered if he'd be calling the ASPCA; I half-wished he would.

Although determined to wait Dolly out, I surrendered again that day by unclipping the leash from her collar. She immediately sprang back to life, victory gleaming in her round brown eyes. Off she scampered, looking back over her shoulder at me. Gloating.

Who's training whom?

At my wit's end, I shared my dilemma with the plumber adjusting my heating system. A breeder and trainer of hunting dogs, he told me to start with something small trailing behind Dolly to get her used to the concept: "First, tie a short string around her collar, then a thin rope, eventually working up to a leash as she adjusts."

I half-listened, all the while silently screaming, *Are you freakin' kidding me? Who has time for this shit?*

But it worked. After two days, Dolly tired of trying to ensnare the simulated leash. *My wild mustang has been broken*, I thought, not without some remorse. Prematurely, I'd soon discover.

The next step was housebreaking.

"Puppies can only hold their urine one hour for each month of life. It's not her fault she wets in the house," a puppy consultant explained. "She's not even three months old."

Not her fault? There's only one rug here. One hand-woven area rug I'd chosen to create a tranquil ambiance in my studio, where I write, practice yoga and Reiki, and meditate. Upon arrival, Dolly selected it as her special rug too – for indoor toileting. Her personal canine litter box. Even after performing both functions outdoors (*Good girl, Dolly!*), she'd run back into the house, ears flapping like Dumbo, to do them again – on that rug.

"NOOOOOOOOOOOOOO!" I'd scream, louder than Jamie Lee Curtis. Just once I made the mistake of picking Dolly up mid-stream.

She likely thought her full name was *Damn-it-Dolly* because that's how it usually came out of my mouth. Knowing I'd lived a solitary existence for four years without man, child, or beast, a friend offered her perspective: "I decided long ago that I could either have a clean home or a dog. I chose a dog."

I didn't confess which I'd have chosen right then.

Upon the advice of other dog experts, I bought a crate

because puppies feel safe and protected in simulated dens and, most important to me, won't soil where they sleep. So Dolly slept in her crate in the laundry room. And proved the experts wrong.

"The crate must be too large," friends counseled. I bought a smaller one; she wet that too. This recent retiree dutifully washed the urine-soaked towels and pads each morning. Spraying a *no-smell-no-stain* product all over my new home. My stepdaughter, a dog-devotee, suggested I take Dolly out several times during the night; I set my alarm for 2am and 5am. My puppy and I went into the dark woods, alone and vulnerable, listening to branches crack and seeing shadows move in the still-dark hours of morning.

Might some creature snatch up my puppy?

It would be karmic justice because my puppy snatched up everything else. Dolly preferred to graze in the wild. My yard became her salad bar, well-stocked with sticks, wild mushrooms, pine cones, bark, grass, and dandelions. No vegetation was safe from this furry Pac-Man. She also ate things that aren't considered food by any species. She snapped at tulips as she raced by, yellow and purple petals dangling from her red tongue. Gulped down before I could pull them from her mouth.

"Puppies have special stomach enzymes that can break down the non-food items they consume," yet another dog trainer told me. (I'd engaged several by this time.) "Not to worry."

"Not to worry? Really? What about the diarrhea and vomiting? In my new home. On my only rug!"

"She's a puppy," the unsympathetic response.

Menu planning was more of a challenge than I could have imagined. Having lost three goldens to cancer, devastating yet not uncommon for the breed, I was determined to do all I could to break that cycle of disease for Dolly. No dog or pet-parent should have to go through that horrific disease cycle.

I interviewed sales representatives and pet store owners.

I researched top-of-the-line pet food brands and bought the most expensive ones. Yet every kibble-based protein – lamb, chicken, turkey, beef, duck – caused loose stools. And plenty of them. Eventually, I settled on a fish-based kibble, which she best tolerated, although it gave her a cat-like essence.

Dolly's stomach continued to be ultra-sensitive, despite the so-called *special enzymes* she supposedly had. I often had to cook rice with chicken or cottage cheese for her. So I was also working as her chef. Again, I had to ask myself, *Who has time for this?*

Damn-It-Dolly did. Puppies have all the time in the world.

My eventual capstone achievement in the dog-training category was to train Dolly to only "go" in one location in my yard – when she eliminated outside, that is. I owed this success to bribing her with a ridiculous number of treats. I scooped up all her droppings so neither she nor I would step in them, thereby working as Dolly's grounds crew as well, illustrating Jerry Seinfeld's point that if aliens observed humans picking up dog poop, they'd assume dogs are *our* masters. Which may be true.

A neighbor caught me scooping up Dolly's poop just minutes after I was interviewed live on National Public Radio about my first book. "You may be a big radio star," he shouted across the lots. "But you're still picking up dog poop. Humbling, isn't it?" Within seconds, a wasp flew up my nose, stinging me numerous times, causing instantaneous swelling, *a face made for radio*. Simultaneously, Dolly began to projectile vomit her bad dietary choices: sticks, wild mushrooms, pine cones, bark, grass, dandelions. Tulips.

Humbling indeed. Yet not my first such experience related to dog poop.

As a young girl, I'd volunteered to pick up Gypsy's poop. Gypsy was our neighbor's brown and white, overweight cocker spaniel who toileted in our yard. "Why the hell does that damn dog have to crap all over our yard? I've had enough of this!" my father boomed one day. I didn't give a hoot about Gypsy but knew all about Dad's explosive temper when he'd "had enough." I begged him not to pick a fight with our neighbors; he made a pact with me that if I picked up Gypsy's poop, he'd not confront them.

It was worth it to me to suffer that indignation, much preferred to him alienating another neighbor. My sister signed on as well.

I held the brown paper bag while she dumped poop into it. I can't imagine why my dad took home-movies of this, which I recently found in a box of my parents' stuff. He zoomed in on my face, scrunched up from the stench. I'm wearing a little bonnet, adding to the absurdity of the black-and-white footage.

Decades later, when taking my own dogs outside to do their "business," I often thought of Gypsy and my dad, the path we travel on this journey called life, and how hard we try not to "step in it" along the way.

* * *

Punkin, the puppy I'd raised with my husband, was smart but not well-behaved. As a single pet-parent, I needed Dolly to be both. So I registered her for a puppy training course, fully aware that I'd be the student. Despite experience with three prior dogs, Dolly was my first puppy in over twenty years. Puppies hadn't changed much, but I had. Like Peter Pan's Wendy, I'd become older and less tolerant of antics and messes – especially in my new home.

We traveled an hour to join other puppies and their exhausted-looking nursemaids, many of whom brought their human children to instill responsibility. From what I saw, the kids weren't necessarily a good influence on the pups. And vice versa. (A couple more leashes might have come in handy.) *Silly puppies need silly children*, I concluded. *It's a better match than Dolly and me.*

As the other puppies chased each other around the room, Dolly cowered under my chair. Despite how crazy-active she was at home, she hadn't been with other puppies since left behind by her littermates so lacked canine socialization skills. The trainer instructed us to put our puppies on our laps and touch them everywhere: between the toes, in the ears, in the mouth. Dolly deferentially let me claim dominion over her, although in the past, she'd been prone to fending me off by snapping. This desensitization exercise would prove invaluable when object removal from Dolly's orifices became necessary.

With pride, I noted that Dolly was cuter than most of her classmates, with a sweet face and deep-set droopy eyes that some said resembled those of Emmett Kelly or Robert Mitchum – due respect to them all.

On occasion, Dolly had her own cheering section when Christine and Kathy showed up. They gushed over how their former charge had grown, inspiring her rear end to wag as it recalled those early Bohemian days in their home. I wished I could be as impressed as they were over Dolly's incremental progress, which included waddling around with other puppies, not pooping or peeing inside, and interacting with strange humans.

Basic commands weren't part of the puppy curriculum, and Dolly remained a wild child. *Damn it, Dolly* wasn't my only expression of frustration; her stylized nickname became *Jesus-Christ-What-The-Hell-Are-You-Doing-Now*? Overall, rearing her was proving to be more challenging than my professional career had been. For decades, I'd worked more than 50 hours per week, including weekends and evenings. I dealt with many diverse stakeholders, often at odds with each other. I negotiated with unions and tried to assuage taxpayers. Yet the 24/7 responsibility for feeding, toileting, and monitoring this puppy's indiscretions was exhausting me. I needed respite – a dog-free zone; Dolly needed a home-away-from-home.

"She's not going to dampen my ability to travel in retirement," I told myself and others, attempting to minimize her disruption of my life. "I refuse to be constrained by this... this...gift."

Yet I could remember how much I dreaded boarding my previous dogs – sending them off to "doggie prison." We'd always chosen nice kennels, but the dogs were still confined to cold, concrete floors in small spaces. I couldn't bear to hear their pitiful cries as the gates closed behind us. To witness the betrayal registered on their faces as we walked away. And how badly they smelled when we picked them up. We usually resorted to paying sitters to stay in our home with our spoiled dogs. This was going to be different, and I told her so.

"Tough luck, Dolly. You're a puppy – NOT A BABY – and I must remember that. You have to go to a kennel when I go away, and I'm not going to feel guilty about leaving you behind for a few days. I'm not!"

My research of area kennels began in earnest to ensure I'd have several options for dropping her off at a moment's notice when the time came. I asked dog-walking strangers where they boarded; I asked friends. And then began a tour of recommended facilities.

Not exactly the wine tours I'd envisioned for my retirement years. Instead, I was touring doggie prisons.

I soon realized I was looking for a kennel that wasn't a kennel. There was no way I could leave Dolly in any of the places I visited. She was too little, too young. Too Dolly.

Damn it, Dolly! I'm NEVER going to get away from you, am I? You're holding me hostage in my own home.

Then I stumbled upon a small, private kennel in the basement of a well-appointed home. The boarding accommodations for each dog were bigger than my bathroom, with linoleum and a doggie couch. It cost three times what a typical kennel cost but was convenient and worth my peace of mind.

It's MY turn to be untethered, I mistakenly thought. I fantasized about dropping her off when she got a little older.

Instead, Dolly has now dropped off the deck – wearing that still-too-large royal blue collar. I wish she were simply playing possum; I'd never try to put a leash on her again.

Baptism

For when the disciple is ready, the master is ready also.
                                                    - Mabel Collins

Dolly continues to whimper and shake as I hold her. Tears stream down my cheeks as I begin to give her Reiki, a Japanese healing modality administered by the laying on of hands. Hands that once pushed Dolly away out of frustration and resentment now seek to heal her.

"I bless the Divine within you," I whisper into her soft, floppy ear. "I offer you this gift of healing energy with love. When you accept it, you will use it for your highest good."

Over and over, I repeat that incantation, punctuated by my sobs and interspersed with desperate pleas for mercy from the heavens. My hand shakes as I cup Dolly's delicate hips.

At the same time, I wrestle with my self-doubt and guilt: *This accident is my fault. What makes me think I can help her now? She needs medical attention. And I need a miracle!*

Raised in a Roman Catholic home with Italian influences, there was a little altar in my bedroom with statues, a votive candle, rosary, crucifix, and scapula. I prayed on my chubby knees every night – to my Infant of Prague (replete with his splendid garments) and the Blessed Virgin. I certainly knew about miracles – the ones Jesus did: changing water into wine, providing enough loaves and fishes to feed the multitudes, healing the sick, raising the dead. Jesus was God so, of course, he could do those things.

But, as a young girl, I wanted no part of miracles; I didn't want any supernatural powers that I'd have to keep under wraps, like Samantha on *Bewitched*. Not wanting to be different, I repeatedly tried to prove to myself that I wasn't capable of making bizarre things happen. I took comfort in that innate feeling of powerlessness most young children rebel against. Because if I were indeed powerless, then maybe I wasn't to blame for discord in our home. For my dad's rage, for my mom's seeming disregard for what would predictably enrage him.

To test myself, I'd periodically command inanimate objects to move. Not because I wanted them to but because I *didn't* want them to. Sitting on the living room floor, my little round face level with the coffee table, my eyes laser-focused, I'd silently tell the ashtray, *Move. Move!*

It wouldn't move.

Phew! All is well.

As an adolescent, I set my sights on higher-stakes evidence that I was poltergeist-free. I'd try to make airplanes fall out of the sky – not crash, just nosedive a little, although I had no plan to rescue them should I succeed. I'd be relieved each time my attempted psycho-jacking was unsuccessful. I needed to know I wasn't one of those weirdos who could bend spoons on the Ed Sullivan Show, which, in retrospect, probably made me an even greater weirdo.

No psychokinesis or telepathy for me, please.

Like most kids, however, I did paradoxically dabble in some tools of the trade. Nuns warned us that ouija boards were an instrument of the devil; we shouldn't just throw them away – we must burn them! After all, they'd killed people...or something like that. But I hung onto mine with some impressive results that were not easily explainable. I also participated in levitations and séances until the night we ran screaming out of the dark windowless basement.

Where had that red light come from?

Toward the end of our marriage, my husband's unsolicited diagnosis was that my birth family had numerous issues so I sought proof I was "normal." A therapist suggested I'd been afraid of my own power.

* * *

By the time my first dog, Punkin, was diagnosed with terminal cancer, he was already in deep pain. My husband, Peter, and I were too grief-stricken to conduct business-as-usual, so I called our insurance agent to cancel an appointment. My voice broke as I told John our dog was dying. The dog who'd crashed through the storm door when

John had rung the bell for our first meeting, covering his navy-blue suit with shards of glass. The dog who'd stepped into his open briefcase on the floor and licked an entire roll of stamps, which then hung in a spiral from his wet tongue like a Cootie bug in that children's game.

That dog.

I was surprised when John asked if he could still come; I was certain he'd gladly postpone until Punkin was no longer with us. "I do healing touch," he told me. "I might not be able to cure him, but I'm sure I can make him more comfortable."

I'd never met anyone who claimed to have healing powers, and John seemed a most unlikely envoy. I still resisted paranormal activities, but desperate people do desperate things: I welcomed John to our home that evening.

John got down on the floor – in his pristine, navy-blue suit – and placed his large, manicured hands on Punkin's back. Within seconds, Punkin stretched his legs and began breathing more evenly. John continued the laying on of hands for almost thirty minutes, creating a visible difference in Punkin's comfort level.

We held our breath.

"Can I feel your hands?" John asked when finished with our dog. He told Peter that he, too, had the ability to heal. He didn't sense any "buzzing" in my hands but told us everyone has the ability to heal themselves and others if they focus on it over time.

I was okay with that.

Punkin was not healed, but his discomfort was visibly reduced over the next three months, thanks to subsequent treatments by Peter, who was also able to alleviate my back pain.

Confirmation that I, too, could be a conduit for healing energy came fifteen years later from an unexpected source: a colleague.

Kate had been waiting for me after a contentious meeting during which district administrators and building principals had butted heads. Again. Despite common goals, our vantage points were different, so we often disagreed.

Seeing her outside my office door, I went through a mental Rolodex of what her current concern might be. Kate's vast experience as a well-respected high school principal – and her uber-direct communication style – intimidated this decidedly-less experienced administrator. When we'd try to jointly resolve an issue, my dominant right brain would bang up against her dominant left brain, which worked to her advantage. She was so damn logical!

"I was wondering if you'd be interested in attending a weekend Reiki training with me the end of this month. It's right in Saratoga, and I've heard it's pretty good," Kate said.

I'd never even heard the word *Reiki* before – had no clue what it was. But I didn't want to look ignorant. And I couldn't believe Kate was inviting me to do anything with her.

Shield up. "Uh, maybe. Can you send me more information?"

"Sure. It's a form of hands-on healing, you know."

"Yeah, I know. I just want to know more about this *specific* training."

My face likely betrayed my bluff. But I wasn't going to let on to Kate. Not after that meeting we'd just left.

That evening, I went online to research Reiki (pronounced *RAY-kee*), a challenge as I didn't even know how to spell it. I learned it's a form of energy medicine, similar to therapeutic or healing touch. Although there are differences among these three practices in training and application, all are based on the premise that universal life-force energy flows through all living things. Balancing this energy promotes health.

I was surprised that former math teacher Kate would have any interest in such hocus-pocus. As far as I knew, Kate played golf in her spare time; she didn't do this kind of stuff. It was the second time I'd been astounded to discover an unlikely energy healer in my midst. *Is there an underground network of professionals secretly practicing the occult?* I wondered. *What made her think I'd be open to learning how to heal myself and others through a laying on of hands to shift energy fields?*

I remembered what the insurance agent had said: "Everyone has the ability to heal themselves and others if they focus on it."

Simply out of curiosity, as much about Kate as about Reiki, I accepted her invitation.

Two weeks later, with little idea what to expect, I joined Kate and six others in the Reiki instructor's home. We were taught the history of this healing technique, originated in the late 1800s by Dr. Mikao Usui of Japan. They'd instructed that those seeking to heal others must first take responsibility for their own health and well-being, not unlike the proverb found in the *New Testament*'s book of *Luke*: *Physician, heal thyself.*

The practice includes five simple life principles. Each only requires a one-day-at-a-time commitment.

Just for today, do not be angry.
Just for today, do not worry.
Just for today, show gratitude.
Just for today, live with integrity.
Just for today, practice kindness.

Deceptively simple, not easily attainable. I've struggled with each of these principles on an on-going basis.

We learned seven basic hand placements corresponding with the seven primary energy centers in the body called chakras, running from the base of our spines to our crowns. They mirror the colors of the rainbow, which school kids learn as ROYGBIV, starting at our tailbones. Essential for good health, Reiki balances and aligns these chakras along the fourteen primary energy pathways between them (meridians).

"I bless the Divine within you. I offer you this gift of healing energy with love," I learned to say following my attunement, during which my meridians were opened by the Reiki master, enabling energy to freely flow throughout my body. This Doubting Thomas could feel heat and vibrations in my hands, in my body. On others' bodies. And something within me shifted; possibilities opened up.

By Sunday evening, it no longer felt scary or weird to harness energy to make something happen. I'd entered the realm of believer and practitioner. My awakening was a form of baptism – transcendence into a new belief system, allowing me to cast off my fears and embrace the power of what spirit, mind, and body can do when working in concert.

Among the best conversions that weekend was that Kate and I became good friends, bonded by something more powerful than bureaucratic red tape. In the months and years to come, we'd work together to help heal others. And ourselves.

My first "patient" was my elderly mother who'd had a persistent open wound on her gossamer skin. Repeated visits to the doctor hadn't helped, and she was getting anxious about contracting an infection. Although skeptical about Reiki, she was desperate enough to let me try to heal her leg. No one was more surprised than I (except maybe her) when a scab appeared the next morning. Years later, after she died, hospice assured me I'd spared my mother considerable discomfort by placing my hands on her bald head every day. Even with three tumors pressing against her cranium, she didn't even need aspirin for pain-reduction.

It took me more than a decade to ask Kate why she invited me to attend Reiki training with her. She smiled broadly, her blue eyes sparkling, and responded, "I really don't know. I've wondered myself."

My Reiki master believes more and more people are being called to be healers because our world is messed up. Thanks to religious scholars, we know Jesus walked this Earth during Pax Romana – a spiritual version of the Renaissance. Healers were prevalent, miracles abundant and commonplace. That awareness, coupled with clerical hypocrisy, sparked my resentment toward the religion of my birth for all the ways it diminishes the potential and power everyone has to manifest miracles, to heal. For all the ways it made me feel less-than as a woman and a seeker. Ways that had left me feeling spiritually rudderless until guided to another path.

* * *

My puppy now needs a healing miracle. Although she's starting to squirm, her hind legs remain limp, causing her to collapse when placed back on the ground. Under the rapidly-darkening sky, I scoop her up and run down to the shore. Fully clothed, I wade into the water and kneel on the sandy bottom. I sprinkle water on Dolly's furry little face, as if a baptism; droplets fall from her blonde eyelashes as she blinks. "I bless the Divine within you," I repeat.

I douse her hind legs with lake water, again turning my face upward: "I beg you: Please don't let Dolly be paralyzed. This wasn't her fault; I'm to blame for calling her down those steps. If you heal her, I promise she'll do something good in this world; we both will. Heal her in this water under this night sky. Please. I...I...love her so."

In that moment, I realize I do. And have all along. I was just afraid to admit it. Afraid to love and lose again.

Canis Spiritus

Dogs come into our lives to teach us about love and loyalty. They depart to teach us about loss. A new dog never replaces an old dog; it merely expands the heart. If you have loved many dogs, your heart is very big.

- Erica Jong

Dolly is not my first golden retriever but is the first puppy I've single-parented.

I didn't become acquainted with *dogginess* until my early thirties. As a young girl, I had a sweet kitty named Twinkle – until I didn't; I don't remember how that story ended. She was followed by a beautiful Persian cat that didn't even pretend to like us, although he was allowed to sleep on the dining room table in an antique bowl within striking distance of Tweety, our canary. Fluffy hid under beds, diabolically lunging at ankles when we walked by. His long white fur became matted because he scratched us when we tried to brush him, so he had to be professionally shaved twice a year. He scarred my dad's face, barely missing his eye. My dad forgave it all, despite his well-deserved reputation as a master grudge-holder. At a ripe old age, Fluffy was hit by a car, yet had nary a scratch on him; we speculated he died of a heart attack.

Neighbors on both sides had dogs, but I had little contact with them (except for Gypsy's poop, of course). As aggressive as Fluffy was, canine was the species that confounded me. Not because I'd ever been injured by a dog; I just didn't understand dogs' symbiotic relationship with humans coupled with their ability to kill like jackals. Like the dingo who reportedly crept into the campsite in Australia to steal a baby.

Shortly after moving into our first marital home, my husband began to plead so desperately for a puppy that I had to consent: "Okay, but only a floppy-eared puppy. Pointy-eared dogs look threatening. And you'll have to take care of it." Peter readily agreed to the same conditions under which every twelve-year-old boy gets his first dog.

"That dog will be a handful," my colleague warned when told we were going to look at a litter of golden retriever/Irish setter puppies.

"Nah. The ad said these puppies are really sweet," I confidently replied. "Plus, we've only started looking. This will take a while."

I didn't realize puppies cast a spell that makes it impossible to walk away empty-handed.

My colleague's warning was prophetic: Punkin grew to be a beautiful 85-pound dog with a setter's silky red coat, a solid retriever body, and irrepressible *joie de vivre*. He was smart and perceptive. He looked at what you pointed to. He barked at the second hand as it moved around the face of the wall clock. He tried to get behind the television to find the dogs on the screen.

"Bored by traditional commands," we'd rationalize when he wouldn't sit, come, down, or heel. Like all gifted children.

Punkin was best known in the neighborhood for his obsession with Nicholas, a large, lumbering sheep dog who lived around the corner. Punkin would do anything to express his disdain for this dog whose hair covered his eyes. He once dove through a large screen on our wrap-around porch to get to Nicholas, only to be faced down by the larger dog with a deeper growl. Not learning his lesson, days later he blew out a double-pane window in our living room by taking a flying leap off an antique chair, strewing glass inside and out.

A novice pet-parent, I didn't realize he wasn't functioning within an acceptable range of canine behavior until a dog trainer tried unsuccessfully to make an example of him to prove any dog can be rehabilitated. "You can't hurt this dog," he sputtered. "I've tried." An unacceptable technique, but Punkin's spirit was hard to break. His outrageous behavior only made us love him more. Admire him, even.

I came home from work one day, and Punkin was gone.

I looked for him upstairs and down, calling a neighbor to report that someone had stolen our dog. Phil flatly responded, "No one would steal that dog." When I hung up, I spotted Punkin in the front yard; he'd figured out how to unlatch the locked screen door. Another time, he took himself to a nearby health care facility after chewing through his tether and being grazed by a car. He was unscathed.

In his twelfth year, we received the dreaded diagnosis that afflicts 50% of dogs over ten years of age: cancer. On his last walk, so weak he could barely stand, he tugged his leash toward Nicholas' house, where he let his bladder loose on the front stoop. Punkin was put to sleep in front of our fireplace on his favorite blanket, his deep red coat still soft and silky. I wailed in the backyard, a grief so deep I thought it would split me wide open. A grief like none I'd ever before experienced.

After twelve years with Punkin's big personality, it was surreal to be in our home without him. His essence was felt in every room. My grief made it impossible for me to see the area in front of our fireplace as anything but sacred.

Only five weeks into dog deprivation, we found Dryphuss Alexis, a purebred three-year-old golden, listed in the *Free to Good Home* section of the newspaper. He was being displaced by a baby who was allergic to dogs. "Maybe they should give up the baby instead," we joked. The father seemed to have considered that option as he actively discouraged us from adopting Dryphuss, warning, "We can't keep him off the furniture. He slobbers when he drinks. And he sheds all over." But when we spotted Dryphuss standing on the couch, we knew we had to have him: He was Punkin's doppelganger – a bonus and a liability for him and us.

His mom visited us to make sure he'd be going to "a good home," a conscientious decision since goldens' gentle disposition makes them attractive for medical research. She noted our large yard, spacious living quarters, and doggie-tude. The father opted to not be present when we took away his dog the following weekend. As would most goldens,

Dryphuss eagerly jumped into our car.

Ironically, although Dryphuss' arrival helped fill the hole in our hearts, we created a hole in his. He began a year-long bereavement period. Dogs are so shameless and unabashed in expressing emotion that we considered producing a video about bereavement starring visibly-grieving Dryphuss. He'd stand by our car, leash in mouth, seemingly begging for a ride home. His face was contorted – red eyes, deep-knitted brows, skin stretched taut over his facial muscles. He whimpered and cried. We unwittingly offended his former family by asking, "Does Dryphuss know his name?" because he wouldn't acknowledge our calling him, thereby denying us legitimacy. We finally consulted a golden retriever expert who told us, "Dryphuss will always wonder why he was taken from his pack, what he did wrong. And he'll always be anxious that it might happen again. Try to be patient as he works through this."

Easier said than done. Dryph's resemblance to Punkin caused us to expect him to be Punkin. To be the uber-zealous dog who knew our routines – routines Punkin knew but ignored. To immediately adopt and embrace us as his family. But Dryph didn't meet us at the door. He didn't eat with gusto, especially food stolen off the kitchen counter. He didn't race us upstairs or play hide-and-seek. No, he stood around as if in shock, showing no interest in his surroundings. Our backyard was not a place to play; it only served as his toilet. Nicholas daring to walk past our house was a non-event.

Dryph may have sensed our disappointment that he couldn't immediately slip into the role of our family dog. And his continued detachment signaled his frustration that we didn't know his routines either. Escaping the tension, he bolted out the door one afternoon, taking advantage of a visitor who mistakenly let him out. We notified the village police, who told us someone a few blocks away had him. When I drove to their house, Dryphuss showed no recognition of me or his name. The rescuers were hesitant to turn him over because he didn't act like he belonged to me. After I told them the history behind our strained bond, they released him, recording my name and phone number just in case.

Had we short-circuited our grieving process by replacing our beloved Punkin too soon? We'd placed much pressure and many expectations on ourselves and Dryphuss to make everything okay again because we no longer wanted to hurt. Maybe we should have chosen a different breed to prevent such an unhealthy transference. Yet most dog owners are loyal to a specific breed. I wouldn't have given up on my floppy-ears requirement; for my husband, a large dog was a non-negotiable criterion. We'd chosen a quick fix, something Dryph's mom couldn't detect when assessing our suitability. We learned we couldn't heal our emotional wounds with a replacement dog, any more than one can replace a child or spouse to stem the grief.

Structured time in obedience training healed us as a family. Dryph's red eyes cleared up; his brow softened as we established new routines together. A common language. His face looked fuller, no longer drawn. The leash was retired because he stayed right by our side, responsive to every command. He became so well-behaved that I wondered why I'd put up with Punkin's antics. Dryphuss brought us unadulterated joy, not by replacing Punkin but by affirming our deep affinity for the species. His first mom sent cards and called periodically; we sent photos and learned the couple had separated. We wondered if the strain of surrendering their dog had come between them. We'd later discover for ourselves how fragile marriage can be in the wake of deep, personal loss.

At eleven years of age, a mast cell tumor had deteriorated Dryph's quality of life. We'd been reassured for months that the small bump on his paw was nothing, until the cancer spread to his organs – one of my first lessons in the importance of questioning both canine and human diagnoses. At the end, I selfishly told the vet, "I'm not ready to lose him." He sympathetically responded, "I love people who don't give up. But the problem with people who don't give up is that they don't know *when* to give up. Dryphuss is suffering – it's time to let him go." Afterward, Dryph's motionless body wrenched my heart out, but his pain was gone. I was grateful his first mom had come to say goodbye and that he'd graced her with recognition.

Love endures.

Eight years earlier, Dryphuss had arrived to ease our grief, eventually becoming the catalyst for similar grief. My pain was no less the second time around – perhaps even greater because I knew how much and for how long it would hurt. More consequential, Dryph's death was bookended by my parents' deaths. When friends tried to console me by labeling it a loving act to end my dog's life, I kept thinking it paradoxical that I was able to arrange "humane" euthanasia for my dog but not for my mother who'd been suffering with brain cancer far longer than even her stalwart Catholic faith could justify.

We adopted Rusty Maloney two years later, perhaps hoping this new-baby-equivalent could hold our twenty-plus-year marriage together. Rusty was approximately two years old when found wandering the streets of central New York by a golden retriever rescue organization. A deep red color, he was the most photogenic of our dogs, always eager to pose for a camera. His teeth were decayed, yet he bit through leather leashes and nylon ties in seconds. On walks, he'd pull us over to look inside parked cars, as if his *real* family might be in there waiting for him. That made us suspect he'd been booted out of a car; with rescued pets, you're always trying to piece together their history based on observed behaviors.

We'd rescued Rusty but were unable to rescue our marriage. It suffered collateral damage from two years of continual loss, including Peter's parents. We agreed the dog would remain with Peter in the house with a big yard; I wasn't prepared to single-parent a rescued dog in a small townhouse while working full time. I also knew I'd be okay alone; I wasn't sure how Peter would fare. Our separation agreement spelled out the terms of our shared responsibility for our last co-parented dog. With sad, knowing eyes, Rusty watched me move out when my husband was unable to bear witness. Locking the door and leaving the key – with my dog and marriage inside – was one of the hardest things I'd ever done.

When Rusty died at only four years of age, the victim of an aggressive neck tumor, Peter and I were temporarily reunited in our grief. It would be our last shared loss; we'd each end up with our own golden in the future.

Each time our dog departed, a phantom dog appeared – sometimes for months. I could hear the clicking of their nails on the floor, the jingle of their collars. I could see them out of the corner of my eye. I believe our grief held them here for a while. We were never ready to say goodbye. One never is.

Yes, I know what it's like to love a dog only to lose a dog. And my parents. And my marriage. That's why I tried to protect myself from getting too involved, from caring too much about this new puppy named Dolly. I've been afraid to emotionally invest in her only to lose her. Afraid to love so deeply that my heart would break again when death wins; my recent experiences had convinced me it always does.

Even I find it odd that I wasn't as concerned about all this when planning to adopt an adult dog, who would likely depart sooner. I wonder why a puppy presents so differently. Perhaps Dolly's vulnerability reminds me of my own.

I often wonder what my childhood might have been like if I'd had a dog. Would I have been thinner from running around with her? Less scared and lonely? Less wounded by my older sister's resentment? Would I have told my dog my secrets? Would I have buried my face in her fur and cried while the yelling went on around me? Losing such a beloved companion in childhood would have been my first brush with death and might have affected how I handled my parents' deaths decades later. Rather than tightly holding on, perhaps I'd have better accepted transience if I'd experienced a dog's death as a child.

My mother had never cared for my dogs, never even seemed to know their species much less their names. When she'd inquire as to their well-being, only to be polite, she'd say, "How's your animal?" In contrast, my father had loved our goldens because they provided unconditional love – something he neither gave nor got.

All my dogs were cremated, their ashes mixed together and spread on the shore of this lake because they'd all loved water. Reflecting on their fidelity, I now invoke their canine spirits to help this puppy heal.

As I continue to soothe Dolly with cool lake water, she stops whimpering; her hind legs begin to wiggle. Encouraged, I gently set her down. She again collapses, forcing me to make a decision.

I know what I must do. But I'm not thinking clearly enough to determine how. I don't even know where the emergency veterinary clinic is, much less how to get there. Someone once told me it's 45 minutes away, over this mountain and around another. My GPS doesn't work here, and it's night-time dark.

I have to figure this out. And hope it's not too late.

Hugging Dolly snugly to my chest, I run up the hill toward my garage. My lungs struggle to take in enough oxygen. My car is locked, so I gently place her limp body on the gravel driveway while I run into the house to get my car keys.

When I return seconds later, Dolly is missing. Gone! I begin to shake, fearing that a wild animal has snatched up my defenseless puppy.

A coyote? A hawk? A bobcat?

She was wounded. I shouldn't have left her alone.

"Oh, God! Help me! Help meeeeeeeee! I can't do this!" I scream, my plea for intercession laced with rage at the ever-mounting complications. There are no neighbors to answer my cry for help; it's not intended for them anyway.

My last reserve of hope depleted, I call out in little more than a whisper, "Come, Dolly. Come. Please come, Dolly," despite knowing Dolly doesn't do that. I sit on the gravel in my wet jeans and sob, my head in my hands.

I'm so sorry, Dolly. I didn't deserve you.

Resurrection

> *There is healing in the laying on of hands;*
> *in the letting go of fear, in asking for help,*
> *in silence, celebration, prayer.*
>
> - Danna Faulds

Suddenly, the motion-sensor light at the other end of the driveway flashes on, shining down on an orange puppy chasing her tail. Dolly is frolicking under the very night sky to which I'd sent my pleas for mercy.

I'm afraid to believe what I think I see. Just moments before, my puppy was lifeless. Now she's spinning in circles.

She grins at me over her shoulder, inviting me to play. The crescent moon smiles down on us. I see the iridescent stars through a prism of tears. A prism of healing salt water.

My soggy jeans squish on the gravel as I kneel in supplication to the Universe. "Thank you, thank you," I sob. "Thank you for this gift of forgiveness and healing we've been granted. Thank you for a second chance."

Baptism followed by resurrection.

Dolly scampers over...and sinks her needle-teeth into my ankle, disrupting my prayer of gratitude.

"OW!" I cry, a word she's often heard after one of her surgical strikes – most of my socks have small holes in them from exactly this.

Lifting and squeezing her tightly, I whisper in her wet, floppy ear, "Dolly, I'm sorry for not appreciating the many blessings you've brought into my life. Tonight has changed me. Tonight has changed us."

I'd yet to realize how much this night would change everything.

* * *

I'd stopped praying five years ago. When my mother died.

I couldn't even say the word *god* without immediately adding the word *damn.*

Up until my mother's last breath, I had enough faith and

confidence to believe I could save her. That my potions, my prayers, my energy work, my medical advocacy, my sheer will and hers would be enough to cheat death. Under my orchestration, family members, friends, congregations, and prayer circles all stormed the gates of Heaven on her behalf. Prayer coupled with western medicine and Reiki would make those tumors disappear. I was convinced.

Until I came face-to-face with destiny.

"Call this number," a fellow caregiver instructed, handing me a slip of paper. "She'll help your mother. My husband was near death, and she turned him around. She'll give you the recipe for a special concoction that will knock the cancer right out of her."

Grateful for the hope offered, I called the phone number as soon as I returned home. The woman on the other end of the line asked me two questions in a lilting voice: my mother's name and her location.

After a long pause, in a somber tone, she told me, "It will all work out as it's supposed to."

"Can you save her? Can you save my mother?" I pushed in desperation.

She repeated, "It will all work out."

No special concoction was offered. Nothing to "knock the cancer right out of her."

I decided not to beg. I may have already known our fate was sealed, that it was my mother's time, and no amount of intervention could help.

I hung up in a stupor. *What could this stranger discern, based solely on my response to those two questions?* I wished she'd better masked her clairvoyance. I tried to dismiss it as voodoo, a misguided crystal-gazer. But that conversation was seared into my consciousness.

"Miracles are still possible," my uncle encouraged. The movie *What the #$*! Do We Know!?* espouses that most of us stop believing just before the miracle is about to happen. But I no longer believed in prayer, in God, in my ability to facilitate healing. If there were a higher power, he'd have to be cruel to let prayers go unanswered or, worse, be inversely applied. Cruel to let my mother become paralyzed from brain cancer.

God had failed. Reiki and prayers had failed. Western medicine had failed.

I had failed.

The toughest part of failure for me has always been my inability to forgive myself. For not being perfect, for not being able to make everything better. A critical, rageful father and a high-achieving mother had charted my course at a young age, reinforced by a shaming religion and high-profile public career. I had to do things "right." I'd succeeded in most of my endeavors, primarily because I only took calculated risks. When my blood pressure kept spiking, the biofeedback counselor correctly diagnosed, "You suffer from perfectionist disease." A colleague dubbed me "Patty Perfect."

But this had been a BIG miss: My mother had died.

When healing modalities don't work, it's believed (or, some would say, rationalized) that they're not supposed to. There must be a higher purpose to the illness. Everyone has a time and manner when they are to exit this Earth. Isn't that what the clairvoyant had discerned? But this was a bitter pill for me to swallow. Because it's hard to know when to give up.

I rebelled against *The Serenity Prayer*: *God grant me the serenity to accept the things I cannot change, the courage to change the things I can, and the wisdom to know the difference.*

What a lazy cop-out, I thought – we should instead change the things we cannot accept.

Following my disappointment in a so-called God and in myself, I'd relegated Reiki to an interesting phenomenon rather than a legitimate healing practice. Yet when Rusty, the golden my husband had custody of, started limping one year later, I offered to try it on him. Perhaps to compensate Rusty for enduring the strife that accompanied our marital breakup. I wasn't convinced we hadn't caused his *dis-ease*.

Alone in my estranged husband's new residence, surrounded by furnishings that once graced our home, I realized our stuff had a new life. So did Peter. Did I? Or had I simply lost everything?

Freedom's just another word for nothin' left to lose, penned Kris Kristofferson.

I laid my hands on Rusty's back as he snuggled next to me on the floor. When it felt too intense, he'd walk away and stare at me from across the room. We both felt it.

To my great satisfaction, Rusty stopped limping after just one treatment. I felt empowered once more in my healing ability. But a few days later, I paid half the vet bill to get a definitive diagnosis – a tumor between his shoulder blades so horrific we put the four-year-old dog down the same day.

I lost my faith in possibilities. My parents and in-laws had died, Dryphuss and Rusty had died, my marriage had dissolved, and I'd been living alone in a small townhouse. Self-awareness of my shortcomings and perseveration over my failings made it impossible to approach healing with conviction. Since being saddled with this puppy, I'd felt increasingly angry and worried. Angry that my fragile, reconstructed life had been up-ended by this unwanted gift and worried I wasn't enough – couldn't be enough – for her.

Thich Nhat Hanh, a Vietnamese Buddhist monk, teaches that we're all born with anger, instilled by the traumatic birthing process. Anger can cause us to neglect gratitude, kindness, and integrity. As we mature, it's our responsibility to redirect anger in ways that lift us and others up, to channel the energy into a higher vibration. To channel the passion of rage into love.

To love and forgive as unconditionally as dogs.

In retrospect, I believe the Universe has been screaming at me for decades to surrender control; many of my birth family issues had revolved around control, vying to be the most powerful when, in the end, none of us were. Earthly power is an illusion; yet there is a higher consciousness at work and, if my desire is in line with the higher good, it will come to pass. If not, my prayers will be answered in unrecognizable ways, which may appear to be unanswered or even contrary to my intent. Yes, my mother died, but she died without physical pain despite tumors pressing against her cranium. And Rusty was granted a few more good days before leaving us. Perhaps my interventions did make a difference, although the outcomes were not what I'd hoped.

The epic struggle between *what should be* and *what is*. A challenge for me to understand or accept.

"When you lose, don't lose the lesson," the Dalai Lama advises. Acceptance and surrender lead to gratitude and kindness. The path to personal resurrection.

It took a whirling Dolly Lama to resurrect my faith in my personal power as guided by universal energy. Under that vast night sky, I felt small and powerless, face-to-face with my limitations and failures. In my desperation, I intuitively reached for the only options available to me: water, Reiki, and prayer.

And now, Dolly dances in the moonlight.

I pray to be worthy of this precious gift.

Juggling a squirming, wet puppy in my arms, I open the door to my home – our home. I feel the sanctity of the covenant made with, and witnessed by, the heavens: *I'll do anything if you save her.*

Confirmation

> *I could not lie anymore so I decided to call my dog*
> *"God." First, he looked confused, then he started*
> *smiling, then he even danced.*
>
> -Tukaram, Indian Saint, 1608-1649

After what she's just been through, Dolly won't be sleeping in her crate in the laundry room tonight; she'll be sleeping with me.

I'm so grateful to have her warm and still-damp body by my side. In my bed.

I don't even care if this wet puppy wets.

She conks out immediately, snuggled under the sheets – obviously delighted with the upgrade in accommodations. I continue to perform Reiki on her, gently placing my hands on her hips. I, too, am exhausted but don't sleep a wink. I listen for her every breath, monitor her every movement. Give thanks for every twitch of her furry little body.

Periodically, she stands, circles, and plops down again. But she doesn't wet the bed. A lesser, yet important, reason to give thanks.

Lama should be her middle name, I intuit the next morning. *She's my personal guru and guide, here to teach me lessons about what's really important. To teach me about physical and emotional healing. Dolly Lama and I were destined to be together.*

The next morning, Dolly resumes her typical antics as if nothing had happened, making the events of last night seem surreal. The friends I call to tell the tale are conspicuously skeptical. I don't have answers for them – I only know what I witnessed.

But the seed of doubt has been sown, and I begin to worry about internal bleeding.

My heart thumps against my chest wall. Maybe this won't have a happy ending after all. Not willing to take any chances – not after coming so close to losing my puppy – I take her to the veterinarian that morning. When I describe what happened, I intentionally leave out the applied healing interventions of water, Reiki, and prayer.

Am I embarrassed to admit that I believe I was able to marshal higher powers to heal her?

He listens to her heart, palpates her organs, and presses down on her hips. "She seems okay to me. Puppies are resilient. I can take x-rays to confirm if you like, but I'd have to sedate her. She's a wiggly little thing."

A few hours ago, I feared paralysis. Now, to my sheer delight, she wiggles too much.

Go, Dolly!

Dolly's been through enough in the last twenty-four hours, I conclude, declining further medical assessment. I instead pursue a different kind of assessment by calling my friend Marie.

In the interest of time, I abbreviate the story: "Dolly took a tumble off my deck last night and was immobilized for a while. She seems okay now, but I'm wondering if she really is. Can you do a reading?"

Marie instructs me to hold on while she engages her divining crystal. I can hear her ask my question aloud. She quickly reassures me: "Dolly is fine – totally healthy. All damage has been repaired." She then hesitates before adding, "Um...your parents want you to know they were with you at the moment of impact. They were helping and supporting you, and each has a message for you now."

Maybe I'm still in shock from last night, but I'm not surprised my parents have something to say about what happened. I've heard from both of them many times since their deaths. And now that Marie mentions it, I did feel their presence last night but, in my desperation, hadn't fully registered it.

"Okay, I'm ready," I sigh. "They've always been very opinionated and protective, even from the other side. So go on. Let me have it."

"Your dad says you can't do this alone; get some help.

Your mom says Dolly needs more training." I laugh. Right on both counts. Marie had never met my parents, yet the messages she delivers are consistent with what they would have advised had they been physically present.

I then disclose the full story of last night's adventure to Marie. We've been friends for more than thirty years. When she relocated to New England, neither of us was good at staying in touch. We both had families and careers as school administrators. We had no idea there'd be a more powerful connection that would deeply bind us in years to come.

Just the prior weekend, after a long period of limited long-distance contact, Marie had visited and met Dolly. We had much to catch up on. We'd both separated from our long-time spouses. She, too, was a lapsed Catholic; I'd never have guessed her interest or ability in psychic phenomenon. She was far more advanced than I, sharing stories with me about psychic visions, channeling, and angels. Using divining tools, Marie determined that my property had once been sacred to Native Americans who'd been forcefully displaced. She performed a ceremony to release their spirits. She smudged my new home with burning dried sage. This Native American practice of using the smoke of sacred herbs to purify the air removes negative energy, creating a more positive atmosphere and mood, she explained.

My home was definitely in need of smudging after weeks of absorbing my frustration with my rambunctious puppy. Marie had remarked on my unflagging service to Dolly, while appreciating the pup's exuberance.

Marie also helped me create a spirit circle, consisting of a natural stone border, a meditation bench, and a statue of Quan Yin, the Goddess of Compassion. It honors the diversity and unity of the four natural elements essential for life: earth, air, water, and fire. It's a place to connect with the divinity, spiritual wisdom, spirits, angels, and ascended masters.

It was my college boyfriend more than twenty-five years earlier who'd first opened the door for me to seriously entertain the possibility of spirits among us. Three years after we broke up, Michael called to tell me the book *Out on a Limb* had changed the way he looked at life and death. Shirley MacLaine, a well-known dancer and actress, had been declared a self-aggrandizing crack-pot in the 1980s after publishing a book about her supernatural beliefs and experiences. I was surprised Michael, an Irish-Catholic technocrat, would even say MacLaine's name out loud, much less recommend her work. But when the Universe sends you a message through an old boyfriend, you have to pay attention.

I bought *Out on a Limb* the next day.

True to his endorsement, Ms. MacLaine's writing expanded my understanding of the spirit realm, which led me to read other books about contact with those who had died. It seemed plausible to me: The human body consists of energy, and energy doesn't die – it changes form. Basic quantum physics. Life-after-life scholars cite evidence from nature, anthropology, psychology, philosophy, science, and the Bible. But sometimes, in order to believe, we have to experience contact directly, which requires being open to the possibility. And paying attention.

One week after Marie's visit, the messages she channeled from my deceased parents about Dolly's accident again confirmed for me that they live on in a different dimension. And if she hadn't visited the weekend before, I wouldn't have known she could help after Dolly's fall.

As Ms. MacLaine espouses, there are no coincidences.

Although not a believer herself, my mother had always gotten a kick out of my burgeoning interest in the spirit world. As she lay dying, I asked her to promise she'd return to assure me she was okay. She'd kept her word, providing numerous verbal and visual messages that she was doing well on the other side and, in fact, was quite busy. When I railed against God after a friend's baby died, I heard my mother's voice: *There are no tragedies; there's only life*. A self-confessed catastrophizer like me could never conjure up such a belief on my own. My mom had consistently practiced the power of positive thinking, and, in death, has continued to steer me toward a deeper understanding of the cycle of life.

There are no tragedies.

My biggest surprise after both parents died was the frequency and doggedness with which my father appeared. I'd never asked him to; I'd been afraid he'd haunt rather than visit. But by the end of his life, we'd both put aside old wounds. Dementia and medication dissipated his rage, and he was grateful for my Reiki touch on his head. "Keep doing that," he'd say. "It helps me think better." His aphasia did noticeably improve for a short while after each Reiki treatment.

When he died, he apparently was not ready to leave this earthly plane. And still isn't. Perhaps he's trying to make up for past transgressions. Or wants to give me a chance to do so. Despite my strong emotional connection to my mother, it's my father's spirit I see and hear when I'm most in need. In a bizarre way, that makes sense: His behavior had always been more appropriate when there was a crisis because he always functioned in crisis mode. When there was something legitimate to get worked up over, his pervasive fear and paranoia landed his behavior within the normal range.

It's now up to me to internalize, and make manifest in my life, the multi-faceted healing that occurred last night. I wonder if or when I'll learn to fully trust my heart over my head. To trust the power of intention. To trust, without empirical confirmation, the messages the Universe generously offers.

Did I offend cosmic forces by verifying Dolly's condition with a veterinarian, when I'd been granted an unmistakable manifestation of their intervention last night?

Such questions would continue to challenge and guide me. Future lessons would be plentiful, powerful, and sometimes painful as Dolly Lama herds me closer to discovery and affirmation of my spiritual beliefs and healing practices.

When I didn't feel worthy, the night sky shone its beneficence upon us. So I may never forget what happened, I name my new home *Healing Waters*. I momentarily consider spelling it *Heeling* Waters, but that would be too pedestrian a pun for my newly-christened Dolly Lama. Plus, I'm not convinced Dolly will ever learn to heel.

But she may have finally learned to come when called.

Now stay, Dolly. Stay.

Please.

Part II: *Redemption*

Yin and Yang

God is in the roses and the thorns.

-Rosanne Cash

Despite her new exalted title, or maybe because of it, Dolly Lama's behavior doesn't noticeably improve. Foraging is at an all-time high, compliance is optional, and toileting is at her discretion.

She's brought chaos into my tidy existence. Trying to understand the sudden infusion of polarity into my life, I reflect on the yin and yang of living with this puppy:

I don't get much sleep.
I have a reason to get out of bed.

I have to walk her several times each day.
I'm becoming more fit.

She infuriates me when she doesn't obey.
She's taught me so much about patience.

She causes me worry and concern.
She makes me laugh out loud.

My floors are littered with dog toys.
She's taught me how to play again.

I can't leave her for any length of time.
I have someone to come home to.

She's expensive to care for.
She's more precious than gold.

She's a puppy.
She's my puppy.

That's what it comes down to: Dolly's a puppy. A puppy trying to navigate a human's world. Yanked away from others of her species – from those who look and act like her, descended from those who have for centuries survived based on their finely-honed instincts. How hard it must be for Dolly to try to figure it out on her own without modeling by others of her kind.

Indeed, how hard for any minority to singularly navigate a different culture, with informal rules and expectations that aren't intuitive to the outsider and don't make sense based on diverse backgrounds. In employment, new hires' success depends on how quickly they assimilate into the organization's culture. The same is true for pets new to our households. And for any budding relationship.

Perhaps that's why my friend had advised, "Get two puppies. It'll be easier." I've read that dogs learn from each other fifteen times faster than they learn from a human. But shouldn't at least one of two canines in a household be a mature, well-trained dog that can model for a goofball puppy? From observing Dolly, two puppies might spontaneously combust from the friction of fur racing around the house. I marvel when I see people walking two or more dogs when I can barely manage one.

Several expressions are used in our culture to help us make peace with polarities: *Take the bitter with the sweet. Every rose has its thorns. Every cloud has a silver lining. Life's ups and downs.* In Chinese philosophy, yin and yang represent two seemingly opposite forces that are actually complementary. While yin is a negative, passive, dark force, yang is a positive, active, light force. The underlying principle is that all things exist as inseparable and contradictory opposites, and their interconnectedness gives rise to each other. Related theories have been applied in Chinese medicine since 700 BC to balance energy centers (chakras) in the physical body.

Chaos and suffering result when there's an imbalance between these forces. Within our bodies, our lives, our world.

In my home.

No, Dolly hasn't become a dream dog overnight. But my acceptance and appreciation of her continues to grow. Because I've stopped having unrealistic expectations of this puppy – expectations she couldn't meet at her young age. While expectations can establish important standards, they can also lead to disappointment. Psychologists tell us unmet expectations are at the root of anger.

I wish I'd not expected my father to change and, instead, changed my intrinsic belief that his behavior had the power to make me happy or sad. I know now that he couldn't even do that for himself.

I'd always been deeply affected by my father's rage – even when not directed at me. But much more so by his unpredictable behavior. When I walked through the door, I never knew which father I'd find: the funny, playful, and indulgent father; the rageful father infuriated by the most innocuous of comments or actions; or the nurturing, instructive father. I used to wish he were an alcoholic, like my friend's dad. The bottles and acrid whiskey smell alerted her that her father was on a tear, so she knew to stay clear. I had no warning signs; the change could be sudden, like a flipped switch.

Imbalance. Chaos. Suffering.

Yin yang yin yang yin yang.

My older sister and I didn't bond like littermates; she'd enjoyed six years as an only child and grandchild before I came along. She took our father on, challenged his irrationality; I tried to be perfect so as to not upset him. My mother effectively practiced denial, yet tried to assure us it wasn't anything we did, employing Longfellow's poem to explain our dad's behavior: *When he was good, he was very, very good. When he was bad, he was horrid.* Later, my expectations of how a father should behave governed my adult response to him, making it impossible for me to select a Father's Day card without weeping in the store aisle. Cards that thanked fathers for being supportive of their daughters, celebrating the special bond between them. Those cards.

I always chose one that withheld emotion and praise – the two things he craved the most, I now realize. Our responses to each other tended to be the opposite of what we were hoping for or needing. Yin. Yang.

Many years after his death, I concluded that my father was bipolar. The diagnosis, denoting the polar opposite behaviors of mania and depression, was first coined in 1980. Prior to that, as early as the 17th century, the condition was called manic-depressive disorder. Counseling helped me realize three sets of behaviors present in a bipolar personality: depression or melancholy; mania or super-excited; and normal. Periods of behavior within the normal range can make loved ones hesitant to seek treatment for the ill person because they witness him functioning appropriately at times so conclude it's a behavioral choice. It's not.

The condition is caused by an imbalance in brain chemistry, which triggers behavioral swings that can be dangerous for the ill person and those around him. Medication can stabilize symptoms if the right "cocktail" is prescribed. It's also hereditary, with up to 90% of those diagnosed having a relative with the same disorder.

Medication for depression at the end of my father's life leveled off the mood swings and, despite challenging circumstances, we were able to forge a relationship months before he died. For that reconciliation, I'm grateful to modern medicine. But I regret not confronting his mental illness sooner, regret time lost. Most of us wait too long.

My yoga practice provides a model for me to better manage my own reaction to external stimuli. (It's either that or plentiful adult beverages.) Yoga's tall and steady *Mountain* pose reminds me that mountains remain immoveable and solid despite storms and catastrophes swirling around them. The *Tree* pose of standing on one leg helps me stay centered and balanced. Bearing in mind that it's possible to maintain my equilibrium in the face of chaos, I begin to view Dolly's antics differently and seek ways for these polarities to coexist. Watching her barrel down the hallway with her squeaky Harpo-Marx-sounding ball, I smile. It's still annoying when she chooses to play with this noisy toy at my feet when I'm on the phone, which is by far her favorite time to do so. But I now frame that squeak as the sound of fun and companionship. Sounds that have been missing since I left my marital home.

SQUEAK! SQUEAK!

"Not now, Dolly. I'm on the phone. Stop it!"

SQUEAK! SQUEAK! SQUEAK!

Who bought her that noisy toy, anyway?

I laugh, knowing the answer. There's no one to blame but myself. I've started to overindulge her, a consequence of the accident. Overcompensating for past misdeeds.

This unwanted puppy has wormed her way into my well-guarded human heart. How did I sleep these last four years without her lying next to my bed? Hearing her deep sighs and stirrings that signal I'm not alone any more. How did I awaken to emptiness before I had Dolly's precious face staring at me, ready for her day to begin? Her small cuddly body taking up so little physical – yet so much emotional – space in my new home. How did I meet new friends without Dolly as a conversation-starter? Impatiently waiting for strangers to pet her, lunging and leaping, her red tongue shamelessly hanging out of her mouth in anticipation. How did I come home without a furry friend anxiously awaiting my arrival? All four paws simultaneously off the floor, unbridled enthusiasm whether I'm gone for ten minutes or three hours.

Yes, now I remember why I love having a dog. Plus, as they mature, their behavior is relatively predictable – a mandatory quality for me in any companion these days.

Dogs have commonly been referred to as "pack animals." That descriptor is now under dispute, arguing that dogs have evolved beyond the pack to fully become social creatures. This transpired because dogs no longer have to hunt together in order to survive. Dolly's attempts at self-service aside, dogs have become dependent on humans for food. Lizi Angel, a canine behavior psychologist in the United Kingdom, also claims that the notion of having to teach a dog that you are the in-charge Alpha is no longer conventional wisdom – taking charge is not a natural instinct of dogs. Even wolf packs don't have Alphas; for purposes of hunting, they may have a "breeding pair" leading an egalitarian pack that largely consists of their own offspring. Submissive and dominant are more accurate descriptors of how dogs see the yin and yang of their position in a human family, she writes.

But dogs do need and want leadership, and we fail them if we don't provide it, according to animal trainer Suzanne Clothier in her book *Bones Would Rain from the Sky*. She suggests *status* is a better term for how dogs frame their relationships with humans or other canines. Status affects what a dog views as important; obedience issues may erupt when the dog views his people as deferential to him. (Does picking up poop qualify?)

From the beginning, I knew Dolly was dependent on me for survival. Now I'm becoming dependent on her. My numinous experience with her tells me she's here to show me what I'm capable of, what I'm worthy of. I intend to do the same for her. While I once sought to rid myself of her, I now want to show off this beautiful, innocent creature who found her way to me. I want her to have a "win" after absorbing my displeasure for so long.

This overcorrection from yin to yang leads me to make an embarrassing inquiry on her behalf.

Driving by a sign at a public park announcing the Lioness Dog Show, I shout to the back of my SUV, "Now, Dolly, there's something you could do! Even though you don't obey commands, you DO look like a lion cub." Her large head and paws remind me of Simba, the royal cub in *The Lion King*. This may just be the right event for her, with no expectations as to behavior or performance. She simply has to look the part.

She'll nail this!

I call for more information as soon as I arrive home.

"Hello, I'm calling about the Lioness Dog Show scheduled for the end of the month."

"Yes, how can I help you?"

"Well, I'm wondering if any talent is required, other than resembling a lioness, of course. Like, does the dog have to *sit* or *down* or anything like that?"

Silence.

I prattle on. "My dog is still a puppy, but she does look like a little lioness – you know, with her tufted ears, her color, and stuff. Kinda like the cub of a lioness. Would that qualify her to enter?"

Continued silence. I'd soon realize she was trying not to guffaw.

"I'm not sure what you mean," she cautiously responds. "This is a dog show sponsored by the Lioness Club, the female branch of the Lions Club. The dog does have to perform on command. But it sure doesn't have to look like a lioness."

Her voice breaks. I mumble a thank-you and hang up, feeling literal and stupid. Foolishly eager to have Dolly be successful on her own terms. I hope my name and number didn't appear on this *real* Lioness' caller ID, although I'm sure a reenactment of our phone conversation will brighten many Lioness Club meetings for years to come.

I hold Dolly close and tell her she looks good, smells good, runs good, plays good, catches good, eats good, walks good, sleeps good, barks good, and loves good. She just doesn't obey good (grammar aside). Her puppy-like behavior will continue to challenge my determination to reframe it, although less so, thanks to my increased consciousness about the yin and the yang of it all. (It's theorized that Jesus and Buddha were also poorly behaved youngsters. And they turned out pretty well.)

As my mother had advised through Marie's mediumship, more training is in order. For Dolly and me. No matter how deep my affection and guilt over her mishap, I have the responsibility to provide leadership. To claim status. I'll love her no matter what and want the rest of the world to love her too. That requires she be socialized. As my dad messaged, I can't do it alone. Fortunately, unlike cats and oppositionally-defiant humans, most dogs can be readily trained through the consistent use of edible rewards. Since incidental learning takes place continually, I must pay attention to what I'm inadvertently teaching as well.

Dolly's not mine to claim. She's a living creature unto herself, belonging to the Universe. She'll teach me universal laws – intrinsic, unchanging laws of our Universe originating with ancient cultures – as I'm called to teach her the ways of the human world (although the Lionesses must think I could use some tutelage myself). When I command "Hurry up, Dolly," she speeds up – she hears it frequently enough, impatient as I am. I hope she'll also learn the meaning of the words *I love you*. The phrases aren't polar opposites but can manifest as such if we don't take the time to love.

One *woof* breaks the silence of the still morning – the sound of my pup. Annoying by her intrusion, reassuring by her presence. She is being dog, responding to the call of a neighbor canine who beckons the day too early. She sounds her acknowledgement. Then we both fall back to sleep.

Covenants

There's a divinity that shapes our ends, rough-hew them how we will.

         - William Shakespeare

When we adopt a pet, we make implicit agreements with the Universe in exchange for the vulnerable life entrusted to us. Above all, we agree to love them and accept their unconditional love for us. We agree to be kind to them, feed them, clean up after them. We agree to pet them, groom them. We agree to train and exercise them. We agree to keep them safe and get them prompt medical attention when needed. We agree to allow them to be an intimate part of our lives for as long as we're graced to have them. And we agree to help them leave us when their time comes and to feel the inexorable pain when they're no longer by our side.

In addition, I entered into an explicit covenant when I told the night sky, "If you heal her, I promise she'll do something good in this world; we both will." Dolly's quick recovery from the life-threatening fall, with seemingly no residual effects, has left me with a sense of wonderment and reignited my belief that there's something bigger than I out there, an energy to be tapped when human power isn't enough. Like a survivor of a plane crash, I feel obligated to contribute in a way I'd not before considered. To create something positive and life-affirming of the experience Dolly and I'd shared, with deeper implications for the collective higher good.

In *The Four Agreements: A Personal Guide to Freedom,* don Miguel Ruiz presents a code of personal conduct, passed down to him from Toltec artists and spiritual seekers who went to Mexico more than a thousand years ago to establish a place to connect with their own divinity. Based on these teachings, Ruiz, a shamanic teacher and healer, recommends we make four agreements with ourselves to create love and happiness in our lives:

Be impeccable with your word.
Don't take anything personally.
Don't make assumptions.
Always do your best.

So simple, so practical. Yet his best-selling book explains how and why our minds challenge and resist fulfilling any of these agreements, no matter how motivated we claim to be.

I'm sure my father and I violated all four of them during our time together. I have many regrets about things said and not said, done and not done, over the course of our relationship. But lying to him at the end of his life remains one of the most egregious in my mind.

"Dryphuss was too tired to come with me," I'd say when I stopped bringing my dog to see his "grandfather" in the nursing home. Or "He's home with Peter." I couldn't bring myself to tell this man, who'd recently lost his wife of 63 years, that Dryphuss, too, had died months prior.

My grief weighed heavily; I couldn't carry his as well.

When my father asked for Dryphuss on his deathbed, I substituted our newly-adopted dog, Rusty. He was so similar in color and size that I assumed my dementia-riddled father wouldn't know the difference. But Rusty had never met him, wasn't used to the institutional setting, and, consequently, didn't behave in a familiar way.

Don't make assumptions.

My father's eyes told me he did know the difference, knew I was lying. He had an empathic relationship with Dryphuss, if not with me. He knew my dog by essence, not appearance.

"No, that's not him," he said emphatically, peering into my eyes and shaking his head.

Stopping just short of begging him to accept this ruse, I insisted, "Yes, it is, Daddy. It's Dryphuss. You just haven't seen him in a while."

Be impeccable with your word.

"No, it's not. It's not Dryphuss," he said, his eyes clouding over with a still, gray sadness. He stopped trying to pet fidgety Rusty and rolled toward the wall, turning his back to us.

I've replayed that scene over and over in my head. One of my last conversations with my father was based on a lie – a lie about a dog. After all the strife between us through the years, I was the one feeling guilty in the end.

Don't take anything personally.

Do intentions count when we fabricate stories to protect someone? Is there such a thing as a "white" lie? Or do we always owe someone, and especially ourselves, the truth? Is there such a thing as truth or is it all perspective? Such questions continue to haunt.

Always do your best.

I wonder if Dryphuss and my father commiserated over my duplicity when they met on the other side two days later.

✳ ✳ ✳

With a knowing that mesmerizes me, my friend Luann speaks of agreements beyond this lifetime. Agreements we make with the Universe before being reincarnated back to Earth. Consistent with Eastern theologies, she speaks of discerning the lessons we need to learn in order to evolve to the next level of enlightenment: "Whatever happens to us in this lifetime is something we chose prior to returning. It's all predestined, predetermined."

She worries about what she may have chosen to speed up her own evolution because the faster the track, the harder the lesson. "People who die from cancer are highly evolved because that's a terrible way to go out," she purports. "They chose that tough path as their next karmic step toward nirvana. And those who quickly rise and then crash – like Robin Williams – bought their fame at the cost of losing it all in a relatively short time. But they'd previously decided the cost was worth it."

A Catholic school graduate like I am, Luann's beliefs are now informed by years of shamanic study, Native American rituals, and personal paranormal experiences.

In the last few days of my mother's life, I told her of my

belief that, after we die, our spirits return to those who can teach us the lessons we need to learn in our next lifetime. And that we come back in the same circles, in different configurations.

"I chose you, Mom," I tearfully told her.

That I must have also chosen my father wasn't lost on me.

She stared off wistfully; I was convinced she hadn't heard me. Or didn't want to hear me. *Probably just as well. Why open this can of worms now?* I thought. *Reincarnation is contrary to Roman Catholic doctrine.* But a few minutes later, she looked into my eyes and calmly replied, "I know. You were floating around out there, and I couldn't catch my baby."

I wish I'd asked her to say more: *Had she chosen me too?* But I was too shocked to pursue it; that window to discuss our union closed as quickly as it had opened. I can only assume that as she drew closer to the other side, she caught a glimpse that there's more to this process of birth and death than church dogma can accommodate. Very young children seem to have an unschooled knowing about this, often spontaneously relaying their past-life experiences until rational thought edges out such remembrances. Or until they're instructed not to talk "nonsense." The University of Virginia's Division of Perceptual Studies has studied more than 2,500 young children who talk convincingly about previous lives, then forget about them after age seven.

"There are more things in heaven and earth...than are dreamt of in your philosophy," Hamlet told Horatio, arguing the limitations of human knowledge.

The intersection of pre-birth agreements and destiny fascinates me: We discern our divine purpose and fulfill it in accordance with agreements we made prior to our birth. In accordance with our covenant with the Universe. Considering the unlikely rise of *Queen's* Freddie Mercury from a Tanzanian refugee to a rocking cultural icon or Mozart's ability to write concertos at eleven years of age, I tend to subscribe. Yet still wonder if the notion is simply a shirking of our own responsibility for choices we make. A justification or excuse. If it's all predestined, what difference do our day-to-day actions make? If destiny rules, we'll end up at the same place anyway, despite free-will decisions along the way.

If it is true, I'd like to know what agreements I made before coming back here.

Or maybe not.

During one of my sister's and my many protracted spats over the years, a psychic urged me to reconcile with her because, according to her reading, we'd been together in five prior lifetimes, each ending in the murder of one by the other. We'd taken turns being the perpetrator, from one lifetime to the next but repeatedly chose to come back together. I can't remember who is to kill whom in this lifetime. Better not to know.

Sibling rivalry can be deadly, apparently. The Old Testament story of Cain and Abel drove that home – just one of many reasons I wish my sister and I weren't alienated.

It's not easy to accept that I could be responsible for pre-selecting the messes I find myself in. Yet I do seem to step in the same *stuff* over and over. I'm getting better at reframing life events as lessons to be learned rather than as problems to be overcome. Like reframing Dolly's arrival. And her accident.

Dolly should become a therapy dog, I conclude. It's perfect! She's beautiful, with her silky red coat and white star on her chest. At six months, I can tell she's going to remain relatively small for a golden retriever so she won't be intimidating. Together, we can bring companionship to the elderly in long-term care facilities, alleviate the deep-seated loneliness too evident in their hollowed-out eyes. When they leave their homes for the last time, they give up almost everything – including their beloved pets.

As early as 1859, Florence Nightingale wrote that a small pet is "often an excellent companion for the sick, for long chronic cases especially." In fact, it's because of an injured dog that she began to practice the healing arts. Studies demonstrate that pet companionship has measurable positive outcomes, such as reduced need for medication, lower stress, improved physical activity, and improved vital signs. They also help us stick to routines and feel safer in our homes. Simply petting a dog or cat releases mood-altering hormones that alleviate depression and agitation, and increase overall well-being – not just for the elderly but for all.

I can attest to Dolly's mood-altering powers.

That's why I frequently brought Dryphuss to the nursing home to see my father even though he wasn't an official therapy dog, A big smile would light up my dad's wizened face when he saw the big red dog on the end of my leash. "Yes, yes, yes," he'd say as he bent over to pet Dryphuss who'd be looking for a treat after helping himself to the globs of food on the floor next to residents' wheelchairs. Everyone in the dementia ward loved Dryphuss, their thin translucent arms reaching out to touch him as he made the rounds.

Yes, Dolly's destiny is to be a therapy dog. It's what she's meant to do – this is her raison d'être. And I would never have considered it if she hadn't taken that tumble.

Is it possible that Dolly also made agreements before coming to be with me? Did she choose me? Am I an instrument to help her fulfill her destiny? Did she fall to bring me closer to enlightenment?

However we got here, in order to fulfill the promise I made, my playful pup will have to forego most of the behaviors she overenjoys.

"It's time to get serious, Dolly Lama," I tell her as she prances around refusing to relinquish the tennis ball in her mouth.

After graduating from puppy school, the metric for which was *the-puppy-doesn't-pee-indoors-and-the-human-doesn't-use-the-puppy's-name-in-the-reprimand-when-the-puppy-does-pee-indoors*, I enroll Dolly in a beginner obedience course. She cowers behind me when the Rottweiler towers over her, and she shakes when encountering the smaller corgi. The corgi behaves as if he is indeed the Royal Canine, refusing to perform any of those silly tricks expected of the common dogs beneath his station. He sits on his royal rump, staring down the peons.

He makes Queen Elizabeth seem effusive.

Goldens, on the other hand, are considered one of the easiest breeds to train because they're eager to please. By some calculations (not mine), it takes them less than five repetitions to understand a new command.

For training purposes, all the dogs are fitted with tight nylon slip collars that, when correctly positioned, run from their throats to behind their ears. Dolly hates it – we both do – but it does focus her attention on the job at hand. Dolly learns pretty quickly to *sit, stand, down,* and *stay* in response to hand signals and verbalizations. The commands *come* and *heel* remain a challenge, causing the trainer to remind me, "If your dog doesn't come when called, you don't have a dog."

Those were the days, I wistfully recall.

Although I'm pleased with Dolly's progress (she graduates handily), part of me feels bad that she can be easily bought. Treats in her soft mouth are Dolly's wages for conforming to human expectations. She eagerly performs commands just to chomp on a treat for two seconds. I'm embarrassed for her that she surrenders her liberties so cheaply. For a tasty morsel at the veterinarian's office, for instance, she passively stands still while a needle is stuck into her leg.

When I share this perspective with the veterinarian, she disagrees: "Dogs don't sell out. They have the upper hand in that they get paid for everything we want them to do." I pay her as if it were my privilege to take care of her. I pay her to go potty, to be brushed, to let me wipe her feet, to turn around when we walk, to drop the stick. Suzanne Clothier calls this *trading* – giving the dog something in exchange for what we want. That's how dogs initially became domesticated: They traded their liberties for the right to hang around for grub. It beat chasing those damn gazelles. It's especially useful when we want them to surrender something in their mouths. Like tennis balls. Or worse.

I think about the times I have sold out – for approval, for keeping the peace, for getting what I want. Despite our theoretically more highly-developed moral composition, most of us have sold out. For even less than what Dolly earns in her bartering process.

I'll admit that sometimes I admire her for choosing to "go rogue" like the corgi, dismissing me as irrelevant to her canine existence, no matter what bribe is offered. Erica Jong writes that although we've domesticated them, dogs still help us reclaim the feral in ourselves. "They remind us that in ancient days we had much wisdom that we have since sadly abandoned: the wisdom of touch, the wisdom of smell, the wisdom of the senses.... Listening to the animals, we hear the secrets of the Universe."

* * *

Since Dolly hasn't consistently mastered *come* yet – one of the most important canine life-saving commands – my friend Rick arrives with his 85-year-old-father, Pete, ostensibly to help me train Dolly. She is lying on the back-door stoop when they pull into the driveway. Rick doesn't get out of the car; he stares at the little beast through the windshield. Pete, on the other hand, bounds out of the car, picks her up, and nestles his face in her warm fur while Dolly licks his forehead. Since she hasn't yet killed his father, Rick approaches the two of them, fully extending his arm to pet the tippy-top of Dolly's head with two fingers. She swivels her head around to snap at his hand.

"Oh, she does that," I laugh, remembering the day I picked her up.

Rick isn't laughing.

He asks many questions about how I acquired Dolly, perhaps wondering if I told him that as an excuse to get a dog when I know he's terrified of them. When he was a young boy, he cut through a neighbor's yard on his way home. A snarling German Shepherd chased the roly-poly kid and knocked him down. He vividly remembers the dog's paws on his shoulders and hot breath on the back of his neck. He recalls hearing adults yelling, followed by neighbors helping him to his feet. Although the dog didn't physically harm him, the close encounter was enough to instill a lifelong fear.

I understand Rick's fear of dogs; I was afraid of them until Punkin came into my life, although he also could be scary, biting both my husband and me several times over the years, for which we always made excuses. Pet owners do that, to our own detriment. A bite is a bite.

My wariness started as a child when, at a dinner party, a Chihuahua bit my father in the ankle and hung on. (Perhaps not coincidentally, these family friends had named their nasty dog after my father.) After extricating the dog, we took my dad to the hospital because dog bites can be fatal. The Center for Disease Control reports that there are 4.5 million dog bites annually in the United States, the majority occurring in victims' homes. Over thirty breeds are associated with fatalities.

In days to come, one of the accused breeds will become Dolly's "boyfriend;" the other, her attacker.

After lunch, I hand Rick some dog treats and tell him to stand at one end of the driveway. I go to the opposite end, with my eager pup in tow. I instruct Rick to call her and give her a treat when she comes.

"Um, Dolly? Do you want to come?" he asks so softly that not even a dog's ears could detect a sound.

"That's not how you call a dog," I yell, realizing with dismay that I'm now training two species. "You have to be firm. Make it a command: 'Dolly, come!'"

"Dolly, come," he weakly mimics.

She gallops toward him, ears flapping, tail high. *Good girl!*

Rick starts running too – away from her – attempting to shield himself behind a tree. She follows him, but he's unable to reward her because he's paralyzed with fear.

I call her back to me. She comes and gets paid with a treat. Rick slowly emerges.

What were Rick's agreements from a past life? I wonder. To appreciate a different species? To conquer fear? Or maybe to re-enact Daniel in the lion's den?

* * *

When my visitors leave, Dolly joins me in the space I've designated "my sanctuary." She's the only living being that doesn't have to take shoes off to gain entry; her dirty little paws are welcome anytime. In fact, I listen for them, hoping she'll come in.

I welcome her participation in my spiritual experiences, although sometimes wonder if I'm being disrespectful to my spirit guides. Yet I know Dolly is a spiritual being. Like a cherubic angel, loving and playful, waiting to be engaged. She's part of my spiritual journey on this earthly plane.

The pendulum on a chain in my hand spins clockwise, indicating a good energy flow as it clears and aligns my chakras. A red dog face appears beneath the dangling crystal, her eyes following it around and around, a kitten watching a catnip-stuffed mouse twirl. I burst out laughing wondering if I might be inadvertently hypnotizing her, and I instantly know that the joy she brings me clears my chakras better than any other sacred ritual could.

She rests by my side as I do yoga, then grabs a toy to engage me in play. Yes, there are dog toys in my sanctuary. For what would be more god-like than Dolly's invitation to be joyful? Laughter is sacred, too, essential to balancing our emotions. The Laughing Buddha, modeled after Pu-Tai, a Buddhist monk who lived a thousand years ago, represents the belief that laughing makes problems easier to handle. It not only releases endorphins, it boosts the number of antibody-producing cells and enhances the effectiveness of T-cells, leading to a stronger immune system.

The Dalai Lama describes himself as "a professional laugher." His belly laugh is proof enough for me.

HAHAHAHAHAHA!

Shift Happens

> *God gives us power to get well. He gives us power to*
> *heal sickness... Life and death are in the power of the*
> *tongue. A word is spoken and a chemical change takes*
> *place in the body.*
>
> - Florence Scovel Shinn

It's beyond terrible to walk into the vet's office with a pet and leave without one.

I'm beyond despondent to be doing just that.

Dolly can't keep food down. Recommended dietary changes over the past week haven't curtailed her diarrhea and vomiting. She's listless, weaker by the day.

The veterinarian keeps her for an exploratory, injecting a barium sulfate suspension to observe the path it takes through her digestive tract. She suspects something is lodged there.

A sock? An acorn? A stone? Lord only knows what Dolly might have gobbled down despite being under constant surveillance. She's quick, swallows before I can reach into her mouth and pull it out. Ignoring my commands to "drop it," whatever "it" might be in any given moment.

When I return two hours later, the veterinarian shows me films revealing that Dolly's intestines are filled with gas, her stomach severely bloated. "Although nothing showed up on the scan, she has all the signs of an obstruction. We'll most likely have to cut her open to remove whatever she's ingested. We'll take more x-rays in the morning but, after consulting the other vets, I'm not hopeful surgery can be avoided."

The vet proposes to slice open my six-month-old puppy from stem to sternum since they don't know where the obstruction might be. My response is immediate and resolute.

"No."

I tell the vet I want to bring Dolly home for the night to

consider my options. She agrees to release her since there won't be anyone there overnight to observe her anyway.

"She's young; she'll recover from the surgery quickly," the vet reassures.

She'll recover without surgery. Tonight, I say to myself.

Despite my apparent bravado, I'm not sure what to do. Dolly couldn't have barged into my life only to leave me this soon, could she? What about our agreement? Aren't we supposed to be together?

When we get home, I drop a mattress on the floor where we lie body-to-body. I hold the image and intention of her intestines clearing, a drain unclogging. That imagery had worked for me before.

I'm not willing to let them operate on Dolly any more than I was willing to let the doctor cut into my breast without a fight three years earlier.

* * *

What had started out as a routine mammogram quickly became every woman's nightmare. A lump was discovered on a Thursday that, based on the radiologist's review, warranted a biopsy. Immediately, they said. Monday. I had the weekend to come to terms with my new health status.

Despite wanting to stay under the covers, my Friday work schedule was full. Trying to crawl out of my funk before I headed to the office, I called a friend who let me sob for a while before asking, "Why are you calling me? Susan could actually help you."

That suggestion set something in motion for me; I began to abandon the victim mentality and felt empowered. Susan is a certified energy worker who trained under Donna Eden, arguably the foremost authority on energy medicine. Eden tells us all disease is caused by trapped energy so contacting Susan made sense. She agreed to work with me that same evening.

She performed healing exercises to unblock the trapped energy, assuring me I still have much to do in this lifetime. "It's time to stop living in loss and start celebrating life. This

lump is your body's way of crying out for self-nurturing."
She gave me imagery to make the lump go away: a snowball
melting, a drain unclogging.

I began to understand that this lump may be representative
of a more serious condition: self-neglect and fear. So many
losses in such a short time had left me adrift, unsure of
my core identity. No wonder I needed a biopsy – I had
disappeared. Who was I without my parents, my marriage,
my sister, my dog? That night I wrote in my journal: *I owe
it to myself to clear my stagnant energy, once and for all. No
matter the outcome of this biopsy, this is the path I must take.*
(*What biopsy? They won't even be able to find it on Monday.*)

As I fell asleep, I placed my hand on my left breast,
visioning radiant blue light flushing out my lymph nodes,
a healing strategy I'd learned from Norman Vincent Peale's
books on imaging.

Saturday morning, I sought a Reiki treatment. Although
a Level II practitioner myself, my energy was too depleted to
effectively perform Reiki on myself. I randomly called Gina
(who'd later become my Reiki master) because her listing
included the word *healing*. She agreed to see me later that
day, filling me with gratitude for the gift of two healing
professionals making themselves available to this needy
stranger on a weekend.

As I meditated during the day, my mother sent a message
from beyond. I heard her voice clearly intone, *You are perfect;
you are well.* I was buoyed by the support provided in this
and other realms. Like a glider airplane propelled by gusts of
wind, when I started to go down, another gust came along
to keep me afloat.

After Gina did a full Reiki treatment, she told me she
felt no energy moving in my left breast. It was stagnant.
Trapped. "Please go in again and work on it some more," I
pleaded as I lay on her table. "My goal is to have this lump
gone by Monday."

"It doesn't necessarily work like that," she softly
responded.

When she again placed her hand on my breast, I felt pulsating and could feel a shift inside my body. I next felt cramping in my rectal area as if disease were exiting.

Then the sensation was over.

I felt healed. Yet neither of us spoke of that possibility. "Start envisioning healthy breasts instead of diseased breasts," she instructed. An exhortation similar to Susan's the night before.

I went for two more sessions that weekend, feeling calm and healed.

For good measure, Sunday evening, I called my cousin in New Mexico. Marianne agreed to do hypnosis over the phone to ease my anxiety and aid my healing. She took me through a guided meditation, where a bubble of light would reveal the one who'd best help me through this ordeal. I smiled to myself, confident my mother would appear.

As the bubble opened, I saw my mother – and then my father bumped her out of the way, announcing, "Don't worry, honey. It'll be okay." I laughed – he always did compete with his wife for their daughters' attention. And he excelled at physical comedy as well as crises. I went to bed that night confident my father would be there for me, despite our contentious history. Perhaps our relationship would further heal during this experience. Perhaps this was all part of my emotional healing.

Monday morning found me filled with angst. Despite my best efforts to believe and to beat back fear, I was no longer confident anything had changed. I lay in bed with a knotted stomach and looked around my bedroom as if for the last time. I would be safe if I didn't leave my bed.

My eyes landed on a book given to me by a departing employee a few years before. When she'd handed it to me, she'd said, "I've always found what I need in this book." I'd placed it on my bookshelf because, frankly, it looked too religious for me. But that morning, I was guided to read, finding life-altering messages on its pages. I recorded them in my journal as quickly as I could move my pen across the page:

*Negative thoughts always defeat the manifestations
of your heart's desire...Prepare for your blessings,
rejoice and give thanks, and it will come to pass...
The God-power is within you, your superconscious
mind. It is the realm of miracles and wonders. Quick
and seemingly impossible changes take place for your
good...God's gift to us is power...Choose faith over
fear.*

Choose faith over fear. Florence Scovel Shinn had written
these words in the 1920s. She was an artist-turned-
metaphysicist and spiritual teacher whom Louise Hay
acknowledged as an early influence on her own more
contemporary work. In that moment, it seemed Shinn had
written that book just for me and had been waiting for me
to discover it.

I somehow got myself showered and eventually behind
the wheel, headed to the hospital. Determined to apply one
more modality to keep fear at bay, I played Dr. Andrew Weil's
sound healing music. Also called vibrational medicine,
sound waves can attune the brain to relax and heal the body.

"What's that crap?" I heard a familiar voice say. "Let's
listen to something fun, like Dean Martin."

My father appeared in the passenger seat, wearing his
iconic straw hat, plaid pants, and yellow shirt. At first startled
by his three-dimensional presence, I then remembered
he'd promised during hypnosis to accompany me to the
biopsy. Although it wasn't the soundtrack I'd intended for
my somber ride, I fumbled around to find my Dean Martin
CD as I drove. When my dad was alive, Dino was our
compromise musical artist, bridging the generation gap. We
couldn't argue when we were singing *That's Amore.*

My mood lifted; my dad and I sang *Volare* over and over
again, all the way to the hospital. To the stereotactic biopsy.

At the hospital, I nervously undressed, feeling foolish for
believing I could impact the outcome. I climbed onto the
cool table and waited. The doctor arrived and set out with

the probe to find the suspicious lump. He stared long and hard at the screen. I watched his face anxiously, my left hand behind my head, my sheet-draped body turned to the right. He sighed and scowled as he moved the probe around.

"What's the matter?" I asked, beginning to shake on the table.

"Oh, he's just trying to find the best place to approach the lump from," the dutiful technician chirped.

"It's gone, isn't it?" More a statement of affirmation than a question for the doctor.

"No, it's not gone," the doctor responded with annoyance. "I just don't see anything warranting a biopsy."

"I won't be disappointed if you tell me I can leave," I said, holding my breath.

What biopsy? They won't even be able to find it on Monday.

My dad, who I could now see sitting in a chair – his yellow shirt a beacon in the antiseptic room – rose to stand beside the table. "C'mon. Let's go," he commanded in his characteristically-demanding tone. I wondered if others could see or hear him.

"What I see is clearly benign," the doctor slowly uttered. "We could biopsy it anyway, but I don't see any reason to...." He shook his head, murmuring to the technician that I should return in three months because of his colleague's concern, not because of his findings.

They left the room, and I fell to my knees in gratitude, the sheet draping my prayerful form. I sobbed with joy and then left the exam room to get dressed. On my way out, I pulled the curtain back and peeked into the examining room to emblazon on my brain the memory of what had transpired.

I was startled to see my father back in the chair, waiting for me. It had seemed like a stress-induced illusion before, but there he was again. "Let's go, Dad," I said out loud with a laugh. He grinned, stood up, and followed me out. He disappeared before I reached the car, having fulfilled his promise to support me through the process.

I called Gina from the parking lot. "I knew the lump

had cleared after that first session – I felt it break up – but didn't want to tell you in case you'd cancel the biopsy," she admitted. "It's important to verify results using medical technology."

Trust, but verify.

"And, by the way," she adds. "Your dad is often present at our Reiki sessions."

I called Susan and select friends who'd supported me along the way. They each told me what they'd done energetically to influence the outcome. I'd not realized so many friends believed in energy healing; it hadn't been openly acknowledged previously.

But over the next few weeks, I was approached by others who didn't trust the results, thought I'd put too much faith in energy healing. Voicemails and emails telegraphed their advice to get another opinion – some quite resolute. I began to doubt my experience, to question my own reality. So I conferred with the hospital's director of imaging who reviewed my records: "If you want another opinion, go somewhere else because this report is quite clear. No concern is warranted."

At the follow-up exam three months later, after on-going energy work, visioning, and prayer, no lump was detected. In fact, other benign cysts that had previously been detected in the mammogram had disappeared.

Before leaving the exam room, I told the medical staff of my healing journey, including my belief that my deceased dad had been with me at the previous visit. The two women stared at me in silence until one mumbled, "Well, whatever you did seemed to work."

It doesn't matter if they didn't believe me; it was my truth. Maybe if more people confessed to holistic and spiritual healings, energy medicine would be more readily accepted.

When I shared the outcome with Rick on the phone, he flatly responded, "That's wonderful...but it was already true before they verified it for you. You didn't have to wait for those results to be well."

Rick is hard-wired that way; he believes *all is well* even in the face of adversity. He's right, of course: It was already true before the doctor declared it, but I doubted my own intuition, being so dependent on medical professionals to diagnose what's happening in my own body. I wish I hadn't needed the doctor to confirm it in order to trust what I felt, wish I could have trusted the messages from the Universe. *Do I offend the Universe by continuing to doubt, despite powerful manifestations?* This remains a recurring theme of my faith journey.

Although I wasn't as brave as I wanted to be, I was stronger than I'd been in the past. I learned fear can be beaten back, and healing can occur, with faith and intention. I posted health affirmations by Florence Scovel Shinn to my bedside bookcase:

> *In nothing be anxious.*
> *My divine design is perfect.*
> *Divine love floods my consciousness with health.*
> *Every cell in my body is filled with divine light.*
> *I give thanks for this perfect day. Miracles shall*
> *follow miracles, and wonders shall never cease.*
> *Let me now express the divine design in my mind,*
> *body, and actions.*
> *Infinite Spirit, reveal to me the way.*

I integrated Donna Eden's *5-Minute Energy Routine* into my morning and continued to go for Reiki treatments. They were calming, helping to balance my compulsive psyche. To still my monkey brain. Gina encouraged me to enter master-level Reiki training to deepen my understanding and spiritual practice. To fill the void where hope had been vanquished.

Signing-on was a major risk because it meant I had to walk the talk. It was time for me to get serious. Thus, began my journey seeking a deeper consciousness of, and connection to, the healing power of the divinity, whatever or wherever one conceives it to be. I recreated an altar – an inclusive altar. My childhood statue of Mary, her head cracked and glued, stands beside Quan Yin who stands next to a replica of the Brazilian statue of Christ the Redeemer with outstretched arms as a symbol of peace.

My own healing experience coupled with the master-level attunement was perfect training for what I must now do to address my puppy's obstruction.

＊ ＊ ＊

As we lie on our shared mattress on the floor, I whisper to Dolly, "Blue light running through your intestines, dissipating...dissipating." I'm not exactly sure what those words mean, but the phrasing intuitively comes to me as I place my hands on her abdomen.

All night, I lie awake tracing her intestinal track with my hand. Up and down her warm body. She lies motionless, tonight not the active puppy I've grown to love.

I petition her in the words of Ernest Hemingway: "Be strong in all the broken places."

I hear a bubbling sound: *POP-POP-POP-POP-POP-POP.* I wonder if it's my heating system or something else mechanical, so regular the rhythm. Every fifteen seconds: *POP!* But there's no noise source nearby; it must be her body or mine making that sound.

My own stomach then gurgles from hunger as if to show me what that sounds like. It's not what I heard. I watch Dolly's mouth, wondering if she could be making those noises. She's not. It's a sound unlike any I've ever heard from a living creature. I decide to believe it sprang from her body: Her energy shifted when she accepted and absorbed the healing energy from my hands.

Without a wink of sleep, I return Dolly to the vet the next morning to confirm what I believe is already true.

Trust, but verify.

They conduct more tests while I sit in the waiting room. "The x-rays show her intestines have cleared," the vet reports. "She must've passed a lot of gas last night."

Having been snugly on a mattress beside her all night, I wasn't aware of her expelling gas; every dog owner knows what dog farts sound and smell like. Nor was that the mechanical popping sound I heard.

I'm allowed a moment of relief and gratitude before the vet adds, "But her stomach remains bloated, indicating there's still an obstruction."

DAMN IT! I'd only directed healing energy to her intestines, not to her stomach.

"Be specific with your intentions," Gina always advises. "Be crystal clear to avoid unintended consequences. Be demanding." That's what the Law of Attraction is all about: Know your intention and put it forth to the Universe.

But be demanding with God and angels? Really? The *Our Father* prayer imploring *Your will be done* suggests it shouldn't be about what we want. Then there's *Matthew* 6:26: "Look at the birds of the air; they do not sow or reap or store away in barns, and yet your heavenly Father feeds them. Are you not much more valuable than they?" In Catholic school, I was taught this means God knows what's best for us so we shouldn't be telling "him" what to do. Yet reading a little further, *Matthew* 7:7-8 instructs, "Ask, and you will receive; seek, and you will find; knock, and the door will be opened to you. For everyone who asks will receive, and anyone who seeks will find, and the door will be opened to those who knock."

Doesn't this contradict the "birds of the air" thing?

I've struggled my entire life to accept the notion of *Let go, let God.* It seems too risky to leave the outcome to someone else, even if that someone else happens to be God. But what if the recipient of the prayerful benefits has to be the one to sort it out for themselves? This is more consistent with the Reiki blessing I was taught – and have successfully used: "I offer you this gift of healing energy with love. When you accept it, you will use it for your highest good." Because our highest good is often not what we're hoping for, sometimes quite the contrary.

Perhaps it's up to the intercessor to simply draw attention to the situation, like flagging down a police officer when someone's in an accident. I wouldn't tell the cop what to do – I'd just expect him to summon needed resources.

At this age, how can it be that I don't know the right way to pray? Is there a right way?

Feeling defeated, I ask the vet for more time before consenting to cutting Dolly open. They agree to do more testing before proceeding. I leave Dolly there once more, resolving to send her Reiki while we're apart. I ask Gina to send healing to Dolly as well, and she agrees, although admittedly not a dog-person.

Ethically and spiritually, a recipient's permission should be obtained before sending healing energy. Some consider it a karmic violation to not do so. My own attempts have met with noticeable rejection when I didn't consult the object of my well-intended, yet misguided, efforts. My wrist painfully cramped when I tried to send healing to my dad the night before he died. It was his time to go – no intervention called for. My estranged sister has also energetically rejected my attempted sends over the years.

Animals can't grant permission but, depending on their own karmic journey, can reject healing energy. If they're open to it, the results lend greater credibility to the practice since pets aren't susceptible to the placebo effect. According to Dr. Doreen Virtue in her book *Angel Medicine*, "Animals respond very quickly to healing energy that's sent to them." Anxiety, doubt, and defensiveness don't get in their way. Mind games don't kick in; their response is purely visceral.

In Reiki, sending healing energy to another involves invoking the distance symbol while envisioning the recipient's face and saying their name. One hand then draws the remaining symbols in the opposite hand, and the intended recipient is energetically held between both hands. Consistent with the butterfly effect – chaos theory's premise that a small localized change in a complex system can cause larger changes elsewhere in the system – most

Reiki recipients can feel the infusion of healing energy no matter the distance.

As Gina had taught me, I write out my intention for the send: *A perfect gastrointestinal system for Dolly. All clear.* I intone the now-familiar words: "I bless the Divine within you. I offer you this gift of healing energy with love..." My hands start shaking – back and forth, back and forth – until the written intention falls from my hands into my lap.

Exhausted after a sleepless night, I fall into a peaceful slumber after the send. It takes energy to send energy.

Waking from my nap, I immediately call the vet – earlier than they'd instructed. I'm told the barium is now moving freely throughout Dolly's entire system.

All clear!

Surgery is not needed. Dolly is healed.

The vet isn't sure what made the difference because they hadn't treated her – only conducted more diagnostics. But I know: Reiki shifted her energy.

I take my Dolly home, where she will continue to shift my consciousness.

Each morning now, I conduct a morning ritual of "sweeping" her. I run my hands from her head to her tail, telling her I'm brushing off anything she doesn't want in or on her body. Things like disease and pain. I rid her of any negative energy that might be clinging to her from a past experience or might attach as a result of a new issue. I also perform what Donna Eden terms a *spinal flush* to clear Dolly's neurolymphatic reflex points.

Dolly lies there and seems to "get it." Like waiting patiently when I smudge her with burning sage. Perhaps all I'm really doing is showering her with attention. Whatever it is, it seems to be working, like the radiology nurse had reluctantly offered three years before. Despite setbacks, Dolly is generally a healthy, happy young dog.

Today, she reciprocates – another common practice in Reiki: The recipient is expected to give something in exchange for receiving. Reiki shares are quite common

– a group of people get together to take turns giving and receiving treatments. I wasn't aware of the inter-species possibility until now, however.

While I'm on the floor giving myself Reiki after yoga, Dolly nudges my arm. By now, I know just to give in and pet her – she's persistent. But I'm annoyed that she's interrupting my own self-care routine, given all the effort I expend on her well-being.

I stroke her chest as her red head looms over me, saliva dripping from her mouth. Onto my face.

I tell her to lie down. She does, always a pleasant surprise.

Her left paw lands on my chest – displacing my hand, which had been encouraging my heart and breast health. I reciprocate and put that hand on her spine, creating a circuit of energy between us. She next puts her head where my other hand had been.

The warmth from her body permeates mine – in exactly the places I'd been tending to myself. *Be strong in all the broken places.* It feels loving and therapeutic. Dolly didn't interrupt anything; she initiated a Reiki share. We're proof-positive that *shift happens.*

Left Behind

A mass movement is afoot in the world today,
spiritual in nature and radical in its implications...
Things we thought were primitive beliefs turn out to
be more sophisticated than we are.
                                        - Marianne Williamson

Cell phones start beeping in rapid succession signaling notices from the National Weather Service. Sirens from local firehouses begin to blare.

The training on healing with essential oils is suspended; attendees are instructed to relocate to an interior room with no windows.

I have to get home to Dolly.

Racing toward the exit door, I'm stopped several times by strangers warning that this storm is very dangerous, so I shouldn't be on the road. I tell them I must get home to my dog, although I know it sounds lame, like an eccentric old woman living alone with nine cats.

They insist the storm is moving quickly in our direction; I resent them costing me precious time. Pushing past the self-appointed gatekeepers, I run to my car in a torrential downpour, splashing through two-inch puddles. Thunder roars and lightning cracks the black sky as I pray I won't encounter fallen trees. Grave warnings emit from my car radio: *Stay off the roads. Seek shelter in a basement immediately.*

My Dolly needs me; she'll be frightened alone. If I don't get there, who will take care of her? One of the many hazards of single-parenting anything.

Dolly meets me at the door, wide-eyed and panting. On my knees, I hug her, saying I could never leave her behind. The paths of several potential tornadoes are being tracked on television, two headed in our direction. The meteorologist again sounds the alarm: *Seek shelter in a basement immediately, if possible.*

Upstate New York, like the rest of the world, has been

experiencing increasingly violent weather as a result of climate change. Some storms have left a swath more than a mile wide, devastating entire communities. I can hear the deafening, howling wind. With no time to waste, I grab Dolly and carry her down the basement steps. I run back up to get her water and kibble in case of a long siege. After getting her settled, I begin to think about what else I might want to save in the eventuality of a funnel cloud touching down, scattering my possessions to Kingdom Come. As if filming a documentary, my eyes scan my living room in slow motion. I see my stuff fused with my parents' stuff. Stuff they left behind that I can't yet bear to part with.

After they died, I hauled boxes of their belongings to my basement; there was no time to be selective. I've fondled each piece and reminisced about its role in my parents' lives, in my life. The dusty treasures only had meaning because of the people with whom they were associated. Stuff holds no inherent memories, except for the people who touched it - and you - along the way. People give stuff life; people give it value.

The desk I coveted – nearly came to blows over with my sister – is cracked and scratched. Hardly worth the additional damage it did to our relationship. Stuff can ruin relationships, as well as recall them.

Things are just that: things. We all have too many; we all want more. But they're nothing in the end. How sad to part with, but how ludicrous to have, so much stuff. After all, memories are intangible, aren't they?

It would be devastating to lose any belongings in a storm, but there's only one thing I couldn't bear to lose – my journals, the only "documents" I keep in fireproof boxes. They provide me with a roadmap of where I've been and contemplations about where I'm going. They tell my life story, biblio-photography of my journey.

Complicit with truth's mercurial nature, journaling is a forgiving practice, allowing us to question and contradict ourselves and others. It helps us stop believing what we think. To peel back the layers of an experience toward a greater understanding of what happened. To leave trauma behind, in a safe place that neutralizes its power over us. Correspondingly, benefits include personal growth and a significant reduction in stress-related illnesses.

I run to my bedroom, grab the two heavy fireproof boxes from under the bed, and lug them down the basement steps. I secure my laptop next, as some of my musings are recorded electronically.

A few cookies and a pitcher of water, and I'm ready for what the storm may bring. I have my dog and my journals.

Dolly lies at my feet as we wait, listening to the thrashing and crashing of the storm outside. I feel gratitude for having a roof over my head. And a dog I love enough to risk my life for.

Two hours later, a friend calls to give the "all clear." Dolly and I emerge from our refuge, but I leave my journals in the basement – just in case.

* * *

As fall blankets the mountains, Dolly and I leave the lake and woods behind, returning to a development on a dead-end lane – a two-bedroom residence I maintain for the more desolate winter months. She readily adjusts to this townhouse near Saratoga Springs, New York. Wall-to-wall carpeting enables her to dash around the antique furnishings without wiping out; she can graze-at-will in the grass like the billy goat she is. But mostly, she's enamored with Kevin – a neighbor tending his thirteen-year-old dog, Corey, who's nearing the Rainbow Bridge.

I first learned of the Rainbow Bridge from a book our veterinarian sent when Punkin died. It's a fabled after-life destination where deceased dogs wait for their masters to cross over:

> *The dogs all run and play together, but the day comes*
> *when one suddenly stops and looks into the distance.*
> *Her bright eyes are intent; her eager body begins to*

quiver. Suddenly she begins to run from the group,
flying over the green grass, her legs carrying her faster
and faster. You have been spotted, and when you and
your special friend finally meet, you cling together in
joyous reunion. The happy kisses rain upon your face;
your hands again caress the beloved head, and you
look once more into the trusting eyes of your pet, so
long gone from your life but never absent from your
heart.

Pet owners take comfort believing they'll be reunited with their loyal companions one day. It helps us get through the long days and longer nights when they leave us. Many mediums claim to channel messages from pets who have passed. I've received a few direct messages myself. Unsolicited, my dogs have "come through," playful and happy – and want me to be too.

If there is a Rainbow Bridge where pets all gather, I wonder if Punkin could get along with Dryphuss and Rusty. He liked being an only child and is now likely a troll who won't let others cross the bridge until he's exacted a toll. Especially from Nicholas!

Peering out a living room window, Dolly sits for hours hoping "Uncle Kevin" will appear. I rearrange the furniture so she has an unobstructed view. She barks excitedly the minute he steps out his door, enjoining me to unite them by letting her out. Kevin loves Dolly too. He laughs at her antics and scoops her up in his arms, hugging her close. He ignores the discipline I'm trying to instill, causing his wife, Doris, to chide him. Corey, however, isn't at all smitten with this young, energetic competitor. He pretends Dolly doesn't exist as he ambles past our house on their now-short walks. Every once in a while, I hear a low growl, meant for oblivious Dolly, from this canine patriarch of our lane. But Dolly doesn't care about Corey; she runs past him to get to Kevin.

It's a good thing she has Kevin because I've recently accepted a part-time administrative position with a local school district. There's a shortage of certified administrators in public education, so retirees are often asked to serve as interims until suitable hires can be recruited. This opportunity comes at a good time: Dolly can be left for a few hours without toileting.

Dolly's elimination schedule dictates my work schedule. Fitting somehow. In fact, the majority of dog owners admit they plan their free time around their dog's eating and toileting routines.

Returning home after a busy afternoon reviewing teacher tenure recommendations, I find Dolly lying by the couch, even though I'm later than intended. I'm so proud of her. So proud, in fact, I decide it's okay to leave her again to meet a friend for dinner. I feed and toilet her, breathing a sigh of relief that she's on her way to being that adult dog I'd intended to get...someday. Perhaps the worst is behind us.

"Bye, Dolly," I breezily say as I leave again. "Be a good girl." Words every dog hates to hear. Words Dolly will choose to ignore.

When I return two hours later, a corner of the living room carpeting is between Dolly's teeth. She's pulling it toward her while looking at me sideways, inviting me to join this game of tug.

I maniacally scream at her, causing her to run from the room. The corner of the wall-to-wall is chewed up. Slobbery. She didn't ingest much of it – just unraveled it beyond salvation.

I curse myself as much as I curse her. I should have known that boredom would get the best of this still-immature pup. She'd been left alone too long today. And I'd prematurely stopped using the crate, allowing her free rein in the house. My fault, not hers, I reconcile.

For the next few weeks, I stick closer to home. My furry warden demands I remain under house arrest, only allowing me time off to go to work for short stints.

The following week, after a few grueling hours of policy review, I return home to see brown bamboo shafts jutting out of Dolly's crumpled mouth when she jauntily greets me. She'd treated herself to the new basket I'd bought yesterday to hold her toys. I didn't realize it would also serve as a culinary delight. But she did – eating one-quarter of the basket in my absence. Dry heaves and stomach-churning follow, then diarrhea. And more diarrhea. In my carpeted townhouse.

This after recently avoiding surgery for an obstruction.

Concerned about toxins, such as melamine, that the Made-in-China weave might contain, I consider calling the vet or taking her to the emergency clinic. Thousands of pets have died over the years, presumably from food and treats made with ingredients sourced from China. Although the FDA has yet to pinpoint the exact cause, large pet food retailers are pulling such food from shelves.

Instead of rushing off for medical intervention, I decide to apply what I've been researching since Dolly's last issue: using one's own energy, as well as that of the natural and supernatural worlds, to rid the body of disease. To shift energy, a practice that's been applied in domains as diverse as churches and operating rooms.

In 1879, Mary Eddy Baker founded the Christian Science religion, which chooses prayer over western medicine – directing intentions for good health and healing to God. Similarly, prayer circles and prayer chains are organized by other faiths because they've been shown to be effective healing applications. Prayer is distinct from positive thinking (but not mutually exclusive), as the former invokes a divinity while the latter requires an internal shift in perception. Norman Cousins' 1979 groundbreaking book on self-healing, entitled *Anatomy of an Illness,* told the story of how this highly-regarded journalist and professor cured himself of a perceived irreversible disease through positive thinking and laughter. Shifting his own energy. Renowned surgeon Dr. Bernie Siegel has written dozens of books testifying to the power of *love, medicine and miracles.* He applies all three and touts their combined efficacy. Recent studies on the power of placebos support the belief in mind over matter, thereby validating the Law of Attraction as a form of energy healing.

Donna Eden, too, teaches that our bodies are capable of healing themselves. But our increasingly toxic environment interferes with their ability to do so, requiring us to boost our immunity through "practices that are natural, friendly, and familiar to body, mind and soul." Practices western medicine has left behind.

Eden's and Feinstein's seminal book, *Energy Medicine: How to Use Your Body's Energies for Optimum Health and Vitality,* defines this as "the art and science of fostering physical, psychological, and spiritual health and well-being. It combines a rational knowledge and intuitive understanding of the energies in the body and in the environment." The goal is to realign our energy systems back to their natural state of health. Shifting our energy.

Healing modalities to do so include visioning/imaging, prayer/meditation, sound waves/music, laying on of hands (Reiki, healing touch, massage), gentle body movement (yoga, tai chi, qi gong), Traditional Chinese Medicine (acupuncture and herbs), homeopathy crystals, aromatherapy, and magnetic therapy. They may seem primitive compared to the hallmarks of western medicine – synthetic drugs and technology. Studies have shown that most patients feel they haven't been effectively treated without getting at least one allopathic prescription, a consequence of our fear-based western practices and our medicalized lives.

It's incorrect to label these healing modalities "alternative" medicine because they are the *original* medicine – traditional curatives discovered by shaman and other indigenous people. They're not "New Age" either, since many have been effectively used prior to the Middle Ages. *Complementary, natural, holistic,* or *integrative* treatments are more accurate descriptors.

My basket-case dog needs my intervention after ingesting so much bamboo. First making sure bamboo isn't poisonous to dogs, I choose a combination of modalities. Instead of withholding food until the diarrhea clears, I fill her bowl and draw Reiki symbols over it, reciting, "I bless the Divine within you. I offer you this gift of healing energy with love..." As Dolly gobbles the food, I visualize little soldiers chasing after toxins. Imaging.

I next smudge her and the house with burning sage so her surroundings support healing. She stands still as the fragrant smoke swirls around her head. I expect she might cough, but she breathes it in with no adverse reaction.

The healing ceremony over, she runs around with no obvious discomfort. She sleeps through the night and when I take her outside the next morning, she eliminates the basket weavings in a "normal" fashion.

The healing power of energy medicine is still new to me as a practice, so I'm hesitant to give voice to it, not wanting to be thought strange or weird, my lifelong trepidation of being different surfacing again. But Dolly is a safe and silent partner in these age-old practices, giving me plenty of opportunities to experiment. A mixed blessing.

As work demands intensify, I realize I need more formal puppy care. Part-time jobs never fit into part-time hours. Although Kevin is willing to take Dolly out when I get stranded, he reports that she gazes up at him adoringly instead of doing her business. "I'm out there with her so long, people think I'm a homeless man in a field with a dog," he quips. "Dolly seems to be waiting for ME to poop."

Some well-meaning friends have pointed out that Dolly prefers people to other dogs. To be a therapy dog, she'll also need to relate to other pets, so I enroll her in doggie daycare. It's offered nearby one day a week; I rearrange my schedule to put in a full day's work on Mondays and only a few hours the rest of the week. Problem solved. Supervision and new playmates for Dolly. And a day away from Dolly for me.

Each Monday, Dolly eagerly runs to the door of the daycare center, which is a good thing because I'm always running late. The owner takes her leash, and off I dash shouting over my shoulder, "Have fun! Be a good girl." But after a few weeks, I notice Dolly's face is taut and her eyes are red when I pick her up, a sign of canine stress Dryphuss exhibited when first adopted. She runs to me panting, tugging on her leash to leave. So the following week, I stay to observe.

I watch Dolly hesitantly enter the large pen, and I sharply inhale when the other dogs begin to chase her. Both smaller and larger dogs – six in all – chase a panting Dolly. Like a wild pack of wolves. Her tail is tucked between her legs as she's cornered by them. Some growl as they face her down.

She's shaking and whining. So am I when I ask the owner what's going on.

"That's what happens when Dolly's late," she tells me matter-of-factly. "Dogs are territorial, and they've already claimed the pen by the time she shows up. She's an intruder, so they go after her."

Dolly couldn't tell me herself, but I should have remembered her hiding under my chair, away from the other puppies, at her first puppy training class. I'm remorseful that my habitual tardiness has created this situation for her; I should have brought her earlier. I should have made sure she was okay. I should have been on time, not always doing one more thing before leaving the house.

SHOULD HAVE!

SHOULD HAVE!

SHOULD HAVE!

Always do your best.

But mostly, I'm annoyed I wasn't advised sooner that daycare hasn't been going well for her.

"What can we do about that now?" I ask, my vocal cords about to snap.

"Bring her early from now on so she goes into the pen first. Let her claim the space as her own. Then she'll have dominance over the territory, and it'll balance power among the dogs."

In truth, I don't want to bring Dolly back here or anywhere

– ever. I think about parents putting their young children on the school bus for the first time, surrendering control over what happens to them for the next eight hours. After five years of protecting their children – of having primary sway over them – parents bear witness as their precious little ones become subject to outside stimuli that will forever change the ratio of influence between family and the outside world.

I used to emphasize this point at our new employee orientations: *Parents entrust their children to us. It's our job to send them home in the same condition they arrive in. Or better. If not protected from bullies, kids may come home from school battered and bruised. Worse yet, they can be scarred on the inside.*

That's what's been happening to Dolly at daycare.

The owner's explanation and remedy make sense though. And it's important Dolly conquer her fear of other dogs. Trusting the owner's experience with canine socialization, I agree to try her proposed strategy.

But right now, Dolly's going home with me.

It's readily apparent the following week that the plan doesn't work. Suzanne Clothier's book would later help me understand why: Dolly was a new addition to an established group of dogs, and she exuded fear the minute she entered the pen. Dogs target "the unsure, the immature, or the downright frightened," Clothier writes. Dolly met all three criteria. And the bullying had gone on too long for any of the dogs to change their behavior.

No new tricks for them.

Not too long after we withdraw from daycare, a neighbor's terrier sinks her teeth into Dolly's ankle and hangs on, similar to what happened to my dad at that dinner party. And equally horrifying to watch.

These experiences reinforce Dolly's preference for people over others of her species and have created a crisis of confidence for her, the aftershocks of which will be felt for a long time.

They've given me a healthy respect for the lupine instincts

that still stubbornly cling to every domestic dog's DNA. For virtual retribution and empowerment, I buy Dolly a stuffed terrier so she can exact revenge by sinking her teeth into it. I feel like biting it myself. I'm tired of snarly dogs.

Dolly and I become inseparable once again. There seems to be no easy way to leave her behind.

So much for being untethered in my retirement years.

I adjust my schedule to work shorter hours, more days. A friend points out that I now use the pronoun *we* in conversation: "We're good" or "We just got in from a walk." My voicemail message is now plural: "We're not home right now, but if you'd like to leave us a message..."

As testimony to our fusion, when I run into a neighbor shopping, he asks, "Where's your dog?"

That's an odd question, I thought. *After all, I am in a store.*

"She's home?" I respond with that upspeak that should never be used at the end of a declarative sentence.

"Oh. I don't think I've ever seen you without her."

Ain't that the truth.

However, neighbors in the mountains believe they see Dolly without me.

"We have your dog," their voicemail announces. "We've brought her into our house, so come get her when you can."

This message is so out of context that it seems like a ransom note gone wrong. Even though Dolly's sitting right next to me, the thought of not knowing where she is terrifies me. I can't allow myself to even consider a time when she'd no longer be my charge, as restrictive as that might feel to both of us at times. For a second, I wonder if it's possible she isn't really here, and I just think she is, like a phantom or hologram.

I'm transported back to the night my cat Twinkle didn't come home. A young girl in a pink flannel nightgown, I called her repeatedly from the back porch: "Here, Twinkle. Come, Twinkle." But unlike every other night, my tabby didn't come. I cried myself to sleep after being told I couldn't stay up to wait for her. The next morning, I ran downstairs, certain she'd be there.

"Here, Twinkle. Here, kitty, kitty, kitty."

I put out her food in anticipation. I called her name out the porch door for three days and nights until my parents told me to stop – she was gone, they declared.

I didn't give up. On the fourth morning, I called for her again, my throat raw, my eyes red from crying.

"Here, Twinkle. Here, kitty. Please? Please?"

And Twinkle appeared! There she was, running from my swing set to the porch. Twinkle came home!

The memory of that silence, calling a name into an abyss with no response, lingers. The vastness of a dark night can swallow up almost everything. Except the memory of loss.

Although I always know where Dolly is, she must watch me leave without knowing what might happen next. She has no choice but to trust I'll return. She doesn't necessarily want to come with me, yet doesn't want to be left behind either.

I know the feeling. Sometimes neither option satisfies.

I like to think she'd miss me if we were separated long-term. Pre-Dolly, I'd traveled to New Orleans to help dogs left behind after Hurricane Katrina. I walked those lucky enough to be rescued. Frankie Blue Eyes, a pit bull mix, would only walk backward, never taking his eyes off the shelter, the one place he felt safe in that decimated city. With a similar attachment, Dolly walks home faster than she leaves home behind. Maybe we all do.

A phone call interrupts my reflections: "The golden we found wasn't yours. But you probably knew that. She belongs to another neighbor. Sorry we bothered you."

It's ridiculous that I'm relieved Dolly isn't the one lost, but I'm happy they found the owner looking for a dog resembling her. Once you've loved a dog, you can't dismiss a lost one. It becomes your obligation to reunite him with his people, just as you hope someone would do for your dog. Like the dog wears a sign reading, *Take care of this dog until we find him.*

Dogs don't intend to leave their families behind – but

adventure calls! My neighbors understood what a rogue dog represents: a family's broken heart. I'd later learn they'd found Dolly's clone covered with mud down by the lake and soon thereafter heard the owners desperately calling for her up and down the road: "Here, Princess. Come, Princess."

Here, Twinkle. Come, Twinkle.

As a reward after a walk, I sometimes unclip my princess' leash to let her run free down the dead-end lane. She hears the click and knows she's liberated to take off at her own pace. To leave me behind. But she often stays right by my side. While I'm grateful for her compliance, her subjugation sometimes saddens me. Dogs are built to run, to explore. Instead, she's learning to mirror my scripted life. My domesticated life.

Suppression and control can do that to a dog...or a person. Even when the yoke is removed, we remain imprisoned in our minds. We need to be re-introduced to the ways of freedom; we need to be mentally released. Because to cope with our captivity, we often let go of our desire to be free. It's too painful to not have what we desperately want. Those who hang onto that desire for freedom, like Nelson Mandela, eventually find their way out of enslavement. Those who find their voice lead others out and reach their true humanity. *Man's Search for Meaning* by Dr. Viktor E. Frankl burned that lesson into my psyche decades ago, a life-changing read.

The term *Stockholm Syndrome* was coined over forty years ago to explain why bank hostages had formed an attachment to their captors. Initially convinced they were going to die, they became grateful for even the smallest acts of kindness. Similarly, a dog brutally beaten by his owner to turn him into a guard dog still eagerly awaits his owner's return for whatever kindness he may offer. Or is that just a dog's forgiving nature?

Judging by her resistance at the time, Dolly must have thought she was going to die when I first buckled the collar around her neck – then became certain of it when I attached a leash. As her jailer, I've been able to earn her compliance with rewards and consequences. Is Dolly's bonding to me simply a way to get her basic needs met? Do we misinterpret or personify dogs' ingratiation as love?

I choose to believe not. I love having a furry shadow, although at times I feel trapped in a scene from *Groundhog Day* during which events predictably repeat themselves.

After Dolly steps in her own poop, skootches her butt on the ground, and lands all four paws in mud as it starts to pour, I tell her, "Dolly, just go, will ya?"

She looks at me in bewilderment, her untethered leash flaccid on the ground.

"Leave, and don't come back! Go where you can be as gross as you want without regard for human decency."

I sound harsh, I know. A single mom at her breaking point. She's a dog – she doesn't care about human decency. I'm not even making sense!

Dolly doesn't budge – doesn't leave my side, even as I flail my arms in exasperation.

If Dolly had heeded my command to run off, there'd be no words to describe my devastation. Perhaps it's a good thing she's not *that* compliant or doesn't know what the hell I'm saying most of the time. I grab her leash, and she follows me to the door. As disgusting as dogs can be, she isn't any happier about this predicament than I am. I tell her she's a good girl and give her treats, realizing I'm not exactly dog-whisperer material. We're both imperfect.

I wash her feet, one paw at a time, in a bucket of warm water, which she tries to kick over. Like a cow.

I recently had a waking dream that if Dolly's paw were stuck in a train track and a train were coming, I'd try to free her for as long as it took, even if it meant I, too, might be crushed. And later dreamt there was a fire in our home and, since I couldn't get Dolly out, chose to stay with her.

I could never leave Dolly behind. Not anymore.

Yet there are still times when my dreams reveal my own wanderlust, the freedom of a dog-free life. And as she lies curled up in her bed, Dolly's frenetic paws expose her own fanciful adventures, upon which she occasionally acts. Leaving me behind.

Fall transitions to winter. Dolly experiences her first snow. And I observe the world through a new lens. The lens of a puppy.

What happened to your world?
Snow-covered grass
Buried twigs, pinecones, leaves
Scents have vanished
Overnight

More surprised by what's falling from the sky
Than what's on the ground
You jump up to meet snowflakes
Catching them in your warm puppy mouth
As clumsy paws slide on boot-tromped snow

You don't mind the icy chill
Your coat serves any season
I close your ear flaps to shield tender skin
They flip again when you prance
Nose-upward, gazing in wonderment

While I mourn gentler weather
You're undeterred by cold winds
Like a native to this land, you bond with nature
Wise to the certainty of change
With no illusions of sameness and forever.

* * *

I'm expecting a package, so I'm waiting for the letter carrier before I head out for the holiday. As I pace, I realize I have no gift for her.

Nothing I can do about it now, I thought.

Then I remember the ornaments with Dolly's photo I'd

purchased as gifts. Karen has a golden of her own. That would be perfect!

But I only have one left, and that's on my own tree.

When her mail truck pulls up a few minutes later, Karen gives me a big grin and shouts, "Merry Christmas!"

That's when I decide to give her my one remaining Dolly ornament. After all, I have the real thing.

While she delivers mail to my neighbors, I run into the house, rip the ornament off my tree, and grab some tissue paper. I run it out to her as she's bringing my mail up my driveway.

"Can I open it now?"

When she does, she starts to cry. "It's beautiful. I love Dolly so much! Thank you."

She hugs me and drives off.

I no longer have a Dolly ornament for my tree. Nor did Karen bring the package I was waiting for. But I have the warm feeling of grace and generosity that's so elusive with the commercialism surrounding the holiday.

A perfect exchange.

On his last Christmas, my father cried when he realized we had gifts for him, and he had nothing to give us. But love shared is the greatest gift. He gave me that our last Christmas together. Finally. Before he left me behind.

Welcome the Stranger

*Do not neglect to show hospitality to strangers for,
by doing that, some have entertained angels without
knowing it.*

-Hebrews 13:2

I want to believe Dolly can do this, but I'm not convinced. Yet that kind of negative thinking can ruin our chances. I should be more like Max, who has every confidence Dolly can and will succeed. I'll deploy the Law of Attraction, sending the Universe thoughts of Dolly's success in hopes of it boomeranging back to us this evening.

For months, we've participated in the American Kennel Club's Canine Good Citizen (CGC) program, considered the gold standard for dog and owner behavior. I drove 50-minutes each way to attend the weekly class with five other dogs and their humans. This in fulfillment of my pledge to the heavens that should Dolly survive the fall from the deck, she'd "do something good in this world." CGC was our next step toward that and, as she approached one year of age, she was (theoretically) mature enough to participate.

I envision her performing perfectly tonight, a dream dog.

But when we arrive at the testing site, Dolly becomes a wild thing, crazier than I've ever seen her. Like she hasn't had one iota of training her entire life. She's practically snorting, a race horse corralled into the starting gate. She ignores even the most basic commands, while leaping and lunging to engage the other dogs in play, getting them riled up, something the test-anxious humans do not appreciate.

Nor do I.

She'd behaved fairly well at the weekly sessions. Why is she so damn rambunctious now that it's time for the test? I wonder if she's reflecting my anxiety, my tension. My quest to be perfect. I took her to the groomer last week so she'd at least look the part. I walked her today to expend some of her energy. I gave her a Reiki treatment and sent Reiki to the testing site asking that Dolly's highest good be achieved. I said a prayer.

It's not about what I want; it's about what's best for her, I remind myself.

Nope. Not tonight, I contradict. *Tonight IS about what I want.*

I kneel next to Dolly. "Don't be a little asshole," I hiss into her floppy ear as I yank on her new royal-blue Martingale collar. It's already a size bigger than the oversized collar she donned as a puppy and looks regal against her deep orange fur. She's acting anything but.

I hope I'm out of earshot of the evaluator, the other contestants, and Max, my nine-year-old assistant, but I don't really care. Dolly's acting like a little jerk at a most inopportune time.

Panting and drooling, wild-eyed, she looks away from me, plotting her escape.

"We've worked too long and hard for this moment to let you blow it tonight, Doll."

When her breathing slows, I release her collar. She apparently knows the *don't-be-an-asshole* command. Perhaps has heard it somewhere before.

I brush off my jeans, trying to pretend that little incident never happened, hoping her drool on my shirt dries before we are center stage.

We head to the registration table to sign the American Kennel Club's *Responsible Dog Owner's Pledge*, stating I'll meet Dolly's health needs, keep her safe, exercise and train her, clean up after her, and provide a good quality of life. That's all I've done for the last eleven months anyway.

We've now completed all requirements for CGC testing. I read the fine print to see if that AKC pledge prohibits me from denying she's my dog.

* * *

At our first Canine Good Citizen class three months ago, we were told all dogs would be tested on the following behaviors. I mentally assessed our chances of passing the course:

Test 1: Accepting a Friendly Stranger – Dolly must allow a stranger to shake my hand and speak with me, while being ignored. She must leave the stranger alone. *Yeah, right. No one is a stranger to this dog. She thinks everyone wants to engage with her.*

Test 2: Sitting Politely for Petting – Dolly must allow a stranger to touch her as she sits by my side. *It won't be good if Dolly tries to put the stranger's hand in her mouth, as she's likely to do.*

Test 3: Appearance and Grooming – Dolly will be inspected to make sure she's clean and groomed. She must then allow the evaluator to brush her, examine her ears, and pick up each foot. *We got this: Dolly's brushed several times each day to reduce airborne dog hair. Since she pees on her rear paws, she's used to having her paws wiped. She'll look good even if she doesn't act good.*

Test 4: Out for a Walk – My ability to control Dolly on a leash will be tested. She must attentively walk by my side as I change direction several times, make turns, and stop. There are dog toys and treats along the corridor to seduce her. *Definitely needs work in this area. Dolly never heels; her walk is primarily free-style. She's more into immediate gratification than resisting temptation. Likely a deal-breaker.*

Test 5: Walking Through a Crowd – Dolly must move about "politely" in pedestrian traffic. On leash, she must walk past at least three people showing some interest but not overexuberance, continuing to pay attention to me. *Simply impossible! She never pays attention to me. See Test 1.*

Test 6: Sit and Down on Command and Staying in Place – Dolly must sit and lie down on command. And then stay in position as I walk 20 feet away and return. *Dolly will typically sit and down, with the promise of mucho treats. Will she stay when I take my watchful gaze off her? Her impetuousness makes this anyone's guess.*

Test 7: Coming When Called – Dolly must stay as I walk 10 feet away and then must come to me when called. *A long shot for sure. She still hasn't mastered that command. And seemingly doesn't want to. Just yesterday, she took off in the opposite direction when called. I should have her hearing tested.*

Test 8: Reaction to Another Dog – From 20 feet away, Dolly and I must approach another handler and his dog. Dolly must show only "casual" interest in the other dog and owner, keeping her distance from them. *No freakin' way! NONE! That's an unnatural act for ANY dog, much less this social creature. See Test 1.*

Test 9: Reaction to Distraction – The evaluator will make a big noise (like dropping a chair). Dolly must not panic and only be slightly startled. *I'm not sure how to predict this one. Success will be critical to her therapeutic services in a nursing home because of dropped metal food trays and metal walkers banged around. I know of what I speak.*

Test 10: Supervised Separation – Dolly must go with a stranger and be away from me for three minutes without barking, whining, or pacing. *No problem; she won't even notice I'm gone. She'll probably welcome the break. Maybe they can keep her a bit longer.*

The first few training sessions were challenging; I drove home thinking it hopeless. We were unable to fully practice between classes because I needed a "friendly stranger" with a dog for many of the exercises. That's when I involved Max, my next-door neighbor who'd just adopted Conor, a small, white, fluffy rescue who regularly punishes her new family by peeing and pooping in their house, usually right after being outside. Max readily agreed to help train Dolly because then he, in turn, could train Conor.

Perfect. Except that little kid called me out every time I swore. Which was often.

"My mom says that's a bad word."

"Then don't tell her I said it."

Max always told her. Then told me he told her.

I also engaged every adult and dog within a one-mile radius of my townhome. No one was safe. I needed a village to pull this off.

Each day, Dolly and I went for a walk stalking *friendly strangers*, asking them to shake my hand and ignore Dolly. Dolly hated that, turning herself inside out to get their attention. A stranger with a dog was an even better find and, as predicted, Dolly couldn't ignore either one. And those poor people could hardly ignore me since I sometimes marched right up their driveways to enlist their participation.

Dolly became known as *Citizen Dolly*, and God-only-knows what I became known as. A *too-friendly stranger*, perhaps?

"It takes a village to train a dog," Kevin would call out when he'd see us coming. She'd choke herself trying to run to him while on the end of the leash.

"Dolly, don't let her break your spirit by making you too good," another neighbor warned. Further encouraging delinquent behavior, he whispered in her ear, "Cheat on the test if you have to." But when he saw her tugging on the leash with her mouth, he gently chided, "That's not how good citizens are supposed to act." His advice to me was, "Remember, she's still a puppy."

All my neighbors were in on the act. We had a common goal: a well-behaved Dolly.

Max practiced with us after school and on weekends, playing various roles with and without Conor. He became totally committed to Dolly's success, so I invited him to accompany us to her final exam.

Praise and encouragement are allowed during testing – no treats. But Dolly's not intrinsically motivated; she only complies for tangible rewards. (I'm still paying her to let me wipe her paws!) I considered smuggling in treats, consistent with the "cheat-if-you-have-to" advice, but abandoned that idea knowing Max would turn me in if I circumvented the rules. But Heaven help me if I'm counting on her to behave without shaking me down.

I decided to rub my hands with kibble just before the test so Dolly would think I have treats. My only concern was her figuring out halfway through that none were forthcoming, which could cause her to go on strike.

Unless only a minor misstep, she'll get one chance per test to get it right. She'll automatically fail should she "eliminate" during the course of the exam.

Should we even show up?

The night before, neighbors lined up to be the distracters and the greeters – the *friendly strangers*. They clapped and cheered when she got it right, and encouraged me when she didn't. As we started home, they wished her good luck, saying, "You can do it, Dolly!" I invited them to stop over when we return from the exam. I stocked up on wine for the presumed celebration, knowing I'd drink it all if it turned out there was no reason to raise a glass to Dolly's success.

I was filled with gratitude for such caring neighbors and to Dolly for bringing us all together. Strangers had become *friendly strangers* and then became friends over the course of Dolly's training.

* * *

We head to the ring, waiting to be called. By now, we're both panting and drooling.

"Next up is Dolly Lama with owner, Patricia Nugent."

I take a deep breath. This is it.

And we're off! She points her muzzle up toward my kibble-laced hands, which makes her look attentive rather than the self-serving pup she is. Test after test, she performs perfectly, although she can't resist a slight lunge toward every treat and toy placed on the course during Test 4. Overall, she does better than any practice we've had, earning the title of *Canine Good Citizen.*

The other dogs pass as well. As we leave, full of self-congratulations, Max charges through the exit door, shouting to no one in particular as he prances around the parking lot, "Dolly won! She won! Dolly won!"

Dolly has indeed "won." She's won hearts and achieved the coveted certification. I say a prayer of gratitude. Dolly is now a Canine Good Citizen!

She "eliminates" in the flowerbed right outside the door, as I cringe and the dog-parents laugh. "That's okay, Dolly," Max says, hugging her. "You still won."

Max wins too: I take him out for French fries and ice cream as he regales me with a blow-by-blow of how she performed on each test. He later chronicles it for his mother before she puts her worn-out boy to bed. We drink a congratulatory toast to the dog who is now leaping and jumping all over Kevin, welcoming that friendly stranger who comes bearing treats – the kind she's not supposed to have. I shouldn't drink this much wine either, but we're celebrating. Enough good behavior for one day.

A truly victorious time for all. On to therapy dog training!

* * *

I spot a mobile dog-grooming van in the neighborhood. Knowing how much Dolly fears going to the doggie salon, evidenced by her uncontrollable shaking that begins as soon as we pull into the parking lot, I ask for the groomer's card, explaining Dolly will soon need a summer haircut. She immediately responds, "Oh, I don't do golden retrievers. They're too rambunctious."

She then looks – really looks – at Dolly, quietly standing by my side, fresh off her CGC Neighborhood Tour. "But I would do her," she concedes. "She's beautiful."

How important not to stereotype a certain breed of dog... or a certain group of people. Corgis; British. Rottweilers; Germans. Poodles; French. Chihuahuas; Mexican. Each person and canine should be individually judged by their behavior, not by breed/ethnicity, gender, size, or color. As with humans, many variables determine a dog's temperament. It's not that some breeds are inherently more dangerous than others; it's how people choose to train certain breeds. Suzanne Clothier reminds readers that *a dog is a dog is a dog*, the difference lying in how readily specific behaviors can be triggered in certain breeds. Animal shelters are filled with pit bull mixes, and the breed is banned in twelve countries including Canada and France. But Murphy, Kevin's new dog after Corey went to The Rainbow Bridge, is a friendly pit bull/boxer mix; we call him Dolly's "boyfriend."

This groomer would later confess, "I'm glad I made an exception to my rule."

I'm glad too. She uses natural, organic products, including essential oils, to keep pets healthy on the inside as well as looking and smelling good on the outside. In days to come, she'll guide me in the use of essential oils for healing, filling in the blanks from the training session suspended due to the storm.

You get what you need, my masseuse always says.

Since Dolly has become a celeb of sorts, being pronounced a Good Citizen and all, neighbors approach, wanting to pet her. Her royal-blue Good Citizen bandana hangs around her neck, matching her collar and my Good Citizen t-shirt. I relish her fans engaging with us as we strut past. But there are also expectations to uphold after going public with her new title.

"That's not how good citizens behave, Dolly," neighbors scold when she jumps on them, tugs on her leash, or runs in the opposite direction when called. But she's been good about staying in her own yard, even when temptation abounds on neighbors' properties. Except for an occasional break for Kevin's house, she's content to stay on our own small strip of land as we play keep-away (her version of *fetch* since she doesn't return the ball once she's got it).

Today, however, with her nose catching a scent, Dolly

takes off up the hill behind my townhome and, within seconds, is gone from sight. A new escape route has been christened. She neither recognizes nor acknowledges her name or my command to "Come."

Off I trudge, up the muddy hillside to once again retrieve my retriever. My *Canine-Good-Citizen* retriever. Every few seconds, I spot an orange blur darting past at break-neck speed.

She climbs the steps to a neighbor's deck and boldly peers through their glass patio door. It's a house she'd been monitoring for months, watching out the back window when not staking out Kevin's house from a side window. She'd even had the audacity to bark at the residents for shoveling the same deck she's now on. Their deck.

They're fairly new to the neighborhood; we've never met.

Out of breath, I position myself as a human barrier at the bottom of the steps and stage-whisper for her to come down, hoping the inhabitants won't hear me. I don't want to appear in their patio door window as well – my panting marauder is bad enough.

After sniffing every square inch of their deck, Dolly heads toward the stairs but won't climb down because there are no risers. She starts whining, so up I climb to help her down, in full view of the horrified occupants who must believe we're conducting a hostile takeover of their deck. Behind them, they shield their young daughter, who's pointing and screaming at us.

I hook Dolly to her leash and drag her butt home, giving a backward wave to the traumatized people behind the glass. I'm too embarrassed to introduce myself, forgetting they'll be able to trace my footprints in the soft earth leading back to the townhome behind theirs.

Once home, Dolly settles into a deep sleep, snug in her bed. But that doesn't stop my barrage: "Sure, you're tired, Dolly, after causing all that commotion. Going rogue is dangerous. Why didn't you come when I called you? It's embarrassing to call you *Dolly* when you don't act like a dolly should."

All she hears is *Blah, blah, Dolly, blah, blah! Blah, blah, come, blah, blah? Blah, blah, Dolly, blah, blah, Dolly, blah.*

As she gently snores, I write her a letter in my journal. It's what I do when no one wants to hear what I have to say.

Dear Dolly,

I know you love to run. And I must admit, I like seeing you in your natural state, using your strong leg muscles without restraint. I can see it in your eyes just before it happens. Suddenly there's a look of wanderlust; you scan your surroundings, nose in the air. As you begin to edge away, I sense there's a moment when you still might decide to stay with me. Yet freedom usually wins out, once you get the notion that adventure awaits.

Although you seem content most of the time, the wolf in you must see my protection as inhibiting. It's those times you choose to escape – to feel the wind in your fur, whistling in your ears, chill in your teeth. The earth giving way beneath your paws.

I trust that if it's up to you, you'll return to me. But, my little Dolly, you don't know what's out there. You don't know about coyotes. Or dog catchers. Or mean people. What if those neighbors had a gun? You've been sheltered from all that in this safe, domesticated life we share.

Sleep the sleep of the innocent, your front paws twitching as you dream of your escape. I'll be here when you wake up.

Although her strategy lacked aplomb, Dolly had tried to meet our new neighbors after months of surveillance. It's more than I've done to welcome the strangers whose backyard borders mine. Maybe Dolly should be the *Welcome*

Wagon mascot. If I ever let her out of the house again. Which isn't likely.

But next week, Dolly will be spending a day at another neighbor's house while I'm at an all-day meeting. I bring her over a few days ahead of time to become familiar with Debbie's two small dogs.

When we enter, Dolly hangs back. But when Lola and Penny appear, Dolly is ready to engage. Lola's ready, too, but Penny – a Chihuahua – is decidedly not. A little smaller than Dolly's head, she sits on Debbie's lap and snarls, growls, and snaps at Dolly's face – which to Penny must be a mass of red fur with eyes.

Dolly doesn't get that Penny wants nothing to do with her. When Penny is banished to her bed for being anti-social, Dolly approaches the bed wagging, despite the continued snarls and snaps. She won't give up on making that stranger friendly. Like Abraham Lincoln who reportedly said, "I don't like that man. I must get to know him better."

I'd have thought instinct would've prompted Dolly to keep her distance. But dogs are shameless – they go after what they want when at liberty to do so. (They should star in a training video for sales people titled *Never Take "No" for an Answer.*) What motivates Dolly to continue seeking acceptance, to insist these strangers welcome her? It seems codependent. That's one reason it's easy to train dogs – they desperately seek approval, will work hard for that "Good dog!" Plus treats, of course.

Shortly after delivering Dolly to Debbie's for the day, I receive a text: "Dolly seems too nervous to stay here." So Debbie sits with Dolly in our home, where Dolly snubs her, prompting another text: "She doesn't seem to want me here."

Is this payback for being unwelcomed by her dogs?

GRRRRRRRRRRRRRRR.

I respond, with embarrassment, that Debbie can leave Dolly and just check on her periodically.

Dolly was waiting at the door, incident-free, when I arrived home.

* * *

We're all capable of being inhospitable, unwelcoming. I'm reminded of that when Dolly and I move back to the Adirondacks the following summer. A stray dog appears on my property, stiff and watchful, tail erect, one leg ahead of the other, poised to advance. His gaze is locked on us. Without benefit of eyeglasses, I determine he could be a wolf/German Shepherd mix. He looks dangerous, unlike my golden retriever with her silky feathers. He doesn't belong here; I want him gone.

"Go away," I shout at the intruder. "Get out of here." I call Dolly to my side to protect her, but, true to form, Dolly moves further away, so I lunge after her to hook her leash, while closely watching the menacing presence.

"Go!" I continue to shout, waving my arms. Without fanfare, the canine trespasser turns and ambles up my gravel driveway toward the road.

Dolly remains oblivious to the averted threat. Breathing a sigh of relief, I usher her into the house. And begin to worry that the dog I'd chased away might get hit by a car.

When the dog reappears in my neighbor's yard two hours later, I grab a handful of treats and head over, still wary but penitent. Up close, the dog is not at all what I'd assumed when I'd looked at him through the eyes of fear. He's old, overweight, panting, and obviously frightened. He scurries past me without making eye contact, more afraid of me than I of him. He heads up their driveway back to the road, having been shunned by those property owners as well.

Guilt overcomes me for having chased him away, for assuming the worst rather than rationally assessing the situation. Fear prevents us from being our best selves, our highest selves. Fear of rejection, of looking foolish. Fear of being hurt, physically or emotionally. Fear of taking a risk, fear of those different than we are. That dog needed help. But my interest in protecting Dolly – and myself – made me blind to his needs. Yet a strange dog on the loose in the mountains is nothing to be taken lightly; our lives could have been in danger. But weren't.

By protecting my own, had I caused harm to another? How do we balance our need for self-protection with compassion for others? Risks associated with trusting too much can be great. But the risks of losing our humanity due to fear are much greater. Because of a growing fear of abduction and terrorism, we're indoctrinating our children with *Stranger Danger*, so much so that kids often don't acknowledge adults they encounter. This creates a dangerous "Other" – the one to fear – and reinforces anti-social behavior, which will have long-term consequences for our culture. Better we take calculated risks than become paranoid.

Dogs are an antidote; they can build bridges between strangers. It's easy to ignore another person; it's hard to ignore someone with a dog. Dogs won't stand for it. (Yes, even those with their Canine Good Citizen certification.) They're eager to meet and greet, scrambling to make contact. Likewise, dog lovers can't resist an encounter with a dog.

No one is a stranger when Dolly's around. She's a conduit for meeting new people on our walks, who help me see her differently by appreciating her *joie de vivre*. Should she spot someone ahead of us, she pulls me forward, not resting until we catch up – no matter how far away they might be. They must hear her (and me) panting and clawing as we gain on them, no doubt a scary proposition. Breathless, I always call out, "Friendly dog approaching."

Similarly, if someone's in their front yard or getting out of a car, she stops, won't budge, until they approach or blatantly ignore her. Her neediness embarrasses me. "C'mon, Dolly," I command. "We gotta go." Tugging her collar doesn't help – her desire for attention overrides the collar yank and obedience to me. "I'm sorry," I say to her target. "She thinks everyone wants to meet her."

Most do. Her positive thinking and stubbornness pay off, with the majority of people giving her what she wants, reinforcing her attention-seeking behavior. Stalking people is now a fully ingrained habit because sometimes it works.

And sometimes is enough for her.

Perhaps it's enough for all of us. Although our actions may not always bear fruit, the times they do make our attempts worth it. Skinner's conditioning experiments with rats proved that even irregular patterns of reward increased the likelihood of the desired activity. Because sometimes when you hit the bar, a pellet of food comes out. Sometimes when you stand there long enough and shamelessly stare, someone will pet you. Since more than half of United States' households have at least one dog, Dolly has a 50-50 chance of being warmly greeted by the object of her desire. Kids who are typically afraid of *Stranger Danger* run up to pet her, usually savvy enough to ask permission first. Because some dogs (and some people) are not friendly.

Dolly forces me to confront my own sense of *Stranger Danger* when a tall, thin man with a stiff gait is shuffling ahead of us. I'm always nervous walking alone on a remote road, and his Frankenstein-ish walk adds to my angst. I decide to turn around.

Dolly will have none of my elitism, playing possum when I try to turn her around. She becomes a dead weight. If I yank any harder on the leash, her head will pop off.

Despite trainers' advice to *never let a dog win*, we quickly catch up to the man.

"My dog has dragged me here to meet you," I breathlessly sing out as we get close, trying to mask my fear. He stares at me in silence, no doubt wondering if that's a compliment.

He looks down, sees Dolly, and breaks into a big grin.

"Oh, I'm glad she did," he replies. "I always have a tough time not approaching a friendly dog myself." He bends over to pet Dolly who's leaping and assuming the play position, risking knocking him over.

"Where you headed?" I ask, my fear having subsided with his grin. He tells me he's walking to meet his daughter and her husband who live up the road. Dolly and I slow down to match his stilted pace. He tells me of his early career as a minister, his work in Greece, and later years as a teacher.

I'd been afraid of a minister/teacher. Sheesh. Good thing Dolly knew better.

We continue to walk together, easily chatting. "I retired after I had a stroke. I can't see my right hand," he confesses.

His daughter and son-in-law come into view, and he cheerfully introduces us, including Dolly. The look on his daughter's face tells me she isn't pleased her dad befriended a stranger. A stranger who'd been afraid of her father who'd been a stranger. *Stranger Danger!* She quickly dismisses Dolly and me, and we part ways.

I feel rejected, scorned. Unfairly judged as someone who might cause her father harm. But *turnaround is fair play* since I'd initially judged her father unfairly. Sometimes we're the stranger.

Because I chose, or rather Dolly chose, to walk with this stranger, I didn't get the physical exercise or the cardio workout intended. But, for me, a greater loss would have been to be so paranoid and insular that I missed the opportunity to meet a kind man who helped debunk my irrational bias. And reminded me that judgment can be more crippling than a stroke.

Judgment is a hard vice to quit; it comes easily to us. Yet when we are most critical, it's often because of our own feeling of inadequacy. *First cast out the beam from your eye, and then you will see clearly to cast out the splinter from the eye of your brother (Matthew 7:5).*

* * *

My goofball has turned into a beautiful one-year-old pup. She has a delicate narrow face with round, dark-rimmed golden-brown eyes and long red eyelashes. Her strawberry-blond coat is shiny – more like hair than fur – with a white star on her chest and flowing feathers on her core, legs, and tail. I've started calling her "My Beauty Queen," definitely a step up from "Damn-It-Dolly." Still petite for her breed at fifty-two pounds, she looks (and acts) very much the puppy, CGC certificate aside.

Strangers often declare, "She's so beautiful" or "She's

adorable." Car drivers shout compliments out their windows as they pass us. A contractor burst out upon seeing her, "She's perfect! She could do television commercials!" As he wrote up the quote, she sat quietly by his side, gently nudging his arm with her muzzle to induce some hands-on-fur contact. (And, of course, succeeded.) Compliments and positive reinforcement are important, no matter the species. They keep us buoyed, combating so much else that tears us down, including our negative self-talk. Especially our negative self-talk.

My mother was beautiful. Dark hair with soft curls, green eyes, creamy complexion. Even into her ninth decade. But her illness took its toll: her hair and smile gone, her eyes sunken, her complexion sallow. Her once dancer-shaped legs that had engendered compliments from strangers lost all muscle tone; together, we watched them wither away. Yet one day as I left her room, an aide approached to say, "Your mother is so beautiful."

Assuming she was referencing photos on the dresser, I wistfully responded, "Yeah, she really was."

"No, I mean she's beautiful still...now. She *is* beautiful."

"I'm glad you can still see it."

"It's still there," she insisted.

That stranger – a substitute worker that evening – took time out of her harrowing schedule to help me once again see my mother as beautiful. To help me relate to her as the woman I knew, not the shell she'd become. Nurturing the soul of the caregiver is as important as feeding the patient – to boost our stamina, to help us face another day of our loved one's infirmity. That compliment changed what I saw when I looked at my mother, languid in her hospital bed. It prompted me to repeatedly tell her, as I stroked her head the last few days of life, "You are so beautiful." She was unable to acknowledge my words.

One of my father's most supreme acts of kindness was telling my mother that the salt-and-pepper fuzz growing on her head after thirty-two radiation treatments was beautiful.

I assumed he was making fun of her, being insensitive. She did too.

"Really?" she asked him in cautious disbelief, searching his face for a clue while I held my breath.

"Yes, beautiful," he responded with conviction as he stroked her bald head.

A few weeks after she died, wracked with the exhaustion and heartache of loss, standing in line at the convenience store, I couldn't have felt more unattractive and pathetic. Buying my dinner – a meal for one to be consumed alone after nine months of feeding my mother each evening. I fumbled with my wallet, continuing my negative self-talk about being invisible and old and frighteningly like my mother in her advanced years.

I imagined what the people in line behind me must be thinking to themselves about the figure I cast. Dark circles under my eyes, limp hair, no makeup, wearing old sweats. I had nothing left to give myself or anyone else.

When I hurriedly exited the store clutching my frozen dinner (*no-bag-thank-you-just-get-me-the-hell-out-of-here*). the man who'd been behind me in line was close in tow. I heard him say something in Spanish, but I kept walking because I feared the stranger. He repeated it louder, so I turned around with annoyance to face my presumed stalker.

"I guess no one speaks Spanish around here," the tall, dark-haired, thirty-something man said. I apologized that I did not, to which he responded, "Well, what I said was, 'You are so beautiful. Truly beautiful.' I just wanted you to know that."

Frozen in place, I stared at him. He turned around, heading to his car, and all I could muster was a feeble unacknowledged, "Gracias." I got into my car and cried, my forehead against the steering wheel. Cried for the kindness of strangers who are often gentler with us than we are with ourselves. Cried because perhaps the ravages of caregiving and age had not yet fully taken their toll on me. Cried because just a few days before, I'd seen an older woman whom I thought beautiful and wanted to tell her but held back, afraid of offending or violating her space. Now I regretted not approaching her because I'd experienced firsthand the impact a compliment from a stranger can make on one's psyche.

I arrived home with a new spring in my step. My self-image had turned around with four little words: "You are so beautiful." I didn't care if my Don-Juan-of-the-Convenience-Store meant it or not; it didn't matter if he said it because I looked so pitiful and wretched that he felt sorry for me. He gave me an unexpected compliment, exactly what I needed to dust myself off after so much loss. And he kick-started my emotional healing.

You get what you need.

I'd later wonder if that *perfect* stranger had served as a channel through which my mother had communicated, repeating back to me the last words I'd whispered to her while she lay in a coma unable to speak: "You are so beautiful."

Mother Nature

> *Every single creature is full of God and is a book about God.*
>
> > - Meister Eckhart

Fifty hours at work each week prior to retirement had separated me from the natural world. I still spend too much time at my keyboard – looking at the world through a window. Evenings spent snugly-wrapped indoors unless I have a social engagement. Even as I write this, I'm missing a brilliant orange and pink sunset.

Dolly is changing that though. She forces me to go outside – not just to toilet her but to spend time in the Great Outdoors. To feel sunlight on my face unfiltered by glass. To breathe air not cycled through heating and cooling machines. To feel the ground beneath my feet. To throw a tennis ball.

Dolly trots out in her all-weather fur coat no matter the season. By serving as her chaperone, I have experiences I wouldn't otherwise, as recorded in my journal:

If not for you, I wouldn't be out in this exhilarating air.

I wouldn't see the red blinking lights of an airplane, marvel at the science that made flight possible, and wonder what journey the passengers are on.

I wouldn't notice the dramatic white clouds huddled together in one corner of the infinite sky.

I wouldn't gaze at the deep, blue heavens, ablaze with stars.

I wouldn't think to ask the moon for a blessing.

To seek the Divine, some believe we must begin with the mysteries of nature. Saint Francis of Assisi, the patron saint of animals and the environment, claimed to have discovered more about God and himself through the prolonged practice of contemplative prayer in nature. Being intimately connected to Creation helped him grow more fully into the mystery of God.

We manifest our higher selves when we care for the ecosystem rather than expecting it to serve us. Those who disregard our interconnectedness with the natural world, who embrace a literal interpretation of *Genesis* that "man... should have dominion over...every creeping thing that creepeth upon the earth," do so at their descendants' peril.

What if, through subsequent translations of the Bible – from Aramaic to Hebrew to Greek to Latin to dozens of English variations as well as other languages – the word interpreted as *dominion* was actually closer to *responsible for*, as in *Man should be responsible for the fish of the sea and the birds of the heavens*? (And, of course, everything that creepeth.) How would that change our concept of stewardship of the Earth? How might that halt our dumping toxic waste into the oceans, for instance? Or accepting that up to 200 species of plants, birds, and mammals become extinct daily, which is 1000 to 10,000 times the natural extinction rate?

On our morning walk, Dolly and I come upon two fawns. Reddish-brown fur with big white spots. Side-by-side. Glassy eyes, wide open. In a ditch. Legs mangled.

Population surges in outlying areas have added automobiles to the list of wildlife's not-so-natural predators. *Road kill*, we casually call carcasses strewn along the road, as we try not to look - but can't seem to help ourselves.

The sight of those fawns is deeply disturbing. I tell Dolly about them as I lead her quickly past so she won't smell death. "Dolly, those fawns didn't know about cars and having to be careful crossing the street. They're babies, like you – even your size and color. Their mama must've been heartbroken to see them get killed because she was, no doubt, with them, trying to protect them as best she could. That's why I'm always trying to keep you safe, as frustrating as my vigilance must be for you."

A few days later, the fawn bodies are gone – a meal for lucky scavengers. Nature's balance.

Despite my good intentions toward the natural world, I

contribute to the imbalance. I spray the wasp nest behind my window shutter. I curse the mice seeking refuge in my woodpile, the waddling woodchuck under my deck, and the gaunt deer eating my lilies. I chase away the barn swallows nesting over my window – baby birds are messy!

The universal Law of Noninterference states it's wrong to try to control another life. (One of the reasons Reiki practitioners request permission to send healing.) Yet we often interfere – intentionally or unintentionally through ignorance. When we do, another spiritual law – karma – kicks in: Our actions and intent affect our future. Everyone has a path to walk, and it's up to each of us to figure out what we're here to do, a.k.a. "You do you." If we don't interfere, we can focus on living our own lives.

I'd need a lobotomy to fully comply with that universal law. My then-husband used to joke that my mantra was "Let go, let me." True enough. And probably not intended as a *HA-HA* joke. He'd watched in dismay when I sprayed water on baby birds in their nest because they looked hot and thirsty. Following that unnatural shower, their mother circled for twenty minutes with food in her mouth before landing. We almost lost the little tweeters, thanks to my "helpfulness."

Lessons don't come easy. And sometimes don't stick. Dolly gave me another tutorial on our morning walk when a stir in the bushes turns out to be a cat stalking something. A bird, I assume; *that's okay, it can fly away,* I reason. Then I spot the object of the cat's undivided attention: a Walt-Disney-cartoon-looking chipmunk. Tail straight up, iconic white stripe. A scared and confused baby chipmunk who wandered too far from safety, ending up vulnerable to a feline predator.

Dolly and I will save it, Me-Channeling-Sir-Galahad decides. *Dolly can scare away the cat. Lucky we came along at this time!* I pull disinclined Dolly on her leash toward the cat. The feline stalker warily watches us, intrigued rather than alarmed by the figure Dolly casts. (Her countenance is hardly frightening.) The cat stands his ground as we continue toward him – scaring the little chipmunk right into his jaws.

Just prior to our "intervention," the chipmunk had started to run in the opposite direction, away from the cat. And perhaps would have made it to freedom. If only...

It clearly wasn't what I'd intended by inserting myself – and my clueless dog – into the situation. A reminder that too often our interventions – our attempts to help – can have the opposite effect. Unintended consequences are consequences just the same.

Dolly wanted nothing to do with the cat and chipmunk. She better understands the laws of nature even though she's been separated from the natural world through the selective breeding process. But I struggle to reconcile the Biblical message that *his eye is on the sparrow* (interpreted as God will provide for all creatures) with my inclination to "fix" things, to make them "right." It's the curse of someone who feels the need to compensate for what she perceives as failings. The curse of someone who hates the *Serenity Prayer*, yet is continually reminded of its wisdom (which is assuredly not a coincidence).

Whenever I come across a nature show in which an animal attacks and devours another, I wonder why videographers don't save poor innocents instead of capturing their demise on film. They're right there – why don't they intervene?

Danger and impracticality aside, how naïve and, yes, arrogant to think it's up to humans to show animals the way – we've not done such a great job of managing our own entanglements. Animals likely have more to teach us than the other way around. A proverb of the Nez Perce native tribe summarizes this belief as *Every animal knows more than you do.*

But the interlopers who "discovered" this continent had that dominion-thing going, even though the Bible commanded them to "Ask the beasts, and they will teach you; the birds of the heavens, and they will tell you" (*Job* 12:7).

Ecclesiastes 3:19 draws an inexorable connection: "Surely the fate of human beings is like that of the animals; the same fate awaits them both: As one dies, so dies the other. All have the same breath; humans have no advantage over animals."

How do the rapidly rising extinction rates bode for the planet? Bode for us? If we seek to better understand the wisdom of the animal kingdom, we might all be better served. Because, animals can outsmart us. And often do.

* * *

Hosting a weekend spiritual retreat, I ask Marie to take Dolly out. "She'll show you the way," I tell her. "We always go to the same spot. Just follow her."

Off they go. As the weekend progresses, Marie volunteers to continue being responsible for Dolly's toileting to free me up to tend to guests.

"We've got it down," she assures me. "She always takes me to the same place."

Phew. One less thing to worry about. I'm grateful Dolly's becoming a responsible dog who can take care of herself. And appreciate Marie's willingness to pitch in.

On Sunday afternoon, with everyone gone, I resume toileting Dolly. I open the door, and she blithely trots over to the neighbor's lot to pee. I call her back to her designated toileting area, telling myself it's a fluke she went to the wrong place. But the next time I take her out, she again heads to the neighbor's. I also notice that instead of walking around the flowerbed as we've always done, her clumsy lioness paws stomp right through. She's never done that before either.

I call Marie, not sure how to ease into the interrogation of my generous-but-naïve friend. "Um, when you took Dolly out, where did she go exactly?"

Admittedly not a dog-person, Marie proudly describes how Dolly led her across the driveway to the property on the other side. Just as I'd thought: the neighbor's lot. And, *why, yes!* Dolly had cut across the flowerbed each time: "Wasn't she supposed to do that? She acted like that was the drill. I just followed her like you said."

My sneaky little Dolly. Since a ten-week-old pup, she's been taken out at least five times a day, around the flowerbed to her potty area. But she apparently knew she had a novice on the other end of the leash so went where she damn-well pleased. Like students with a substitute teacher. I chuckle to think Marie can channel those who have died but couldn't see through Dolly.

Even though creatures may seem compliant, that doesn't mean they surrender their desire for what they really want to do and how they want to do it – to manifest their own destiny. In my career, I saw a vast difference between employees who were compliant and those who were committed to a process, policy, or philosophy. It's important for leaders to inspire commitment. Yet somehow, I'd missed the mark with Dolly who's apparently only compliant when supervised.

Instead of being annoyed, I'm proud and amazed that inside this beautiful red-furred dog, there lurks a wolf yearning to live life as she pleases. "The domestication of dogs was one of the most extraordinary events in human history," writes Dr. Brian Hare, evolutionary anthropologist.

Except sometimes.

"Why do I even bother?" I ask Dolly the next time I catch her with a stick hanging out of her mouth. Her grazing will inevitably be followed by dry heaves. Or worse.

I know that; why doesn't she? After all we've been through with her digestive maladies.

"Drop it," I command. She continues to chomp away, gulping it down, despite my exhortations.

Although I'd heightened my vigilance, which didn't seem possible, Dolly has stayed the course, considering all things edible. "Are you *kidding* me? *Really?*" I rant, clearly more traumatized by her near-miss surgery than she.

Despite the top-shelf kibble, filtered water, and vitamins I provide, Dolly seems to have different ideas about what she needs. Are the choices I've made for her in contrast to her instincts? Does she need more of the nutrients Mother

Nature provides? Although not food in my book, most of what Dolly eats in the Great Outdoors is considered edible; those stranded in the wilderness survive on that stuff. And essential oils used for healing are extracted from plants with powerful immune systems – from the same type of raw materials Dolly eats.

Or is she hungry for more than food? For attention, maybe? Because I certainly come running when I hear the snap of a twig between her jaws.

Sometimes I'm more tolerant than other times – based on the quality or quantity of what she snatches up. My tolerance is nil when I see my few remaining flower petals falling from her mouth.

From Dolly's freaking mouth.

"No!" I yell. "No! Drop it. Bad dog."

She looks in my direction, then turns her head back toward the lone remaining blossom, opening her Pac-man mouth over it. I grab her collar and send her toward the house, berating her as we walk.

"Why can't I trust you, Dolly? Why do you have to devour everything all the time?"

Although that might sound like hyperbole, with Dolly it's not.

My friend Jonathan laughs when I tell him how distraught I am over losing one of my last remembrances of summer.

"Tell me. Was it worth getting all worked up over that? What's the lesson for you?"

Not in the mood for his Eastern sensibilities, I shout, "Lesson? Bullshit! The only lesson is Dolly's a little jerk!"

He's silent, Buddha-like, waiting for me to come around.

"So what do you think the goddamn lesson is?" I eventually ask in a quiet voice.

He's known me for over forty years. He's also a therapist, infinitely patient with my impatience. "I think it's about the ephemeral nature of beauty. We have to appreciate it while it's here – which you do – because you never know when it'll disappear. You'll remember it and, in that way, you'll still have it. Dolly can't destroy that memory. And someday it may remind you of her."

I take a deep breath. Coping with the fleeting nature of our existence is one of my primordial lessons in this lifetime. But why does Dolly's pedagogy have to include wrecking things?

Dolly tastes life, like a baby whose instinct is to put everything in her mouth. Despite domestication, she's still one with the natural world. She even blends in, her color indistinguishable from nature's hues. Her coat the color of sunsets, of fallen leaves, of weathered pine needles. No need for pretense; she just belongs.

I must remember she does not belong to me.

* * *

Back in Saratoga in anticipation of another winter that will come too soon, Dolly and I encounter more wildlife than in the Adirondacks. That's because a microchip factory was recently built two miles away, taking more than 220 acres of what was previously a forest. Wildlife desperately fled their habitat, with nowhere to go but into suburban neighborhoods. And black-legged ticks hitchhiked on the backs of their displaced hosts into our development, seeking new blood. Spreading disease indiscriminately to pets and people.

When the facility was first proposed, I'd walk down the dirt road drawing Reiki symbols in the air to protect the animals and vegetation from losing their coveted place in this world. My attempts to energetically derail the project failed, although I took some satisfaction – maybe even some credit – when the project was stalled longer than expected due to zoning issues. (Maybe I should have sent Reiki in the zoning board's direction although it's unlikely members would have granted me permission.)

The dirt road is now paved and lined with high-voltage power lines, memorializing Joni Mitchell's warning about paving paradise. Thousands of jobs have been created, a needed boost for a lagging economy. Yet twinkling stars are now obscured by the glow of lights from the 1.7 million-square-foot facility. The constant droning hum from the factory cuts through the nighttime tranquility.

Fox is one of the species that's lost refuge. A litter of six kits with a mature fox arrived in our neighborhood after construction began on the chip plant. They were beautiful – so regal. A lone kit would occasionally appear outside my study window, resembling Dolly with red fur and a bushy tail. (Foxes and dogs share the same taxonomy.)

Some neighbors panicked, but the Environmental Protection Agency assured us it's not unusual to see foxes during the day. Unless rabid, they flee when they encounter humans.

Today, Kevin stops by with sad news. "Our last-remaining fox was ripped apart by a coyote last night. Not eaten, just slaughtered because they competed for food. Now, they're all gone."

Those screams I heard must have come from that fox. A cry in the wilderness, followed by silence.

"Keep an eye on that pup of yours. Don't let her out alone with these coyotes around," Dolly's village warns after she finds a femur bone on our front lawn. When I walk her that night, I feel death permeating my suburban neighborhood. The air is thick with the scent of brutality; I can almost taste the spilled blood.

Hunger games.

My sensitivity to negative energy has heightened my sadness over the loss of "our" last fox. Intellectually, I understand it's the way of the natural world – necessary for natural selection, part of the food chain. Although we're taught that nature has a way of balancing itself, that might have only been true before humans screwed up the ecosystem. We're causing imbalances; shouldn't we try to stabilize them? Or is that like spraying the baby birds? Where's that fine line between helping and interfering?

Dolly doesn't know it's a dog-eat-dog world, although most dangers she might face would come from humans. I trade her royal blue collar for a bright orange one so hunters won't mistake her for the hunted.

Despite the impending cold weather, I dream of Dolly in the lake. I give her a nudge to swim rather than letting her just stand idle in the lake as she often does. She starts doggie-paddling, but her head gets yanked under. She comes up for air but is then pulled from behind, disappearing under the water. It's as if a shark pulled her down and away. But we're in a lake...what creature could have taken her? I struggle to make my legs move against the waves to get to the spot where I last saw her.

She's gone.

By daylight, I wonder what it represents, this message from my subconscious. Does the "creature" represent my pushing myself or others to be or do more? Or is the message more basic: *Keep Dolly close by. There are dangers lurking that could harm that innocent being if she isn't protected. Don't allow her too much freedom in the natural world.*

To give her more experience fending for herself, I decide to again provide Dolly with supervised exposure to her species and their people. We arrive at the dog park where I hesitate to open the gate: *What if these dogs are mean to her like at daycare?*

When we enter, her ears go back, and her tail retreats under her back legs. I want to turn right around, but Jonathan's there with his puppy and would likely tease me about being overprotective. Yet dogs can get hurt in dog parks; some vets warn against them due to potentially aggressive pack activity. And neglectful owners not paying attention.

The other dogs smell her fear and, just like in daycare, gang up on her, corralling this newbie. She runs away, seeking refuge among the humans, with the dogs in pursuit. But when another dog arrives, the pack leaves Dolly to initiate that newcomer.

And who runs after them? Dolly, eager to continue her canine connections. The break gave her time to regain confidence – they didn't kill her, after all – and she actively seeks interaction with her canine cousins.

I wonder if I did the right thing pulling her out of daycare when I did. Perhaps she needed more time with her species to figure them out, without my interference. There's that fine line again.

The brisk air chills my bones as I stand around with other dog-parents, so I take Dolly out to walk the trail surrounding the park. She runs like a gazelle, legs fully extended on the leaf-covered trail, circling back every few minutes to make sure I'm following. Or to make sure I still have treats. She doesn't stop to forage, although the wooded trail offers plentiful Dolly-snacks.

My little Dolly obviously needs more canine contact and freedom to run. More natural connections.

We go twice around the trail and, as we exit, a woman and her son are trying to move something off the path with a stick.

"My dog just killed this squirrel," she tells me in tears. "He's never done anything like that." Her young daughter bears witness in silence. Her son speaks up, to give his mother succor or to make himself feel better. "I think the squirrel died of fright. There aren't any marks or blood on him."

Probably because the dog snapped the squirrel's neck.

Another reminder that as much as we may personify our dogs, they are still animals, driven more by instinct than reason. Maybe we are too.

"Dogs are not people dressed up in fur coats, and to deny them their nature is to do them great harm," writes Jeanne Schinto, editor of *The Literary Dog.*

Nature rules.

* * *

We wake to the first snowstorm of the season. Pristine, white, and sparkly, a soft blanket covering my yard.

"Damn! The forecast was right," I mutter. "And I gotta take this dog out."

Grumbling, I drag out all my snow gear – hat, hooded scarf, ski jacket (making sure there are treats in the pocket), and tall boots. I put them on, one by one, as Dolly waits patiently, ears primed to hear the words, "Okay. Let's go, little girl."

I pull on my mittens and open the door. And then...dog feet. Dog feet go running out of my house, the proverbial *dashing through the snow.* Leaving dog prints, pounding down the white coverlet.

Dog feet. Everywhere. Running, leaping, playing. Dog feet excited by the opportunity snow offers. It's crunchy, it hides toys, it gets between toes. Best yet, it's edible – like everything else!

Her first winter, I begrudged Dolly destroying the smooth glistening appearance of my marshmallow-coated yard. I wasn't ready for everything a dog can do in the snow. To the snow. But now, I chuckle and join in. Dog feet aren't the only ones trampling it; I've learned that play makes snow better. How else to deal with harsh, unforgiving winters in the Northeast?

Dolly remembers why I took her outside, and then prances and twirls all over again. She looks to me to play, so I throw a tennis ball for which she'll dig to China if I don't intervene.

I wouldn't have gone outside in this fresh snowfall were it not for her. My lungs wouldn't have filled with fresh cold air. I wouldn't have witnessed the tall pines with delicate snow-kissed branches. I wouldn't have playfully chased a ball in my makeshift snowsuit, reminiscent of much younger days. I wouldn't have laughed with pure delight at my exuberant fur-faced companion.

When I tell her it's time to go in, she reluctantly heads toward the door, ball in her mouth for safe-keeping. I'm grateful to have a dog to force me to experience all four seasons in their rawest moments. She and nature continue to teach me the ways of the world. Trees complicitly drop pine cone and twig offerings on top of the snow for her to snatch up as I implore, "Leave it."

She doesn't.

I strive to respect the delicate balance of our coexistence with nature. Upon waking each morning, I go to the window to see who's visited. Deer, or sometimes smaller creatures, gently explore the grounds around my home, seeking sustenance while I sleep, unaware of their trespass. I scan their footprints to see where they went, encircling plants and shrubs. The tracks seem to come from out of nowhere and disappear where snow cannot disclose their passage. Cresting over and then retreating to the hillside, they seemingly slip away as quietly as they came. And I wonder why I never get to see the interlopers that visit silently in the night.

In contrast, my own footprints look heavy and imposing. Deliberate moves compared with nomadic wanderings. For I am the visitor on this land, and they're the natives whose habitat I have confiscated.

Silence is Golden

*If you talk to the animals, they will talk with you and
you will know each other.*

- Chief Dan George

Prior to Dolly's arrival, I'd lived alone for four years. Primarily in silence. Seldom did I turn on the radio or television because, as a writer, I tend to live in my head. Makes me wonder if Dolly's reluctance to comply with certain commands could be because I don't talk to her that much. If Dolly is to respond to me, I need to use language with her more. Turn her into the RCA dog, Nipper, with his head cocked listening for "His Master's Voice."

It's estimated that dogs, on average, can learn up to 165 words including gestures and hand signals. Sometimes I only use hand signals, as taught in obedience class, when commanding Dolly to do something. It's important that dogs learn hand signals in case the dog can see you but can't hear the command – such as "stay" if you find yourselves on opposite sides of the street.

My father was proficient in American Sign Language, also called fingerspelling. A teacher of the deaf, he taught me how to silently communicate; we'd often fingerspell at the dinner table to the exclusion of my mother, mostly about her lack of culinary skills. In his darker moods, my father communicated by deftly substituting a dirty look, a thrown object, a slamming door, or bulging neck veins.

He and I never did talk openly about the issues that had plagued us through the decades. When I became his caregiver, he'd still lash out at me on occasion, but words to do the job right eluded him. He'd stammer and stutter, and then fall silent. I'd pretend I didn't notice his attempt and would hold him until he fell asleep. The frail man's fists would slowly unclench.

Over those months, I silently forgave him...and silently asked his forgiveness for being distant and not coping well with his attempts to express his feelings of rejection and disappointment with how his life turned out. I didn't realize until he died how out of control he must have felt.

Ignoring past transgressions isn't necessarily healthy – perhaps that's why they figure prominently in my memory today. But my dad and I eventually reached a silent, unspoken truce.

His "deaf kids," as we called them, showed up at the funeral parlor en masse to pay their respects. Through interpreters, they told me what a wonderful teacher and mentor he'd been to them forty years prior. They especially loved his slapstick humor, as did I. Physical comedy holds a special place in the deaf community because no language is needed. I was surprised at how many commented on his compulsive humming; even though they couldn't hear him, they could feel the vibration. My neighbors once told me that when my father visited, it sounded like killer bees were swarming.

Not too far off.

My sister and I stopped speaking to each other the day of our father's funeral. We'd had a mini-brawl in a hotel lobby just prior. "You die the way you live," I whispered to my father in the coffin, quoting a hospice worker. "Now your two daughters are at odds with each other, just like you fought with everyone." The strain of simultaneously caregiving both our parents had deteriorated our already-fragile sibling relationship. Or maybe it was the natural extension of unresolved childhood issues.

Children of the same mother do not always agree, warns the Nigerian proverb.

Silence can be deafening. My husband and I lived in relative silence much of the time. My stepdaughter, who lived with us, blamed our large house – it was easy for us to live together and not *be* together. As an advertising executive, Peter understood the power of language. He'd masterfully use words to promote products – some with questionable social impact. He could make a General Electric generator sing and dance, yet struggled to find the words to encourage or compliment me. He'd rationalize that I didn't need it, which he thought itself a compliment. When I'd press for affirmation, desperate for approval from this man eleven years my senior, he'd dismiss the benefit: "Mere words," he'd say. "Mere words."

In marriage counseling years later, we couldn't find the right words to salvage our marriage. Yet neither of us saw divorce coming. It silently crept up on us; we'd thought it was just a bad patch.

Silence was a stealth destroyer in the night.

Hadn't we made promises? Hadn't we entered into a covenant? We'd vowed *for better or worse, 'til death do us part.* I'd wept when the judge's decree granting the divorce arrived, innocuously like any other piece of mail stuffed into my box. Then rage set in – irrational rage at the indiscriminate judge. *Why should a secular judge have the power to undo a holy bond consecrated in a church, witnessed by relatives and friends? Witnessed by God!* The judge never asked if we'd tried everything. He never asked if we were sure we wanted to end our decades-long marriage. He didn't review our history or offer alternatives. He simply signed a piece of paper provided by the attorneys.

I emailed Peter the night it became official: "How are you?"

"Divorced," he responded.

Mere words.

Marriage, and relationships in general, require more nurturing than I'd ever imagined; I didn't have good models for being a partner. When I asked my mother why she stayed with my father despite his volatility, she responded, "I took the vow 'for better or worse.' I got worse." When George Harrison's widow, Olivia, was asked, "What's the key to a long marriage?" she responded, "Not getting divorced."

That may be the key to a long marriage but not necessarily a long life. My mother often quipped, "I never think about divorce. Murder, often; divorce, never."

I now enjoy my solitude, my quiet home. It feels more natural to be lonely now that I'm alone. I can sit at my keyboard and write for hours with no noise – no talking, no music, no television. And, if I'm lucky, no barking.

I don't even talk to myself.

My silence forces Dolly to rely on my actions more than my words for clues as to what's happening next. If I ask "Want to go for a walk?" she doesn't react. But getting her leash or the car keys signals action; the word "treat" means nothing, but when I go near the treat bin, here she comes!

We hear the stories all the time, stories demonstrating that dogs have a sixth sense about what's going on, despite the language barrier. Doesn't Lassie always save Timmy? "Dogs know everything they need to know," my husband used to say. *Mere words* are apparently not always needed.

When Dolly and I go walking, the leash telegraphs my movements and, thereby, informs hers. The leash she resisted mightily as a young pup but now accepts as a condition of her captivity. She dutifully lets me click it onto her collar, another restriction she once railed against. With no more than an imperceptible tug, I zig, she zigs; I zag, she zags.

She walks fast – as I inadvertently trained her. I've never required her to *heel,* so she walks ahead of me, the leash extending my arm like that of a water-skier. I don't usually mind because it motivates me to walk faster, although my chiropractor admonishes. As does Suzanne Clothier, who writes that a dog pulling his person down the street indicates a lack of respect and/or leadership.

Today, it's hard for my two legs to keep up with Dolly's four. With no expectation of compliance, I suggest, "Dolly, let's just do *A* walk. Not *THE* walk. Let's slow down and enjoy a leisurely pace."

To my shock, she immediately slows her pace, dropping back next to me. We walk home together, side by side.

Did respect and leadership just kick in, along with an expanded vocabulary?

She does seem especially eager to get home though.

Although she never ventures into the guest room, it's where she wants to hang out upon our return. She's riveted to the window facing the driveway. I lead her out several times because I want to keep the room free of dog hair, but she keeps returning to her post.

Mid-afternoon, I hear one bark from the guest room. To Dolly's delight, Peggy has arrived from New York City. Peggy is crazy about Dolly. But how did Dolly know love was on the way to her? There must be a little bit of Lassie in each one of these four-legged creatures.

Dolly's vigil is rewarded with much affection – and two high-performance squeak toys. Dolly is a quiet dog except when excelling in the squeak toy category. I've never heard her growl at anyone or anything. And barking is usually aimed at getting attention or directed at a specific Dolly-determined infraction. She's so quiet that she waits to be noticed when she wants something, silently appearing at my side. Then I have to guess if it's food or toileting she needs. Or attention – the most basic need of every sentient being.

It's been theorized that the bond between canines and humans got stronger with increased television watching, family dysfunction and alienation, and workplace uncertainties. Dogs went from being on a chain in the backyard or roaming the streets to lounging on the couch next to their humans in front of the TV or computer screen. (Both species began to increase BMI about the same time.) I suspect social media may be weakening some of that bond now – we communicate through multiple devices with those who aren't there while ignoring those who are. Walking a dog used to be a time to connect, to share an experience – like those precious moments driving your child to school. Yet most people I see walking their dogs now are communicating with someone on a device instead of interacting with their supposed "best friend." Like a parent talking on a cell phone while her child sits in silence in the backseat. Or worse yet, also stares at an electronic gadget.

Social media enables us to live parallel rather than

cooperative lives. Harvard professor Robert Putnam, in his data-driven national bestseller *Bowling Alone*, documented decades ago how and why our sense of community – our social capital – is plummeting as we increasingly choose solitary and/or virtual activities over community. And it's only getting worse.

Dolly doesn't understand why I'd place an electronic device between us – why I'd ever put anything between us. When she's right there looking into my face, why would I open this gizmo and stare at it instead? She waits patiently, staring at the other side of it, her vision blocked. She hears voices and music sometimes, but there are no new experiences for her. Nothing changes on her side of the screen.

When she realizes this may not be just a quick interlude from togetherness, she begins to whine softly. If that doesn't produce results, she'll nuzzle her face into the crook of my elbow, as if to say, *Hey, look at me! I'm still sitting here. Waiting. Your dog – a real live being who can love you back. You don't have to watch a puppy on that screen. I'm right here!*

Many partners – and parents – can relate to feeling displaced by a computer screen.

Sometimes a paw lands strategically on my leg. But after a while, should I continue to choose virtual contact rather than the-most-loyal-of-companions, she gives up with a big sigh. She lies down and enters her own fantasy world of canine dreams, her head warming my feet.

Suzanne Clothier writes, "Far beyond learning what exact words and phrases mean, dogs listen to the whole picture of what we are telling them. The canine language is an elegant and precise one, where context and congruity – and not the spoken word – reign supreme...It's the whole message of voice and body that tells a dog what is really being communicated."

Interpreting sounds was indispensable to dogs' ancestors' survival. Lizi Angel teaches that dogs have an "evolved understanding of human, non-verbal language," enabling them to communicate with people and to recognize them as social partners. "Dogs know that we are not dogs... Rather than trying to be some kind of awkward, two-legged, pack-leading wolf-dog in a person suit, let's aspire to be the best provider, teacher and companion to our dogs..."

Perhaps it is dogs' silence that makes them endearing. They don't have the words to judge, criticize, curse our imperfections. Carl Rogers termed it *unconditional positive regard* – acceptance and support of others no matter what they say or do. Wouldn't every relationship benefit from just a dose of that? From a dose of dog.

On our morning walk, Dolly drags me over to a stranger putting out his garbage who immediately starts talking directly to her. "It's moving day. Today I leave the lake and mountains behind. This living is too hard for an old man like me." I insert myself into their conversation for a few minutes, but when we go to leave, he again addresses only her. "Thanks for stopping to talk with me. You're a good listener." And she is. She doesn't interrupt, change the subject, or offer opinions. That's why some literacy programs include reading out loud to dogs.

Sometimes I talk for Dolly. I can look at her and imagine what she might say to me. *Don't go...I'm hungry...I'm mad at you...This smells great...Can we go home now?* Her voice is high but not squeaky; whiney but stops short of begging; sweet-tempered but insistent.

There are also times when Dolly speaks for herself through her actions. Or the Universe speaks to and through her. Although she typically bolts away from mishaps so she won't get blamed, today she plants her two front paws in dozens of glass shards from a champagne flute that's just crashed to the hardwood floor.

Of all the places for her to show up.

"Dolly, go! Get away from here. This glass could hurt your feet."

I shoo her away as I fetch the vacuum cleaner. When I return, she, too, has returned, standing on the other side of the wreckage, her front paws again crunching the fine glass.

Like she's bound and determined to be in harm's way.

I look at her incredulously, and she stares back like she doesn't have a clue why she's there either. I lead her away from the glass-covered floor, sitting her down to check her pads for embedded glass. I don't find any glass but do find a sharp stone wedged in between two toes, attached to her fur with a tar-like substance. Even though I'd not noticed a limp or other evidence of discomfort, it must have hurt her during our walks.

If she hadn't taken herself over to the scene of the accident, I wouldn't have thoroughly examined her pads, potentially resulting in torn, tender tissue. By giving me a reason to look at Dolly's feet, did the Universe send a message that she needed help?

I choose not to discount this synchronicity. As Sherlock Holmes is attributed to saying about coincidence, "The Universe is seldom so lazy."

While many people aren't comfortable with silence, some say it gives way to answers – profound answers. Answers derived without spoken language lead us to a deep knowing, a wisdom that goes beyond information. "Where there is silence, one finds the anchor of the Universe" is written in the 6th century BC *Tao Te Ching*. Meister Eckhart, a 13th century mystical theologian, wrote, "Nothing in all creation is so like God as stillness." Max Ehrmann's 1927 poem *Desiderata* advised us to "Go silently amid the noise and the haste, and remember what peace there may be in silence." First Nation leader Dan George wrote, "And, above all, may silence make you strong."

We all need moments for self-reflection in a world that has become so noisy. That's why we meditate, contemplate, and journal. Keep silent vigils. And kneel as supplicants in prayer.

Ecclesiastes 3:7-8 reminds us there's a time to be silent and a time to speak, popularized by Pete Seeger's song *Turn, Turn, Turn.* That's because silence can be dangerous, isolating, and the voice of complicity. Remaining silent in the face of condemnation, injustice, and oppression must surely be a sin – defined as separation from the god in each of us. Many ordinary people became canonized as saints because they refused to be silent, choosing instead to speak out against a cultural practice they recognized as unjust or oppressive. Reverend Martin Niemöller, in his gripping poem about the Nazi rise to power, gave us a grim reminder of the evil that silence can render, ending with "Then they came for me – and there was no one left to speak for me."

As Reverend Dr. Martin Luther King, Jr. warned, "A man dies when he refuses to take a stand for that which is true."

Dolly and I are still navigating around each other, physically and emotionally. She's my silent golden; perhaps love is our common language. The other night, I dreamed I was playing ball with her. Just as I threw the ball, I woke up. And Dolly, in her bed across the room, jumped up as if there really were a ball to catch.

"I love you, Dolly," I told her as we both drifted back to sleep. I believe she understood that those are not mere words.

Balance and Alignment

> *As I see it, every day you do one of two things: build*
> *health or produce disease in yourself.*
>
> - Adelle Davis

A weekend boarding experience was not a good one for Dolly or the kennel owner. Or for me, it turned out. Dolly had repeatedly soiled herself and her temporary living quarters – her stomach extra-nervous over being left behind. She returned to me sullen and stinky. Dogs don't like to soil themselves, subscribing to the maxim, *Don't shit where you sleep.*

Despite hundreds of dollars spent on veterinary treatments for digestive issues, nothing is working. I'm growing despondent for both Dolly and myself. My work schedule, my social engagements, and my appointments all revolve around my dog's bowel movements.

Damn it, Dolly, I reprise. Although I know it's not her fault. Except, of course, for all the crap she still gobbles up.

I call the veterinarian. "Something has to change. I just can't do this anymore! It's not good for either of us." She recommends a prescription diet – expensive and only available from veterinarians. After researching, I know it's not the way to go. It's received the second lowest rating on *The Dog Food Advisor* independent website, primarily because corn is the first ingredient, a difficult and unnatural grain for dogs to digest.

How could that possibly be the answer? But what is?

We schedule an appointment to review options. While sitting in the waiting room with my own nervous stomach, I confide my concerns to a woman sitting next to me. She happens to be a breeder who whispers in a low voice, "Give your dog probiotics. It'll make a huge difference." She writes down the website and phone number for a company that sells holistic canine health products.

I feel like I've been handed contraband, a surreptitious

gift from on high.

Gold for my golden.

You get what you need.

I stash the priceless slip of paper in my pocket. And wonder why the vet hasn't proposed this option.

"I will not put Dolly on that prescription food," I inform the vet. "There has to be a more systemic way to cure her, although I have no clue what that might be." She doesn't either. I leave with a prescription for Lomotil, a synthetic narcotic used to treat acute diarrhea in dogs and known to cause drug-dependency in humans. I'm also told I can give Dolly Pepto-Bismol, which will treat the symptom but not the cause of her loose stool.

Am I to give my dog a narcotic and chalky pink stuff containing aluminum? Treat only the symptoms but not the cause of her disease? The Agency for Toxic Substances and Disease Registry reports that bone disease has occurred in children taking some medicines containing aluminum because aluminum in the stomach prevents the absorption of phosphate, a chemical compound required for healthy bones. Although she's not a human child, she's still young, and I'm not willing to take any chances. Goldens are genetically prone to hip dysplasia, so maintaining bone health is important.

The minute I get home, I call the phone number the breeder gave me. The general manager of Nature's Farmacy in Georgia answers. In the twenty minutes he spends talking with me, I learn more about canine nutrition than I'd learned in over twenty years living with dogs. His mother, Jeanette Pickett, had bred and shown Great Danes for years, with a record number of Best of Breed winners. "But too many of her dogs and other Great Danes had suffered and died from stomach bloat," Jim explained. "Experts told her it was genetic for that large breed, but she didn't accept that; she intuitively knew the breed could live longer and healthier lives with better preventative care." Jeanette challenged those who told her probiotics, which were only given to livestock at that time, weren't appropriate for dogs. Her relentless search for a cure led her to a New Zealand researcher who confirmed that his studies pointed to the relative importance of canine diet over genetics. She not only started using but started formulating and selling probiotics and other nutritional supplements for dogs and other companion animals. "Thirty years later, her dogs continue to outlive the average lifespan of Great Danes by as many as five years," Jim boasted.

After more than a year of trying to resolve Dolly's digestive issues through western medicine, and the near-miss surgery, this conversation motivates me to put Dolly on probiotics and switch to a holistic veterinarian. She's less conveniently located and more expensive than the vet I'd been using. But most of it will be covered by her health insurance, and I'll try anything right now.

This vet incorporates herbs, homeopathic products, nutritional supplements, acupuncture, and spinal adjustments into her treatment plans, providing complementary options primarily based on Traditional Chinese Medicine (TCM).

"Western medicine tends to treat all patients the same, no matter the underlying patterns, which is why it doesn't work for everyone," Dolly's new holistic vet explains. "In traditional Chinese medicine, the body is seen as balancing two opposing forces: yin and yang. Health is achieved by keeping the body in a balanced state because disease results from an imbalance of yin and yang. Imbalances lead to a blockage in the flow of qi [pronounced *chee*] – vital energy – along the meridians. The aim of Chinese veterinary medicine is to restore an animal's balance. If we can restore balance, we can restore health."

She asks me questions related to Dolly's preference for hot or cold, to detect a yin or yang deficiency because Dolly's pulse, as felt in her rear legs, is in a state of imbalance between these opposite but complementary forces. I tell her Dolly seeks hot – she can be found lying in the tiniest sliver of sunlight on the floor. The vet explains that suggests Dolly has a yang deficiency, which can cause a body to feel cold and have poor digestion, loose stools, and lower back pain.

The physical examination of Dolly is unlike any I've ever witnessed. It focuses on her tongue's shape, color, and moisture level, and her pulse, checking for one of fifteen abnormal rhythms commonly seen in animals. She palpates Dolly for sensitivities along her meridians and to gauge her body temperature in her ears and limbs.

The vet is pleased to hear I give Dolly Reiki treatments, which also unblock and balance qi. Despite my familiarity with energy medicine, my resolve is tested as I watch the vet prepare to push short, thin needles into Dolly's furry body. She's so trusting: *Am I subjecting my puppy to torture?*

Seeing me flinch, the vet assures me this won't hurt Dolly. Although needles used in China are thicker and, therefore, more effective, Americans don't tolerate pain well so needles used in America have been scaled back. Dolly calmly sits as the first needle is inserted, placed in a meridian at the top of her head to relax her, giving her a Martian-like appearance. That point is the governing vessel, running midline from under the nose to just under the tail. It's also called the permission point. By the time all twenty needles are inserted – from her head to her tail – Dolly is nearly asleep on the floor while Eastern music plays.

According to the vet's website, "Acupuncture is the 2,300-year-old traditional Chinese medical art and science of using small needles inserted into specific body points to affect healing changes. Acupuncture is known through research in modern times to positively influence immune system function, gastrointestinal function, and internal organ function...Acupuncture may be best known for its positive benefit in a large variety of gastrointestinal disorders including inappetence, vomiting, diarrhea and constipation, and bloating..."

Alignment of energy centers and body rhythms to benefit gastrointestinal disorders.

Please let this be the answer.

Two hours later, I'm armed with a recommendation to feed her grain-free food (as opposed to the corn-based diet recommended by the western vet), vitamins, probiotics, and a gray-green silky powder referred to as *clay*. This clay is a geological material mixed into food to adsorb bacterial toxins and increase the reabsorption of water in the gastrointestinal tract, resulting in normalization of stool quality.

Halleluiah! One dose in, Dolly's stool normalizes in frequency and consistency. Our lives as companions soon begin to normalize as well once the toileting issues abate. My only regret is my delay in seeking holistic remedies.

No shit.

Arriving for future treatments, which include spinal adjustments to further restore her body's balance, Dolly eagerly races to the vet's door. She plays carefree in the waiting room, with no trepidation as to the poking and prodding that will follow. She's rewarded with a large, stuffed frog because "she's the only dog able to make it squeak" – a notable talent of hers, especially when I'm on the phone. But in that veterinarian's office, her squeaking prowess makes me proud.

"You won a prize," I tell her. So what if she didn't qualify for the Lioness Dog Show?

I wish I could find a holistic vet for myself – one who could do it all: homeopathy, acupuncture, visioning, energy balancing, chiropractic, TCM, and vitamin supplementation. But each human practitioner has a specialty – unlike veterinarians who must provide comprehensive care, including surgery. They deserve our utmost respect. Yet their suicide rate is exceedingly high due to compassion fatigue, financial debt, and having the ability and implements to do so. The statistics are highest for female vets who manage small practices.

* * *

When I was thirteen years old, my mother didn't get out of

bed one day. Or the next. My mom – a wellspring of energy, a whirling dervish of activity – stayed in the bedroom with the door closed. My dad told me she needed rest; I was to be quiet. The family doctor – a neighbor – would come over after office hours to check on her. He'd whisper to my dad and shake his head as he left.

I asked permission to see her and found her ensconced in bed, pale and fragile. I saw no evidence of my vibrant mother. She reached out to hold my hand, and her skin was translucent, her touch cold and clammy.

I didn't want to go back in her room after that. *I'm not ready to lose my mother,* I wrote in my journal. Was I going to be left alone with my volatile father?

My dad was obviously worried but tried to act confident to allay my fears. "Your mother's a strong woman. She'll snap out of this."

It was precisely her strength that he'd railed against over the years. From my perspective as an adolescent, my parents should have had one date and then said to each other, as they backed away, "It was nice to meet you. Hope you have a wonderful life." Instead, the only son and last born in an Italian immigrant family married a woman who, as high school valedictorian, made newspaper headlines in 1933 by declaring, "A woman's place is NOT in the home." American women had only been able to vote for thirteen years at the time of her pronouncement.

When this unlikely, star-crossed couple married, their home became the battleground for a clash of cultures. They took "opposites attract" to a whole new level; they were different on every possible continuum. My mom claimed to come from Polish royalty; my dad from Italian shepherds. My mom was an intellectual; my dad an athlete. My mom worked in business and politics; my dad was a teacher and a coach. My mom wore tailor-made business suits; my dad loved polyester leisure suits. My mom was intensely serious; my dad performed physical comedy. My mom was private and reserved; my dad was loud and emotive. My mom was a left-leaning Democrat; my dad served on the local Republican Committee. My mom was a Rosary-toting Catholic; my dad an atheist.

Mega misalignment. Yin yang yin yang yin yang.

They argued all the time. About everything. I begged my mother to divorce my father, although I had no concept what that would mean to our family. I only knew they seemed angry with each other most of the time. And I was often caught in the crossfire.

"We're never going to get a divorce," my mother would brag. "We argue too much."

Certainly, there's something to be said for not keeping concerns bottled up – they come out sideways when we do, in the form of sarcasm or resentment. My own marriage suffered from silence. But my parents didn't have one unspoken thought between them – probably equally detrimental to a healthy relationship.

Two weeks into my mom's illness, her firebrand friend, Mary, showed up unannounced and unexpected. She carried a large brown paper bag and, pushing past me, climbed the stairs to my parents' bedroom. She emerged two hours later to find me sitting at the top of the stairs waiting for her assessment, waiting for reassurance. This messy-looking, eccentric woman, with a faint moustache, southern drawl and an inability to pronounce Ls, told me, without hesitation, "Your mama's gonna be awright. Don't you worry yoursef none." She patted me on the head. Like a dog.

Two days later, my parents' bedroom door creaked open. In her beige chenille bathrobe, my mother wafted downstairs to the kitchen where she grabbed the trash bin. She threw open the refrigerator door and started removing food: bacon, margarine, bologna, hot dogs, white bread, and soda.

"Mom, what are you doing? What's wrong? Stop it!"

My frugal Depression-era mother was throwing away food! *Whatever physical ailment she'd had must have gone to her head,* I thought. *Perhaps a fever?*

"We're not eating this crap anymore!" she declared. "Mary brought me books about natural healing. She brought me vitamins and nutritional supplements. Mary cured me when our doctor couldn't. Eating crap was killing me. It's killing all of us! No more!"

She next purged the cupboard: cookies, Twinkies, candy, sugar, ketchup. Gone. Gone from my childhood home forever.

I never heard an official diagnosis of my mom's illness. Although I overheard much speculation, I didn't want to know. Now that she's gone, I wish I did. But I do know what helped her recover.

My life changed in many ways that day. My mom became a disciple of natural (now labeled *clean*) eating. Sprouts, wheat germ, and lecithin wound up in everything we ate. For Christmas, she'd give friends and relatives unappreciated vitamins. She was an outspoken missionary, preaching to all who'd listen, "You are what you eat" and "The whiter the bread, the sooner you're dead" (her favorite call-out when waitresses brought Parker House rolls to the table).

My mother's guru was Adelle Davis, a pioneer in the study of nutrition who preached against processed food, saturated fats, and pesticides in the 1960s – long before the explosion of fast food...and our waistlines. She was also a forerunner in toxicity awareness. Her book *Let's Get Well*, which messy Mary had brought into our lives, prompted my mother to replace our aluminum pots and pans with stainless steel. Decades later, a study published by the National Center for Biotechnology found that aluminum from cookware can leach into certain foodstuffs – amounts differ based on the chemical composition of the food. Some studies suggest a correlation between aluminum exposure and breast cancer. Although not conclusive, the American Cancer Society's website includes this statement: "Some research has suggested that these aluminum compounds may be absorbed by the skin and cause changes in estrogen receptors of breast cells...Some scientists have suggested that using aluminum-based compounds in antiperspirants may be a risk factor for the development of breast cancer."

A possible correlation between aluminum and Alzheimer's has also been suspected. The Agency for Toxic Substances and Disease Registry posts this equivocation on its website: "Some studies show that people exposed to high levels of aluminum may develop Alzheimer's disease, but other studies have not found this to be true. We do not know for certain that aluminum causes Alzheimer's disease."

But they don't deny it could.

A related concern is the leaching of Bisphenol A (BPA) found in plastic food containers, canned goods, and water bottles. Banned from baby bottle components, BPA is a weak synthetic estrogen that acts as a hormone disruptor, affecting estrogen and other hormones, throwing off hormonal balance, another possible trigger for breast cancer.

Dolly's bowls are aluminum, and I supplement her kibble with dog food and pumpkin from BPA-lined cans. Female dogs can get breast cancer. If there's even the slightest risk, shouldn't I try to minimize her exposure to such toxins? And my own.

I'm starting to think I should live in a bubble.

Reflecting back, our already-volatile family's transition to clean eating had been far from easy. I was a sugar-craving teenager; my dad was addicted to fried foods. We both pushed back against supplements. My parents' diametrically-opposed eating habits became another source of tension between them. When left to his own devices, my father ate French fries, hot dogs, and doughnuts. But years later, when my mother was told her 70-year-old husband had a one-year survival prognosis from advanced prostate cancer, she forced a nutritious regimen on him. He was scared enough to comply while repeatedly reminding his pushy wife, "You're not a doctor."

Actually, she'd forbidden his doctor to tell him his prognosis was terminal. She believed in the power of positive thinking, knew if her husband heard his days were numbered, they would be. He was prone to dark thinking.

When she was stricken with brain cancer, my sister and I conspired to not tell her the tumors were malignant. *It had worked for our dad*, we reasoned. *We must now protect her from the truth to give her a reason to keep fighting.* All that healthy living had to count for something! I snuck vitamins and health-food rations into the hospital; we kept promising her that she'd get better soon.

What we told her didn't align with what her body knew: It was her time. I now believe she'd have died sooner, instead of lingering in confused hopefulness, if we'd told her the truth. I wish we had.

I'd lied to both my parents at the end of their lives. They both probably knew because I was never good at it.

Dr. Bernie Siegel writes that no doctor should try to predict how long a patient will live. Too many variables, too many miracles. Too much free will, too much destiny. My father lived twenty years longer than the one-year prognosis, surviving his nutrition-conscious wife by ten months. When she was in a coma just before she died, I caught him inserting a deep-fried onion ring into her slack mouth, a parting gesture that gave me a much-needed laugh at the saddest of times. It was the perfect ending to their misaligned relationship: the yin and yang of it all. Evident right there, in that greasy onion ring.

Yin and yang: Two seemingly opposite forces that are actually complementary.

When Adelle Davis had died years earlier of multiple myeloma at 70 years of age, well-meaning friends tried to convince my mother to abandon her discipleship. My mother's justification was simple, parroting Ms. Davis' own response to her terminal diagnosis: "She would have died younger if she hadn't followed such a healthy lifestyle." My mother forged ahead, gaining momentum like a hurricane over the Gulf. "It's hard to be ahead of your time," she recalled in later years. "No one understands, and you're subject to ridicule. If we do come back for another life, I'm going to come back stupid. It's easier."

My mother was way ahead of her time with clean eating and holistic practices. And she, too, would be subject to lifestyle questioning upon getting ill: *All those sprouts for nothing?*

Our culture is not forgiving of falls from grace. The misalignment of Adelle Davis' and my mother's wellness-based practices with their cancer diagnoses tempts us to *throw the baby out with the bathwater*. We need and want to believe in the infallibility of certain theories or beliefs or people. Or deities. The quick fix. Easy answers. Cause and effect: *Take this pill, and you'll get well. Pray, and you'll be healed.* We want to be able to count on a conditioned response, to have Pavlov's dog salivate when the bell rings. We don't cope well with the unpredictability that results from too many variables. Nor do we have the patience to wait it out.

Yet in the rhythms and bounty of the Earth, we can find answers. Many now seek a re-alignment with Mother Earth, not just in their dietary habits but by physically connecting with the planet. Earthing or grounding is a timeless practice of connecting body, mind, and spirit directly with Earth's electrons. Like other animals, Homo sapiens used to sleep directly on the ground where the magnetic fields recharged their own electromagnetic fields. But, as one theory goes, when we started wearing rubber-soled shoes and built homes with flooring, our physiology began to suffer from the lack of direct exposure to the Earth's energy waves. Beyond the craze of magnetic bracelets, anklets, and mattresses, moving magnetic therapy is gaining scientific recognition long after we've unquestioningly accepted the ability of magnetic resonance (MRI) to diagnose disease. It's different technology, but apparently the concept of using natural elements to heal our bodies is a little harder to accept than their diagnostic utility.

Likewise, food we eat is no longer aligned with the natural rhythms of the seasons, due in part to corporate farms like

Monsanto. Crops have seasons depending on our geography. For example, according to the Environmental Working Group's website, "Strawberries were once a seasonal, limited crop, but heavy use of pesticides has increased yield and stretched the growing season. In California, where most U.S. strawberries are grown, each acre is treated with an astonishing 300 pounds of pesticides." As many as 17 different pesticides have been found on fruit consumers buy. Overall, the artificial conditions under which food is grown and harvested, the use of pesticides during growth and after harvesting, genetic modifications, growth hormones, and antibiotics compromise DNA, making all species more susceptible to disease such as cancer, reproductive and developmental damage, hormone disruption, and neurological problems.

So too, as we seek to re-align with the Earth, we look to the skies to align with natural light. We know that light heals: Jaundiced babies are treated with phototherapy as are those suffering from Seasonal Affective Disorder (SAD), which typically occurs during winter months when daylight is shortest. The current epidemic of Vitamin D deficiency, due to concerns over contracting skin cancer from sun exposure, is now associated with such far-ranging maladies as depression, allergies, osteoporosis, and numerous cancers.

As early as the 1960s, Adelle Davis was writing about the importance of Vitamin D from the sun and various food sources. Today, most doctors recommend supplementation for all genders and ages.

Doreen Virtue is one of many who correlates the invention of the electric light bulb with the onset of disease. Humans were meant to rise with the sun and stop their labor when natural light fades from the sky. This is aligned with circadian rhythms – physical, mental, and behavioral changes that follow a 24-hour cycle of light and darkness. Artificial light has allowed us to extend our waking and working hours, bypassing and even disrupting the natural rhythms essential to maintaining a healthy immune system.

This concern is validated in a report published on the website of Environmental Health Perspectives, quoting Richard Stevens, a cancer epidemiologist at the University of Connecticut Health Center: "...in an environment where there is much artificial light at night – such as Manhattan or Las Vegas – there is much more opportunity for exposure of the retina to photons that might disrupt circadian rhythm..." One Israeli study found a correlation between brightly-lit cities and breast cancer.

Our seven primary chakras mirror the colors of sunrise and sunset, creating a rainbow in our bodies when light (external) and water (internal) combine. Activation and alignment of these chakras is considered critical to balancing our qi, to maintaining our health. But Dr. Virtue maintains that windows filter the full spectrum of natural light provided by the sky, intercepting the light from sunsets, which activates our lower energy centers with red, orange and yellow (base, sacral, and solar plexus chakras, respectively) as well as intercepting moonlight and starlight, which activate our upper energy centers with green, blue, indigo and violet (heart, throat, third eye, and crown chakras, respectively).

When I was a child, my mom would take me outside on clear nights to point out constellations. I didn't want to go, didn't care about the stories she'd tell that relied on imaginary lines connecting the twinkling lights to create characters in the night sky. Orion. Cassiopeia. The Seven Sisters. It didn't matter to me that the North Star was aligned with the outer edge of the Big Dipper.

Now I wish I'd paid more attention.

When I walk Dolly at night, I wistfully look up at that same sky and imagine my mother once again pointing out constellations to me. From a different vantage point. And I wonder if that was part of her spiritual journey that she tried to share with me.

In astrology, the moon governs our subconscious desires and emotions. It's associated with intuition and our ability to nurture ourselves and others. A full moon is celebrated in many traditions as a time to release habits and behaviors not aligned with our higher selves. I have regularly brought Dolly for audiences with the moon, enlisting lunar intervention for both of us, writing this ode to its fullness over several seasons. The moon never disappoints.

I. *Each month you appear*
   Full-faced behind tall pines
   I walk her up the shadowy path
   To behold your brilliance

   Though shadows frighten
   I bring her before you
   We humbly stand prostrate
   Help my puppy feel better

   Pine cones, acorns, sticks
   Gobbled in rapid succession
   Insignificant in the grand scheme
   Shine upon her, grant her mercy

   I know your transcendent power
   Energy of the Universe cradled in your sphere
   You've healed us before
   I seek what you might spare tonight

   She's a good puppy
   With a heart big enough to love all you can see
   Frisky and impatient when I began this plea
   She's now still to prove me not a liar

   This planet needs her purity of spirit
   And your intercession
   Do you have enough alchemy
   To protect us from our bad choices?

Perhaps I ask too much
If so, what you've granted is enough
Accept my gratitude
For letting me bask in your glow

Blue and orange rings surround your creamy center
Ripples of light radiate
My tears serve as prisms
As healing energy rains down from the heavens.

II. You again beckon through the treetops
  Your round face a beacon
  I'm drawn to you
  Compelled like the ocean

  We return to give thanks
  I present her under your fullness
  Look how she's grown!
  She's doing so well

  She's playful now
  Your kindly face beams down
  More patient than I with her antics
  You smile on

  What's that?
  She's eating an acorn!
  Damn it! Drop it!
  I curse into the sacred realm

  This too under your watchful gaze
  Shamed by my own behavior
  Perhaps neither my pup nor I
  Can transcend our waywardness

Forgive our brashness
Help us both make good choices
Your radiance absolves
As I humbly guide her home.

It's in our alignment with the rhythms of the Earth, with planets and stars, with the sun and moon, that we find our healthy center. That both (wo)man and beast discover the Divine within.

Mother and Child

> *...When human mothers view images of their child or
> their dog, a common network of brain areas related
> to emotion, reward, and affiliation is activated. Thus,
> diverse aspects of our biology appear to be tuned into
> dogs and children in remarkably similar ways.*
>
> - Dr. Brian Hare

Dolly is without pedigree papers, so her date of birth is unknown. I'm told she was born on a farm in mid-May, so I designate Mother's Day as her birthday. Today, she's two years old.

I take the birthday girl for a walk, hoping to generate enough serotonin to lift the funk of this motherless child. There are many middle-aged women in my neighborhood but few with visitors' cars in their driveways. From that observation, I surmise that on this day designated to honor our earthly source of life, many mothers are not with their adult children. And many adult children are not with their mothers.

In a bizarre way, this neighborhood scene – all these women alone on Mother's Day – gives me comfort: Even if I'd had children, I might still be alone today. There are no guarantees that offspring will live nearby, be attentive, or even like you as you both age.

But it makes me want to shout out, to rent a billboard, to sound the warning: *If you still have a mother on this earthly plane, spend as much time with her as you can. Because too soon, she'll be gone forever.*

After moving four hours away from my hometown, I seldom saw my mother on Mother's Day. We postponed paying homage to motherhood each year to keep peace in our family. My father's birthday followed by less than two weeks, so we'd celebrate both on the same day – *his* day. To have done the opposite would have been unthinkable...to him. So my mother was one of those women without her children on Mother's Day. She always assured me a phone call would suffice until we gathered for his birthday. "It's not that big a deal to me. Really, honey."

I now wonder if it might have been a bigger deal than she let on. Like most women of that generation, she was used to deferring. Now that my parents are gone, I wish we'd had two celebrations. But at the time, one was all I could handle due to the all-too-predictable family drama.

In contrast, I didn't miss one Father's Day with my dad; the consequences would have been harsh. But I did marry a man who shared his birthday, creating some unwelcome competition between my father and husband on that day. Before the wedding, my mother pondered aloud the wisdom of my marrying someone born on the same day as my father. I never asked if she were concerned with astrological or earthly complications.

* * *

The cross-species connection that humans have with pets is intense, the bond so strong that it feels wrong to use the word *owner*. It's unnatural to think of a loved one as *property* (although American wives legally were until the early 20th century). It feels more like a parent-child relationship. For good reason.

A scientific study by Miho Nagasawa, summarized and popularized in the book *The Genius of Dogs: How Dogs are Smarter than You Think,* reveals a deep evolutionary connection between dogs and humans. Dogs' social intelligence has made them more similar to human infants than to their wolf ancestors. An interspecies chemical loop unites the brains of humans and dogs. Gazing into each other's eyes causes a rise in our oxytocin and theirs, a hormone formerly only associated with the bond between humans and their infants. In the authors' words, "Dogs have hijacked a bonding pathway."

That "discovery" lags way behind empirical evidence offered by pet-parents. We fall hard for dogs. They become our fur-babies, our truest companions, which is why we end up with a big hurt when their short lives come to an end.

When dogs became the first domesticated animal, sometime between 10,000 and 40,000 years ago, they became dependent on humans for their survival. Dolly's totally at the mercy of my deciding how and when her needs will be met. When she has to "go potty," she has to find a way to get my attention; she makes eye contact, nudges my arm, or appears by my side. At 5:30pm sharp, she notifies me it's dinner time, using the same strategies but has no control over whether I feed her then or make her wait until I finish what I'm doing. And she has no say over what ends up in her bowl.

Dolly has to ask and then wait – like very young and very old people. There are only a few fleeting decades of independence and self-determination separating these life stages.

It reminds me of how my parents lost their independence when they became infirm, surrendering control of their lives. They'd never imagined a day when they'd have to ask to go to the bathroom or "hold it" until help arrived. Or that they wouldn't be able to decide what and when to eat, instead having to sit and wait for food to appear. Or be unable to hop in a car and drive away.

As her caregiver, I try to do what's in Dolly's best interest; I take pride in being a conscientious pet-parent. But I can get weary of playing nursemaid to this dependent being who won't advance much beyond this level of functioning. *Your baby will always be your baby*, the puppy ad tells us. *Is that a threat or a promise?* I wonder. Because if my own needs don't get met, I'll be no good to her. I learned that while caring for my parents.

This need for respite is why I signed up for another yoga course, one of the many activities I suspended when Dolly burst upon the scene. A course with dogs is also offered (*doga*), but I choose to go it alone. At our first class, I casually mention that my dog is in the car. "Hope you left the windows open," my yoga instructor cautions.

"I did, of course!" I respond. But from that moment on, the power of suggestion takes flight: *Are the windows open enough? Is the sun beating down on the car? Does Dolly have water left? Could she die from hyperventilating?*

Pets, like babies and small children, can die if left in a hot car for even a short time without ventilation. Although it's late in the afternoon on a mild spring day, concern for Dolly's welfare once again trumps my own self-care, rendering me unable to focus on the various poses. *Downward Facing Dog* sends me into an upside-down tizzy. *What if my dog is facing downward in the car right now?*

Yoga has been shown to improve muscle strength, respiration, metabolism, bone and heart health, and circulation. Although I'm taking this class to help me be more balanced, relaxed, and calm, I'm a wreck wondering how Dolly is faring!

As the group glides into *The Eagle* pose, I rapid-walk several blocks to check on Dolly. I find her lying comfortably in the back of my shady SUV, windows adequately ajar. She stares at me as if to say, *Are you back already? I was enjoying MY respite.*

I again allowed self-doubt, triggered by a reasonable inquiry, to dominate my psyche. My mind had run wild with concern for my little girl dog who has no choice but to trust me with her life.

Who can handle that? One of the reasons I didn't have children.

My mother expended much of her parental energy keeping me safe, perhaps out of guilt. She was generous, however, with words of affirmation, which I, in turn, offer my pup. Dolly, like most dogs, responds to an endearing tone sprinkled with exclamation and question marks to encourage and reinforce good behavior. Sometimes it feels like those words are meant for me too – like a higher power is reinforcing me through my own voice. When I tell Dolly, "You're such a good girl!" I wonder if I'm saying it because I need to hear it to quell my self-doubt. Wherever the message comes from, I accept the praise on Dolly's and my behalf.

My father was much more child-centered than my mother, installing a commercial-grade swing set, basketball hoop, and built-in pool, and flooding the yard for ice skating. He was emotionally dependent on his two daughters, expecting us to affirm him. He turned to us for companionship when my mother was preoccupied with her business and political outlets. Like Peter Pan, he lashed out when we disappointed him by growing up. By moving away. By living our own lives.

At the age of 29, I married a man with two adolescent daughters. When Peter and I agreed to not have children, I had to work up the nerve to tell my mother. "I understand," she quickly responded over the phone. "I didn't want children either." We laughed, but it stung, especially knowing I was born when she was almost forty, six years after her first child. She had no good options; I was an unwanted gift like Dolly. How might her life have been different without me? Perhaps she wouldn't have stayed.

I wasn't a full generation older than my stepdaughters, and they had a nurturing mother and grandmother so didn't need another maternal figure. My relationship with them was more like that of an aunt. Or guidance counselor.

We didn't get together on Mother's Day.

When my mother and I reversed roles at the end of her life – when I parented my parent – I was better at meeting her physical needs than her emotional needs.

She'd modeled that. Because meeting physical needs is neater, easier, quicker.

Less painful.

Less helpful.

"Be her daughter, not her nurse," the chaplain had instructed. I redirected myself in my journal:

> Hold her hand instead of handing her water.
> Hug her instead of feeding her.
> Feed her spirit instead of her body.
> Others can manage her physical needs.
> Your role is to love her.

And I did. Keeping vigil at her deathbed, I told her, "Mom, I probably should've had children so they'd do this for me someday." She slowly turned her head toward me, drolly replying, "You should've thought of that sooner."

I had thought of it sooner – and rejected that option. I knew from the time I learned the facts-of-life (thanks to ten-year-old Georgie who proudly displayed his penis in my playhouse when I was seven years old) that I didn't want to bear children. It made no sense that my belly could stretch like a balloon, and a baby's head could come out of my pee hole. (Georgie obviously didn't have all the facts straight.)

I played with dolls – loved my "babies" – yet never named them. That was the extent of my yearning.

I didn't dare give voice to my lack of maternal instinct, instead hoping it would kick in. At every age milestone, I awaited a change of heart. At 16, I told myself I'd be "ready" at 21. At 21, 25. At 25, 30. At 30, 32. I read books evaluating the binary choice because if your resistance to childbirth is physiological, there's no compromise between zero kids and five. That was part of the undoing of my relationship with my college boyfriend; he wanted a large family. A husband who already had two daughters with no desire for more was a much better match for me.

I was secondarily concerned about how I might parent. My parents loved me dearly – with a full complement of attached strings. I worried about manifesting and magnifying my mother's tendency to hover and overprotect, and my dad's tendency to rage. For that reason, I didn't consider adoption.

Even though I was grappling with this during the second wave of feminism – a time when Gloria Steinem was challenging all stereotypes – I felt abnormal; I was closeted much like gay youth are today. There was, and still is, a stigma attached to being childless-by-choice. People you barely know inquire as to why you didn't have children. To some, it seems selfish; to others, considerate of the overpopulated planet.

When my age made it biologically unwise for me to bear a child, I was relieved. Only once did I wish I'd chosen differently: When my mother died, I felt the yearning for my bloodline to continue. Even that didn't last long.

All those mothers alone on Mother's Day – just like mine used to be.

Dolly and I reverse roles at times, depending on her mood and my behavior. Sometimes she's the child but often the mother – nurturing, demanding, and disappointed. When I was hungover and wanted to sleep it off, she stood next to my bed and barked in my face as if to say, *GET UP! This is your own damn fault.*

Or when I'm late getting home, rather than greeting me in a typical Pavlovian response to hearing the garage door, she lies perfectly still, ignoring my greeting. Looking straight ahead, like I'm not there, punishing me for being away. Sometimes I can almost hear her say, *Oh, it's youuuuuuuuuu.*

Does she drive the nature of our interactions, or do I? Hard to say. Parents and children seem to morph into third entities.

* * *

Rick visits on occasion, slowly becoming more comfortable with Dolly. Her unassuming nature and playful spirit match his own. When he visits, he offers me respite, which every single parent needs. But I find it hard to relinquish guardianship.

Today, I spy out the window when he takes Dolly out. I watch him remove her leash, allowing her to do her own thing – head down, sniffing the ground, sampling new vegetation. She wags enthusiastically and prances. He chooses *happy* over *safe* for her, even though she may later regurgitate her choices. With so much to experience in this world, safe is a limiting criterion for deciding how to spend time.

Better sorry than safe?

"I'd rather have ten minutes of *wonderful* than a lifetime of *just okay*," the daughter declares in the movie *Terms of Endearment*. Perspective colors our interpretation of *wonderful* and repeatedly plays out between Rick and me. Like now.

I run outside, unable to simply observe them any longer. "Look at her! She's filthy! I spent $100 having her groomed last week, and she just ran through mud puddles!"

"She looks like she has little black boots on her feet," Rick laughs. "She's happy. We can always clean her up."

"We" turns out to be me...again. I wash Dolly's feet in a bucket of warm water, realizing she's no worse-for-wear and had fun being a dog. We each should figure out what our *wonderful* is. And try to be taken outside by the person who'll let us pursue it with abandon.

* * *

Dolly loves playing with Kevin's dog, Murphy, when we're in town. She scurries to him as fast as her legs can carry her. But I don't like the way they play. Play-fight, really. Although about the same size, he's muscular compared to her delicate build. He chases her, butting her with his head like a goat. I worry about the impact of this heat-seeking missile on Dolly's hips and back. Yet when she and I play, she wants me to play like that – like another dog. What I consider rough play, she considers fun. She taunts me to chase her, then immediately starts to run sideways like she does to stay upright when Murphy charges at her.

Acting like a dog is good for Dolly. I should play with her as she wants to be played with. But play is not something I do easily or willingly. I prefer to walk Dolly rather than throw a ball thirty times. However, in my defense, I can claim vitreous separations in both eyes, with residual black floaters, from a head collision with Dolly when we both charged the idle tennis ball in a moment of frivolity. She has a hard head in more ways than one.

By investing so much time and energy in Dolly's physical well-being, I sometimes forfeit the opportunity to simply hug a warm puppy. I don't typically roll on the floor with her or snuggle with her for no reason. Independently of each other and years apart, an aura reader and my masseuse both cautioned that I live too much in my head and should work on involving my heart more in choices I make. Even now, I'm opting to write about Dolly rather than stroke her as she sleeps at my feet. I should be gazing into her copper-brown eyes. Get that oxytocin going!

In contrast, Dolly's job is to engage, to connect. While I go about my busy-ness, like my mother, Dolly reminds me there is value to play...especially with her. She interprets my doing yoga on the floor, with my arms extended in the *Child* pose, as an invitation to play, bringing me toys and pawing at me. (Or maybe she just hates yoga since she frequently interrupts my practice.)

When she stands over me or lies by my side, the sight of her kind face is more soothing than the meditative music I play. More loving than my own self-care. And when recently assuming the *Cobra* pose, I asked the Universe to tell me what I need; in response, Dolly dropped a squeak toy on my back. Not too subtle, that Universe.

Obvious to all by now, I harbor guilt over being an imperfect pet-parent. Maybe Dolly would've had a better life had she been given to (or chosen) a different family. Kids to play with and a less formal home environment. Maybe she wouldn't have taken that fall as a pup. Maybe she'd have fewer digestive issues if her family had found the right diet for her sooner. Maybe she'd be more playful if she didn't have such an intense mom. It makes me wonder if adoptive parents ever question whether their adoptee could have done better.

But then I wouldn't have had this transformative experience triggered by her arrival in my life. No one's perfect, despite my quest. She could have done worse.

Can I accept that everything is perfect as it is? That we're where we're supposed to be, for reasons we may not understand? That Dolly and I were meant to be together, for better AND worse? That it's not about luck but about destiny?

If so, we both chose perfectly when choosing to be together.

As I bid Dolly goodnight, I wonder aloud to her about her day:

> *Did you get enough attention?*
> *Did I touch you enough to let you know you're loved?*
> *Did I respond to your invitation to play?*
> *Or did we just exist in the same house?*
> *Me stepping around or over you.*
> *Tomorrow, I'll be more mindful of my responsibility,*
> *Not just to take care of you but to show I care about you.*

Shades of the chaplain's reminder: *Your role is to love her.*

Realizing these are *mere words*, I lie on the floor next to her.

"Is that your stomach gurgling or mine?" I ask. I truly don't know; we are as one being, lying close together as I stroke her silky coat. Our lives, even our bodies, seem indistinguishable in this moment. As if she sprang from my loins.

* * *

Each evening at sunset, I have "Mommy's Time Out" on the dock. By myself. Alone. To honor the setting sun, to read, to align my chakras, to get away from my computer – and away from Dolly. But tonight, as I head toward the lake, I glance back at the deck to see a forlorn pup, her chin perched on the bottom railing. The same railing her little puppy body slipped under that fateful night. Now, her paw barely fits under there.

Guilt kicks in – kids, parents, and puppies have a way of inducing it. I could take her with me, but I cherish my solitary meditative moments by the water, as the floating dock gently rolls with the waves, and the sun takes its leave in a brilliant firestorm of chakra colors. I dread Dolly charging down the hill, eating vegetation all the way, splashing into the water followed by droplets assailing my books and journals when she shakes them off.

But something about that beguiling face this evening compels me to say, "You can come with me, Dolly. Only you're not doing any crazy-dog stuff. You're just going to walk down on a leash, nice and calm, and walk onto the dock, like you're a big girl. We're simply going to watch the sunset. Got it?"

Her leaping doesn't inspire confidence.

I clip on her leash to thwart her would-be free-form race down to the water, about 125 feet away. She calmly walks by my side (sniffing the treats in my beach bag), and together we arrive at the Adirondack chairs, which I employ to block her escape off the dock.

She lies next to my chair, facing the house, watching the waves roll to shore. Dolly, who repeatedly needed rescuing her first summer after falling into the lake, now knows enough to not get too close to the edges of the dock. But by facing the house, she's missing the activity on the water: boats, jet skis, water skiers, swimmers. She doesn't even turn to look at the quacking ducks. I try to get her interested in the many sights and sounds – even turn her head in that direction. She continues to focus on the shore.

"Dolly, don't you know you're a bird dog? You're supposed to be interested in ducks since you were bred to retrieve dead ones."

She's not impressed by her lineage. Or the ducks. She should be – they're the reason she exists. Retrievers came into prominence in the early 1800s because a medium-sized dog was needed for wildfowling. Since game was desirable for food and sport, a lord in Scotland developed the original strain of goldens with soft mouths to fetch water fowl without damaging the goods.

Dolly is a field retriever, which is typically smaller and darker in color, with a narrower head. They're considered better for hunting than conforming to show-ring standards.

No kidding. Conforming is not Dolly's strong suit. I

would put her beauty up against any show dog, though. It's foolish of me to be prideful of Dolly's appearance – I had no part in that, despite my maternal feelings toward her (and our matching brown eyes). Perhaps I have influenced her sweet personality, which does get factored into assessing physical appearance. But this breed has a reputation for being endearing, regardless.

Goldens have always been one of the most popular breeds in America. Because of their intelligence and propensity to please, they're popular guide dogs for the blind. Because of their friendly faces, they're media darlings, appearing frequently in ads and commercials selling everything from baked beans to cars. But taking care of their people's emotional needs is their primary career path these days.

Unfortunately, they've been labeled "The Cancer Dog" – more than 60% of goldens succumb to cancer. That's why I'm doing everything in my power to improve Dolly's odds. A few decades ago, the lifespan of a golden retriever averaged up to 17 years; it's now shrunk to 10-12 years. I know first-hand, having lost three to that insidious disease at or before that age. Studies are being conducted as to why the sudden drop for this breed. An abundance of recessive genes caused by excessive inbreeding is strongly suspected. It seems criminal – golden devotees want answers and solutions.

Dolly's holistic vet agrees we don't have to accept that fate. She also suggests Dolly may not be a purebred despite her classic appearance. I hope that's true since mixed breeds typically carry fewer genetic risks.

As Dolly and I sit together on the square wooden dock, the sun sets, backlighting the clouds with an orange and pink aura. As the sky darkens, we head back to the house, climbing the hill together at a reasonable pace, unlike her usual gallop. I'm proud of her for being such a mature companion this evening.

Gone is my mischievous puppy plotting her escape or eating an errant stick. I feel a bit melancholy, but that's the trade-off: For the butterfly to emerge, the fuzzy caterpillar must be sacrificed. The mature dog displaces the frisky puppy.

Kids and dogs – they grow up fast.

Early the next morning, believing we've turned a corner in Dolly's compliance quotient, I take her with me to skinny-dip. I envision it like swimming with a porpoise, my sweet dog and me, the pine-green mountains reflected in the still, blue water.

A Brigadoon mist envelopes us.

When we're both in the water, Dolly leapfrogs out and bolts up the hill, stopping to chomp on a stick as she looks back at me, seemingly paralyzed in the water. She disappears, shortly re-appearing at a neighbor's dock two lots down, grinning, as I scramble to find my cover-up to traipse over to retrieve my retriever.

Cripes! I do more retrieving than she does.

I apparently still have that irascible puppy I longed for last night.

May your every wish be granted, an ancient Chinese curse.

* * *

Sleeping in close proximity is said to strengthen the canine-human bond. Plus, it's just plain sweet that dogs want to sleep right next to us – if not on the bed, next to the bed. And they sleep through the night with us, even though they've slept much of the day.

When I turn off my reading light at night, I hear Dolly pad into my room. She always brushes up against the bed clothes, dragging the sheet and blanket taut across me before reclining on her bed on the floor next to me. It's as if my mother has tucked me in. And there we sleep, parallel to each other. When I sigh in the middle of night, I often hear her echo it.

Her furry face wakes me every morning around 7am – too early for me but not for a dog who needs some attention and breakfast after a long slumber.

"Lie down. Go to sleep," I command, hoping to buy a few more minutes. And sometimes, she actually does.

Before sunrise this morning, I hear the faintest of whimpers. Only part of Dolly is visible; her other parts are under my bed.

Half-asleep, I get down on the floor and try unsuccessfully to pull her out. Her torso is twisted because she'd tried to pull herself out by her front legs. I don't know how long she's been there – her whimper is so soft that it likely took a while to wake me. Her eyes plead with me to help, but I'm hesitant to tug on her again. A lesser dog might have bitten me by now, out of pain and fear.

I have no choice but to lift the queen-size bed frame off her, with corresponding box spring and mattress. I try with no success – it's way too heavy for me, and there isn't a good position for leverage. The sharp wooden corners cut painfully into my palms.

I recall reading about parents lifting cars off their children when necessary, finding the superhuman strength to do what must be done to save them. I must get my adrenalin pumping to free Dolly. With my fingers, I draw Reiki symbols on my hands and try again, this time successfully lifting the bed frame high enough for her to scramble out.

I sob in gratitude to whatever higher power assisted; I could not have lifted it alone.

Dolly comes right over to me rather than scurrying away – as if she, too, is giving thanks. She sits while I pet and hug her close, and then lies down on the other side of the room. When I wake, she's once again by my side.

Since her fall, I can't let go of my need to protect her. I carry responsibility for her every minute of every day. It's what motivates me to get between my dog and a passing car on the road. To step in front of her when another dog is charging toward her. To dream that I claw the face of a man who tries to steal her from me and offer myself as ransom instead of letting him take her.

I would die for Dolly.

That's the definition of *parent*.

Golden is more than Dolly's breed; it's her value. She's the reason I'm now outside at 5am, having been awakened by her steady gaze, which typically signals distress. It's easy to grumble, to feel sorry for myself standing in the predawn air as Dolly sniffs the ground showing no urgency. *It's always about Dolly's needs*, I reflect. *I come second now.* That's what happens when you become responsible for another life – be it parent or child.

As I turn to go back inside, I glance up at the still-night sky. There shine the brightest stars surrounding a picture-perfect sliver of a moon against a navy-blue backdrop. The same stars my mother used to show me.

That's the beauty and the burden of parenting: You see the world differently through the eyes of one you love deeply.

"May the stars carry your sadness away," Chief Dan George wrote.

The stars aligned to bring Dolly to me. To love, to learn, to laugh. To heal.

I'm where I'm supposed to be. With whom I'm supposed to be. It's perfect as it is.

"Good morning, Mom. Good morning, Dolly."

This, Too, Shall Pass

> *To everything, there is a season.*
>
> *- Ecclesiastes* 3

Too late, I spotted Baby Jesus' feet sticking out of Punkin's mouth – snatched from the tabletop nativity scene. I flew across the room to rescue the Prince of Peace. Punkin took a big gulp, and Jesus disappeared down his gullet.

I'd had that creche since childhood. Each day, I'd hop-scotch the shepherds from table to table across the living room – bringing them closer to the manger where Jesus would be making a grand entrance on Christmas morning. As an adult, I still moved the Wise Men closer, following the star, even though I'd long rejected the literal narrative of his virgin birth. The story still holds magic and nostalgia for me.

But the Savior had disappeared into my dog's stomach. Like Jonah and the whale.

This was unusual behavior for Punkin. Unlike Dolly, he was not a forager. He didn't typically eat our stuff; it was more his style to crash into it. But since a mast cell tumor had invaded his golden body, he'd been on oral chemotherapy, which dramatically altered his behavior. The potential cure turned my joyful, interactive dog into a recluse who hid under the piano rather than interact. Knowing that was no life for Punkin, we discontinued treatment to try to re-kindle some of his spark before he died. The Universe granted us a couple more months.

During that time, he ate Jesus. Seemed fitting in a way.

I called the vet's office: "My dog just ate Baby Jesus from the manger."

Silence. *Crank call?*

I repeated myself.

Laughter.

"I'm serious. It was ceramic – about one square inch. I'm quite sure it went down whole – I didn't see Punkin chew him."

Pause. "Well, that gives a whole new meaning to 'the body of Christ,' doesn't it?"

I allowed myself to laugh, despite concern for my dog and the disappearance of the lead in my childhood nativity scene.

"Unless he shows distress, just watch for Jesus to exit the other end."

"I think he's too big to come out the other end."

"You'd be surprised what Jesus can do. Don't underestimate him. It'll pass."

Laughter in the background tells me I'm being broadcast. That clinic had quite a run (and financial boon) with Punkin's antics over the years.

I hung up and told my husband we had to monitor every poop, searching for the baby. Like King Herod.

"Jeezus," he replied.

"Exactly."

Over the next few days, we watched for the Second Coming. Nothing that appeared was recognizable as the body of Christ. After three days, we had to assume he'd found another way out.

* * *

Because Dolly's had digestive issues since a young pup, every one of her poops has been monitored for both timing and consistency. Probiotics, clay, and pumpkin have improved her condition so much that when she has four straight days of diarrhea, I become alarmed.

It's never lasted this long. And it's gone from bad to better to worse.

A dog – or human – can die from dehydration if diarrhea goes unchecked.

Please not yet is the plea to the heavens of every person fearful of losing a loved one – including pets. *Please not yet.* Because we know how innocuously it can start: a limp, a lump, diarrhea, loss of appetite, blood in the urine, a cough. A dog acts well until she's too sick to fake it. Echoes of their wolf ancestry cause them to not show illness or weakness for fear of being left behind the pack, vulnerable as prey themselves. They bravely persevere, giving rise to the term *sicker than a dog*. By the time they act sick, they're already very sick.

I'd prayed *Please not yet* when my mother was dying, fully aware that I'd never be ready. So much time to prepare for it, so little time to prepare for it. Because there is no preparation for it. Just one day, something starts to go terribly wrong.

Please not yet, I'd prayed for Punkin, Dryphuss, and Rusty.

Please not yet, I pray every time Dolly is symptomatic.

Please not yet, I pray tonight because her condition is getting worse, and I have to leave for a prior commitment. I won't be home for five hours.

Feeling powerless, I do what I should have done on Day One: give her Reiki. From the passenger seat of the car, I send it as Rick drives. I also pray to Archangel Raphael, known for healing minds, spirits, and bodies. I try not to imagine the worst, health or mess-wise.

We race back immediately after the event to find Dolly sleeping with no sign of distress. I take her out, and she only pees. I perform Reiki on her and resolve not to feed her until her bowels clear.

Upon waking, she still has no urge. I again perform Reiki and cast my prayers, wondering if I've overcorrected.

She hangs around the kitchen, begging to be fed. I remind her I'll feed her after a "good" bowel movement. She heads to the door, delivering as soon as we go out. A solid poop, one only a mother could love.

I thank the divine powers that carried healing energy to her when we were apart. That heard and answered my plea even though I can be negligent in doing "the work" and was slow to remember the power of prayer and Reiki. Those modalities seldom fail me – yet they're often my last resort, where I turn when desperate, even though I've been given proof that they help the darkness pass.

I'm guided to use my crystal to determine what had caused her digestive distress. I hold it over each food item and supplement to discover, based on the pendulum's rotation, that the fish oil I'd been putting in her food had become rancid. Why didn't I do that sooner when applied kinesiology (energy testing) was imminently available to me?

Although my healing interventions have proven effective in many ways, *please-not-yet* won't be up to me. If it were, this dog I initially didn't want would be by my side forever. Over and over in this life, I'm forced to confront the reality that *all things must pass.*

Zen master Thich Nhat Hanh reminds us, "It is not impermanence that makes us suffer. What makes us suffer is wanting things to be permanent when they are not." In simpler terms, if we could just accept that everything changes, we wouldn't be unhappy.

One of the most haunting and instructive folktales is the story of King Solomon who commanded his ministers to bring him a ring with magic powers that could quickly change his mood. If he were sad, it would make him happy; if happy, sad. After a six-month search, he was presented with a ring that read, *This, too, shall pass.*

Powerful mantra for staying centered.

As a college freshman, I hand-printed this Robert Frost poem to post on my wall.

Nature's first green is gold,
Her hardest hue to hold.
Her early leaf's a flower;
But only so an hour.
Then leaf subsides to leaf.
So Eden sank to grief,
So dawn goes down to day.
Nothing gold can stay.

Posting such a dark reminder back then was likely inspired by male rejection. But Frost's exquisite interpretation of the ephemeral nature of life takes on a deeper significance for me as an adult. All of life is impermanent – I hate that!

Almost as much as I hate the *Serenity Prayer*. And maybe for the same reason: loss of control. I continue to push to control timing in my life. Like Dolly's toileting schedule.

One thing young children can control to the exclusion of their parents is their toileting behavior; some child behaviorists theorize that kids skillfully use this as a weapon to exert a modicum of control in a world where they have none.

Both Drs. Sigmund Freud and Benjamin Spock claimed that rigid toileting expectations caused stool-withholding and even neuroses later in life. Although new theories have softened their conclusions, I suspect Dolly's behavior may be manifesting the need I've imposed on her to accommodate my schedule.

Simply put, Dolly doesn't poop when I need or want her to. Scientists claim there are legitimate reasons for this, including interest in sniffing other dogs' scents, performance and location anxieties, and distractions. Whatever Dolly's justification, it exasperates me in the same way that toilet-training children frustrates all concerned.

And what about patients in hospitals and nursing homes who are pressured to "go" when the aide has only a few minutes to take them to the bathroom or to bring the bedpan? My mother cried more over having "accidents" than over her creeping paralysis. "I'm not incontinent. I'm not!" she'd sob.

That's what happens when there's no one to take us out.

When Dolly shows no inclination to poop this afternoon, I put her back in the house, telling her she'll have to wait several hours before the next opportunity because I have an appointment. I race home at 5pm to relieve the little dear – still no interest. By now, I'm convinced she's pooped in the house, so I inspect every room, pleased to have judged unfairly.

I feed her dinner, wondering how she can fit anything else in her colon without first dumping something out. An hour later, I take her out again. And double-check the house.

A thunderstorm begins – the perfect storm, in fact, considering Dolly's anxiety coupled with a full colon. I wait for the lightning to abate and rush her out again in the pouring rain. Despite my repeated command to "Poop, Dolly," Dolly does not.

I tell her I've met birds smarter than she when, several years ago, a bird trainer brought her parrots to an elementary school to teach pet care. Of all the interesting things those birds could do and say, the most amazing to me was their ability to poop on command. The trainer perched a bird on her arm over a tarp and said, "Poop!"

The bird pooped.

No *Polly-want-a-cracker* for these show-offs.

I called the Superintendent of Schools to tell him he had to come to the elementary school to see this. "They poop on command!" I exclaimed to my uber-intellectual boss who wouldn't say "poop" if he had a mouthful. He must've wondered what his human resources administrator was doing watching this but came to the performance at my urging.

He was decidedly less impressed than I.

Twice more this evening, I take Dolly out. In the pouring rain. No umbrella – I thought it would be quick this time.

"Poop! Now!" I command. Desperate.

She sniffs the wet ground, raindrops clinging to her eyelashes.

I resolve to call the school in the morning to get that bird trainer's phone number so she can work with my bird-brained dog. I hope someone besides me recalls that demonstration of a few years ago.

At midnight, after my last attempt, we head to bed. Dolly sleeps through the night, convincing me she'll never poop again.

The next morning, she nonchalantly complies.

Crisis over. My self-imposed crisis, that is.

I begin to ponder the concept of pooping on command. I can't do that; why should I expect Dolly to? But those freakin' birds poop on command, and guide dogs for the blind are also trained to poop on command for their owners' safety and convenience. I guess anything can be trained to go against its nature under the right circumstances. When I ask a gastroenterologist about the concept, he's mildly amused, yet sets me straight: "Many people die on the toilet because they strain. Like Elvis. That kind of pushing – *pooping-on-command*, as you call it – can put pressure on the heart, causing a heart attack in humans. Similar to shoveling."

Shit. Apparently, other approaches are in order. Pushing too hard is never good.

To complicate matters, I also want Dolly to pee on command.

Male dogs pee on everything: fire hydrants, trees, stop signs, fences, walls, car tires. They just lift a leg and whiz. They seem to always have something to offload. Dolly is my first female dog – I expected her to do the same. Instead, Dolly seeks out the perfect place to leave her little puddle. She can sniff out ten or more locations to do so and reject them. Site selection is a process, apparently.

I've spent the better part of my life advocating gender equality: *Women deserve the same opportunities as men because there's nothing inherently female or male that should prevent equal access...*and so on. But this female dog is quite different than my three prior male dogs, causing me to re-examine the intersection of nature and nurture. Yet I recognize that many factors contribute to how a dog (or person) turns out.

When my friend Jonathan arrives to pick me up for a movie, I explain I can't leave until Dolly pees. He waits inside so as not to distract Her Highness. She wanders around her toileting area while I feel the mounting pressure of him waiting.

I run inside to explain she's taking her sweet time. He reminds me we have to leave soon, or we'll be late. I run back out to find her standing there. Waiting for me, like I'm the one who's supposed to do something.

"Go pee, Dolly," I command for the millionth time in two

years. "I have to leave. This is your last chance."

The aide trying to quickly toilet patients before her shift ends.

Dolly poops. Not the kind of potty I was aiming for this time.

Oppositional defiance? Withholding?

I take her for a short walk, letting her know my expectations, my voice rising.

When we approach her toileting area again (the place she no longer wants anything to do with), I ask for the angels' intercession. I'm out of earthly options.

Dolly immediately squats and pees.

When I bring her inside, Jonathan announces, "Instead of being irritated you were taking so long, I started praying for her."

It could just be a matter of timing. Or the walk. I choose to believe Dolly's compliance was aided by both of us sending our intentions to the Universe. She didn't need more pressure; she needed positive energy. We all do.

Dolly had two people praying for her to pee. Sheesh.

Yet I remember praying for my mother to urinate, as a sign her kidneys were still working despite the cancer marching through her brain. My supplications worked for a while.

There are certainly more important things to pray for than bodily excretions. But the power of prayer is not finite – there's no such thing as wasted or frivolous prayer. *No intention is too small for the Universe to consider,* I'm learning.

Marianne Williamson recommends this prayer tagline: "All this and more."

Dolly wants all this and more. She swam this morning. Like many mornings. In and out. Smiling as she waded in, wagging her tail until submerged. Smiling as she ran out.

She doesn't know summer is finite. Doesn't know it could be the last time she swims. That cool evenings will give way to cool days. That too soon, the lake will be frozen once more. That this, too, shall pass.

All she knows is that this morning she went swimming.

Because Dolly isn't cursed with such knowing, she suffers no melancholy. But she also isn't blessed with knowing she should savor every moment because it's fleeting – and perhaps should linger a while longer in the cool waters of the mountain lake.

I'm both blessed and cursed with awareness that things change; life is ephemeral. Yet last night, I still fought back my desire to swim in the dark blue water under the stars.

I wish I hadn't.

Be Not Afraid

> *What you pay attention to grows. If your attention is*
> *attracted to negative situations and emotions, then*
> *they will grow in your awareness.*
>
> -Deepak Chopra

The clanging of Dolly's bowl as her tongue heartily chases every morsel has been music to my ears for almost three years now. For each of my prior dogs, I can remember the day I put a bowl down expecting to hear that sound. And didn't. The day I prepared their meal as always, anticipating the usual eager response only to encounter a disinterested dog. A dog who crept over to the bowl, then turned away with a downcast look. Enticements – toast, boiled chicken and rice, peanut butter – didn't do the trick. A trip to the vet, blood work, and terminal diagnoses followed.

Eating had been such a joy for them their entire lives. But they knew when it was time to let go even as I tried to hand-feed them, cheering on every tidbit hesitantly taken. As if that little nibble could make a difference. I never wanted to face the truth of their knowing they were leaving.

Nor did I when my dying parents refused to eat. When they declined nourishment, I brought them food they'd always loved. Hand-fed them in hopeful anticipation of success. Only to have nature overrule me.

After spending a weekend at a kennel, Dolly is refusing to eat. She flinches at any noise associated with her metal bowl. The ping of kibble causes her to tremble and back away.

This dog who ate voraciously – anything and everything, specializing in non-food items – won't even go into the same room as her feeding station, denying herself water as well. Crazy as it sounds, she seems afraid of her food bowls.

Her food bowls. The same bowls she's had most of her life.

I call the kennel, only to be told nothing unusual happened other than Dolly's general inability to cope with the setting. I'm not sure they'd tell me otherwise due to how we'd parted ways.

"She just can't handle it," the kennel owner had declared when I picked Dolly up on Sunday. It's true that Dolly has never adjusted to being boarded, despite attempts to quell her anxiety. Thinking she might feel safer and protected if her "den" were in her stall, I'd lug in her crate. I administered vet-prescribed doggie tranquilizers. They walked her several times a day and played calming music. Nothing was enough to counter her fears manifesting as diarrhea, uncontrollable urination, and constant whimpering, which disturbed other canine boarders.

We were invited not to return; Dolly officially flunked out of boarding.

And now, won't freaking eat.

I'm encouraged reading Internet posts on dogs' food-bowl phobias. It's apparently not that uncommon – a dog can get freaked out seeing her own reflection in a shiny metal bowl. I dutifully replace her metal bowls with plastic bowls, which are quieter but less sanitary as bacteria can hide in the scratches.

She won't go near the plastic bowls either. I try a few different locations before abandoning them.

The veterinary assistant tells me it can be traumatic for a young dog to be boarded because she can hear other dogs nearby in the dark and fear they'll attack. I wonder if it's more than that. When I'd dropped Dolly off at the kennel on Friday, the owner was speaking in harsh tones on her phone, demanding to speak with a supervisor. While still haranguing, she took the leash from me, gave me a quick wave, and pulled Dolly toward the door. Dolly kept looking back at me over her shoulder, causing pangs of guilt. Despite running late to catch a train to New York City, I sat in the parking lot for a few minutes, wondering if I should reclaim my dog instead of leaving for a weekend getaway.

I blame myself for putting my needs first, leaving her behind for the weekend. My caregiver past haunts: "You were away," my dad had said in his trademark accusatory tone. *Yes, Dad, I was away. I needed a break. You fell and broke your hip, and now I feel responsible.*

I feel constrained and tethered by Dolly. *Is there no getting away from her?* Yet my heart breaks when I do leave her. When we're separated, part of me is missing. My schedule has revolved around hers for so long that when we're apart, I think of what she'd be doing. Walking? Eating? Playing? I'm so used to her being in my car that I find myself speaking to her, throwing my voice to the rear of my SUV, saying, "How're you doing back there? You're so quiet." It feels strange when that little red head doesn't pop up over the back seat.

My constant companion – a burden I wouldn't want to be without. Yin yang puppy.

Like the king and queen in *Sleeping Beauty* trying to shield Princess Aurora from the curse of the spinning wheel, I've tried so hard to protect Dolly from harm. The night of her fall from the deck, I made an agreement with the heavens to safeguard and care for her. I've spent significant time and money carefully researching food, kennels, medications, and veterinarians. I've hardly let her out of my sight. Yet just as the princess is pricked by the one spinning wheel remaining in the kingdom after the purge, Dolly experienced a trauma at the kennel in spite of my vigilance.

Young children and pets can't tell us what transpires when they're not with us. We're left trying to piece together the story and undo potential long-term consequences. Like refusing to eat.

I should have trusted my gut reaction, should have taken Dolly back home from the kennel. Our guts never fail us; we fail ourselves when we repeatedly disregard our intuitive nature, substituting our fallible reasoning and intellect. Or capitulating to professionals. Like last spring when I wavered in my conviction to not let a vet tech take Dolly away from me for a simple procedure.

"Why can't you just do it here? I've never had a veterinary

office take my dog away for blood work. My being here won't bother her," I'd vouched. Cripes, I'm always with her.

"Well, sometimes dogs are more difficult when their owners..."

Dolly stood placidly at my side. "Look at her! She won't be difficult."

They pulled rank. "It's our protocol." As if that negated my arguments against it.

My gut told me to not let her go. But they were gentle with her as they led her away on her leash, calling her "Sweet Pea." She willingly went with them.

When they brought her back, she was panting and stiff, tail tucked between her legs.

"What happened?"

"Nothing. She was fine. No problems."

"No problems? Look at her now! She's a nervous wreck."

They held her, trying to calm her. She strained the leash to reach me.

"Let her go," I commanded. "I'll take care of her."

She nestled her head in my lap as I stroked her. My dog who'd never before exuded fear in a veterinary office was shaking.

Protocol be damned. I know what's best for my Dolly. I should have insisted she remain with me; I should have found my voice. And now, after leaving Dolly at the kennel despite my concerns, my dog with a once-insatiable appetite won't eat.

The vet advises me not to worry about Dolly's hunger strike. "She'll eat when she's hungry. Just leave the bowl filled with kibble, and she'll find her way to it eventually. It won't kill her to miss a few meals."

No, but it damn-near kills me when 36 hours later, Dolly still hasn't gone near food or water. And she's already a slender dog. I decide she's fully capable of starving herself to death – more Gandhi than Dolly Lama.

As a child, I'd found my pet canary on his back on the bottom of his cage one morning – his stick legs sticking straight up. Tweety had been my responsibility, and I'd forgotten to feed him for a few days. Despite the expression *eats like a bird,* birds proportionately need a lot of food to satisfy their rapid metabolism. His feeder tray was all shells, no seeds.

The guilt was hard to shake. Such a pretty little yellow bird that trilled beautifully – when our cat Fluffy wasn't perched on the dining room table watching him. Yet Fluffy had only taunted Tweety; I'd killed him.

Out of fear and redemption, I do what must be done to give Dolly sustenance: I hand-feed her, little bits of kibble at a time. When I place it on the floor, she refuses to take it, so I must feed her hand-to-mouth. I then scoop out her canned food and feed it to her in moist chunks. By hand. Totally gross. At least she's eating.

The command Dolly's heard most frequently in her young life has been "No eat" as she nosedives down to snatch up a forest tidbit. Now Dolly *no-eat* period. Had I sent that message out to the Universe so many times that it now ricochets back as a contra-mantra?

After a few days, I grow weary of feeding grapes to Cleopatra. Her behavior seems irrational; I just want her to get over it, which is also irrational. A colleague used to shout "Cheer up" to those who were down-in-the-dumps. "Has that ever worked?" I asked, hoping to sharpen his sensibilities. "Do people cheer up when you tell them to?"

And now, here I am shouting, "Eat!" as I throw kibble in her bowl. *PING! PING! PING!* The sound of the kibble hitting the metal bowl causes Dolly to hide behind the couch. I lead her by her collar toward her food station and command her to eat, a command she's never needed and doesn't know. She shakes with fear, so I let her slink away.

I led her to food but couldn't make her eat. I should've remembered that adage.

I join her on the living room rug and stroke her head as I apologize for bullying her. I worry that there's no solution, that her health will be compromised. I immediately commence hand-feeding her again, and she willingly eats, forgiving my outburst. I wonder if I'm going to be one of those people who takes their dog to a dog shrink.

My would-be therapy dog needs therapy. Or do I?

Punkin went through a brief phase during which he wet the carpet when visitors petted his head. The vet said he was showing submissiveness, and she probed our treatment of him to determine why he felt he had to be. When we told her how outrageously dominant his behavior typically was, she responded, "Perhaps a psychologist might help." When I said I didn't realize there are dog psychologists, she clipped, "I meant for YOU." Although we didn't follow through on that particular recommendation, the solution was to ask guests to kneel and pet Punkin's chest rather than tower over his head. Not all visitors were enamored with our new greeting protocol, but it worked.

There are always reasons behind the reasons for particular behaviors – canine or otherwise.

And now I'm dealing with God-knows-what-kind-of psychosis, which apparently is contagious as I've joined her in being a drama queen. Wish I knew what had transpired at the kennel that fateful weekend.

You were away, my dad had accused.

Yes, I was away, Dolly. And you suffered a trauma.

No one who's loved a dog has ever uttered the words, "She's *just* a dog." But why can't Dolly just be a normal, happy-go-lucky dog? The kind that could live outdoors, eat whatever's on sale at the grocery store, not need grooming, walks, or a battery of veterinarians. My friend Susan's dog, a Lab/border collie mix, lived to be 16 through such benign neglect. She considers my overindulgence to be way over-the-top.

Even Dolly's namesake seems carefree most of the time, despite his burden of bearing witness to the persecution of his people and decades of exile from his Tibetan homeland. In his book *My Spiritual Journey*, the Dalai Lama writes, "Thinking only of the negative aspect doesn't help to find solutions, and it destroys peace of mind...You can see the positive side of even the worst tragedies if you adopt a holistic perspective..."

There's much to learn from his Buddhist practice of seeking contentment. It's about examining the lessons in every situation rather than judging. I'm trying to view Dolly's phobia as part of grander holistic lessons: 1) Accept what is. 2) Transcend debilitating fear.

The Dalai Lama teaches that compassion is more effective than judgment in changing behavior. Certainly, more effective than anger. Dolly Lama has an irrational fear of something that contains the sustenance she needs to survive. Can I relate to her fear with compassion rather than scream at her in frustration? How many times have I been afraid of my figurative food bowl – afraid to do something that will nurture my spirit? It seems an apt metaphor for many fears that have kept me hungry for what I need to grow.

Fear had once been my constant companion – surrounding me, controlling me, robbing me, draining me. I was even afraid of being afraid. As my parents' caregiver for eighteen months, my worried mind fed the beast that was never sated. Because when we wrestle for control, we *have* to worry to make sure everything works out "right." I tried to control what happened to them and couldn't – not without totally surrendering my own life. And not even then. I was exhausted, losing sleep as a self-appointed worry vigilante. There's nothing like spending days in a hospital or nursing home, as a patient or advocate, to make someone feel powerless.

One of the many valuable, yet painful, lessons I learned is that we aren't really in control, despite our illusions. I surrendered to this knowing like Superman to Kryptonite. It liberated me to make personal and professional changes in my life. To face the schoolyard bully and say, "No more." I gradually welcomed in possibilities and divine energy.

I now strive to marginalize fear and replace it with

confidence in my ability to deal with whatever comes my way, with help from a higher source. Sometimes I can't get there from here. It remains a life-long challenge to replace the scared rabbit's racing pulse with a confident lioness's brave heart.

I want to do the same for Dolly – to give her courage. Like the Wizard gave the Cowardly Lion, who had it all along and just had to prove it to himself. When another mealtime rolls around during which Dolly avoids her food and water bowls, I worry I'm conditioning her to only eat from human hands...and won't be able to find anyone who'll do that for her if I ever get a chance to be away from her again. Which right now seems doubtful.

I employ a dog trainer who comes to my home in order to control environmental variables. I ask her about a behavior modification technique I'd read about, which entails removing Dolly's food bowl if she hasn't eaten within fifteen minutes, prompting her to realize her window for chowing down is short. Katie quickly responds, "Dolly has apparently suffered a pretty intense trauma causing irrational, yet deep-seated, fears. Consequences aren't the solution; she needs to feel safe and secure around the bowl. After a few uneventful meals, she'll regain her confidence."

Katie suspects Dolly's fear is related to noise and suggests we desensitize her by giving her lots of positive attention while one of us drops objects on the hardwood floor. We'll start with a teaspoon and work our way up to a soup ladle. The supposition is that if nothing bad happens to her during that racket, she'll realize noise is only noise. No big deal.

But – no surprise – it IS a big deal to Dolly. A *really* big deal. At my insistence, we discontinue the exercise after dropping a tablespoon because Dolly is cowering, panting, and shaking while I hug her and whisper reassurance in her floppy ear.

I have no way to convince Dolly she needn't be afraid of loud noises or be afraid at the groomer's or the kennel. She looks to me for reassurance; I can only comfort. And some purport that by comforting, I'm reinforcing that there *was* something to fear. Probably the same "experts" who advise parents not to pick up a crying baby. While I don't subscribe, the psychology behind caring for dependent creatures can be very confusing.

No miracle cure is forthcoming from the trainer. During a sleepless night, dreading our morning hand-feeding routine, I reframe my response to the situation. I have to change the energy – around her, around me, around us, around the bowl and the room it's in. No matter how angry and frustrated I may be, you can't scream a dog into doing what you want when you want. In fact, it will likely have the opposite effect of making her more afraid and, hence, unable to comply. Same with people.

Deep breaths are in order. Time to execute the Dalai Lama's holistic perspective.

Dolly has always paid it forward by helping to shift my energy. Her quiet presence, bearing witness to the power of unconditional love, has reframed many a day for me. When I'm meditating, her wet nose touches my hand, communicating, *Love surrounds you.* When I'm out-of-sorts, she rests her head on my feet with a big sigh. This morning, I'll repay the favor.

Using my crystal to clear her chakras, sage smudge to cut negative attachments to past events, and Reiki symbols to heal, I work to dispel the fear surrounding her, saying the words that have served her well previously: "I bless the Divine within you. I offer you this gift of healing energy with love. When you accept it, you will use it for your highest good."

Instead of running from the kitchen when meal preparation starts, she lies close by, intently watching. Her face softens, her muscles relax; so do mine. I quietly place the kibble and canned food in her bowl, draw the Reiki symbols over it, place it in her food station, cheerily call her to come...and hold my breath.

Dolly ambles over to her food station and tentatively eats out of her bowl for the first time in more than a week. An errant kibble pinging back into the bowl makes her jump, but she resumes, leaving a little in the bottom that would have required too much clanging to get out.

We've made peace with each other, with the dog food, and with the associated noises. I can't claim to fully understand what brought us to this moment, but I'm grateful for the guidance received.

It's much easier to live this life believing in a higher power – higher energy to be tapped – than living without it. There's nothing to lose by believing – and much to lose by believing it's all up to you. That's *really* scary.

Over the next month, Dolly becomes bolder, approaching her bowls on her own. I'm not allowed to make any background noise – like opening the refrigerator or emptying the dishwasher – or she'll stop eating.

Dolly remains afraid of loud noises in general This had never been an issue before and, for that, I'd been grateful. She could be outside during a thunderstorm and not be overly anxious, unlike Punkin who'd chewed up every window sill in our sunroom when left alone during a storm. Punkin was also fearful of fireworks and had to be put in the "doggie dungeon" in our basement when the simulated bombs were bursting in air. Dolly had always slept through them, a welcome change.

No more.

When an unrecognizable loud noise wakes us both in the middle of the night, Dolly appears at my bedside whimpering and shaking. I get on the floor to soothe her, unintentionally telegraphing my own fear of the unknown. Dogs know what we're feeling, though no words are spoken.

Later, realizing the explosion-like sound was just thunder, I write this in my journal:

> *I hear the night sky roar and crackle*
> *So does my dog*
> *We don't recognize the noise as thunder*
> *and we're both afraid.*

It's as close as I've ever come
to the terror a mother feels
clutching her infant to her breast
as bombs fall out of the sky.

Since her boarding experience, Dolly now also fears bare floors. She used to run through the house, scrambling around corners like the Jetsons' dog, Astro. She now gingerly puts one foot ahead of the other as she navigates uncarpeted areas.

Apparently, many dogs share this phobia, but she's my first. Of course. I trim the fur under her pads, thinking those silky strands might be making her slide. I strew treats on the bare floor to entice her. I sit and encourage her to come. Nothing convinces her. Carpets are her safe haven, and once she "lands" on one, she sits and begs for an escort to the next as she hop-scotches to reach her destination.

Guests assume she's trained to ask permission to walk on the hardwood floors. Neither of us is that good.

Rick suggests I view her fear of navigating floors as a game: *Floor is water, rugs are islands.* "If you reframe how you perceive it, it could be fun." How very Dalai Lama-ish. Easy for Rick to suggest a different perspective: He's in New Jersey while I'm stuck here with the canine mascot of Crazy Town.

Although her demands for an escort are annoying and her fears unreasonable, she deserves compassion. Don't we all fear not having firm footing and falling on our faces? Don't we all want to be on solid ground, to know our feet are firmly planted? To know we're secure and the rug won't be pulled out from under us? Dogs are just more authentic in acting out their fears than humans who mask and dull the pain until it comes out in self-destructive patterns. Suzanne Clothier posits that's because dogs are unable to lie, incapable of dishonesty: "A dog will report faithfully to you in his body language and behavior what he is feeling at the moment." Their tails reveal their true feelings.

Dolly's also more tentative now around other dogs and people. The dog I believed incapable of sufficiently ignoring other dogs during the Canine Good Citizen test now holds back when we encounter another dog. She's not eager to engage and, too often, the other dog snaps at her, perhaps sensing her fear and escalating her reluctance. As I too well know, fear can be a revolving door. A boomerang.

"The lion takes his courage from your fear," Florence Scovel Shinn wrote.

When Dolly encounters our new neighbor's shepherd-mix, the owner assures me Charlie is friendly. Yet he growls at Dolly, who then pulls away. In response, the neighbor says, "Charlie never does that – he has lots of fun with Murphy up the street. But then again, Murphy's a happy-go-lucky dog." Implying Dolly is otherwise. At first, I'm offended, but she's correct: Murphy is a fun-loving dog, while Dolly has become a serious, intense dog who fearfully anticipates. It's theorized that humans are the only species who live with the awareness that they'll someday die. Then why does Dolly react like this? She must suspect some harm can come to her – maybe she just doesn't know the ultimate truth.

How much responsibility do I carry for her fears? I've been her primary influence – did I imprint her with fear of her demise following her accident? It pains me to see myself reflected in her anxious eyes, a mirror of my own. Is Dolly me, made manifest? Perhaps she's a form of biofeedback, alerting me to what stress and anxiety can do.

I wish she were lighter in spirit, like most goldens. I wish I were too. But inadvertently, my mother had transferred her generalized anxieties to me, compensating for not wanting another baby by being overprotective. (I sure understand that now.) If I sneezed, she'd immediately slather *Vicks Vap-o-Rub* on my chest, which could be detected blocks away. I first realized my mother was going to die when I sneezed in her hospice room, and she didn't ask, "Are you getting a cold?" She opened her eyes but remained silent. A decibel-breaking silence that I couldn't comprehend: Why didn't she ask if I were getting a cold? *Ask me, Mama. Ask me! I might be getting a cold, and I want you to know, to care. I want to hear the question again from you. One more time.*

I softly played the hymn *Be Not Afraid* over and over in her room as she lay dying. Because despite my mother's religious fervor, I could tell she was afraid to die. Aren't we all? We fear the unknown. Things we can't understand. Dolly's not alone in being circumspect.

Last winter, I'd been anxious about driving across state with Dolly after it had snowed for almost 24 hours. "What if we get rear-ended?" I asked a friend. "And Dolly gets killed, pinned in the back of my SUV." I immediately regretted giving voice to that fear so did what I could to redirect the Law of Attraction, to bless our trip. But the heaviness lingered from my *awful-izing*.

As I packed the car, Dolly looked like I felt. Her head was down, her eyes droopy. She moved hesitantly to get in the car. Instead of immediately lying down, which she typically does, she looked out the back window for four hours. I wondered if she were being vigilant, warding off cars. Making sure they saw us.

As I prepare to host guests this Fourth of July, I fantasize about how nice it would be if Dolly weren't so anxious, could tolerate loud noises – fireworks, in particular. Like she used to. How nice it would be to sit by the lake with friends, feeding our fire and our faces, chatting, enjoying the bursts of color. How nice it would be to not have to race up the hill to soothe Dolly as soon as the light show starts.

That's the canine paradox for me: I love having a dog and also loved not having a dog, not being responsible for such a needy, dependent being.

When friends arrive, we enjoy the food, adult beverages, view, and conversation. But when the explosives start, I dutifully head up to the house, harboring resentment that I have to leave my own party because of Dolly. As I climb the deck steps, there – in that window – is Dolly's face. That face

I love so much. That sweet, plaintiff face. Looking for me to protect her from the loud noises.

Everything else becomes immaterial. My obligation to take care of her is the greatest honor I've ever been given. Whatever sacrifices I've made are worth the short amount of time I'll have her in my life. It's what enables parents to put their own aspirations and needs on hold for their kids.

A few nights later, I dream Dolly is missing an ear. She doesn't seem to be in pain and isn't bleeding. She looks like a lopsided mouse. I fear that others may laugh at her and that she doesn't look like "My Beauty Queen" anymore. I'd always considered her floppy ears one of her best features.

As I embrace her, my fears vanish. She's still my sweet Dolly despite her deformity. Suddenly the flap of her ear re-appears. She was made whole by my unconditional love.

The frog kissed by the princess.

I awaken from that fractured fairy-tale to the unmistakable squeeze-box sound of Dolly vomiting. (There's no better alarm to bolt me out of bed.) After cleaning it up, I follow her to the rug where she sits. My intent is to apply Reiki to help her feel better.

I choose instead to just be with her. We're eye-level as I stroke her head. She stares into my face as I cup hers with my hands. I want her to see love, acceptance, and kindness when she looks at me. What she likely sees is concern. Our four brown eyes are sad.

What must it do to her psyche to witness my angst? What does it do to others who try to love me when they're faced with my perpetual quest for perfection, to which neither they nor I can ever measure up?

My tears fall as Dolly fixates on my face. I want to do for her what she naturally does for me – selflessly reflect an unconditional *I-would-die-for-you* connection. Because I would.

I force a smile and speak tenderly to her. She becomes playful, grabbing my arm with her soft mouth.

How much better we both feel when one of us lightens up. Dolly is teaching me that relationships can be enhanced when even one of the partners changes how they show up.

I'll soon learn that my neighbor's dog, Charlie, is fearful, too, when left alone in his new home, barking incessantly out the second-floor window. He's re-homed due to his owner's work and travel schedule. Murphy continues to be that happy-go-lucky dog.

Dolly will never be a certified therapy dog. I won't subject her to what it would take for her to tolerate the crashing of food trays and walkers. She's already a therapy dog in every way that counts and has begun the work I promised the Universe she'd do someday. She does it for me on an on-going basis. I'm calmed by petting her silky fur, gazing into her trusting eyes, hugging her warm body. She gives bountiful unconditional attention and love, yet asks for so little.

No certification is needed for a dog to provide comfort and empathy, to re-create a sense of playfulness in adults. Every dog offers that innate gift if given the opportunity (although Dolly did try to nibble the fingers off Rick's 101-year-old great aunt).

Dolly's work will continue.

Solutions present themselves: My former secretary offers to be Dolly's private sitter. She and her family are dog-people who raised dogs for Guiding Eyes for the Blind. They tolerate my detailed written instructions, and Dolly runs to their door with a wagging tail – even though they have hardwood floors. She tries to befriend their three cats and doesn't mind getting her nose swatted. They do call once, however, to report that Dolly won't eat. We quickly figure out it's because they used bowls that slid a little on the floor.

Heaven forbid!

I buy more throw rugs so Dolly can walk from rug to rug over my hardwood floors. Because just maybe *floor IS water,* and *rugs ARE islands.* And when thunderstorms hit,

I play the hymn for Dolly that I'd played for my mother as she lay dying:

Be not afraid.
I go before you always.
Come follow me.
And I will give you rest.

Locusts and Pestilence

The controversies in Lyme disease exist in a setting of incomplete scientific evidence around tick-borne diseases, including a lack of validated direct testing methods...to accurately distinguish infected from uninfected patients.

- International Lyme and
Associated Diseases Society website

Sirens scream. Red lights whirl. An ambulance, accompanied by a police car, races past my townhouse in the middle of the crisp fall night. I know most of my neighbors on this dead-end street but am particularly dismayed that the destination of the emergency vehicles is Doris and Kevin's house, Murphy's pet-parents. My good friends.

The next day, Kevin reports that Doris is in the hospital. She hadn't been feeling well the last few days and had been confined to bed, becoming weaker and weaker. Getting up to use the bathroom, she fell and hit her head on the tub. Kevin called an ambulance; police showed up to make sure it wasn't a case of domestic violence.

For days, no diagnosis is forthcoming as Doris continues to lose ground. I hear it whispered by neighbors that she might not make it. I share that fear when I see her slumped over in a hospital chair. I start to perform Reiki on her and instead choose to comb her strawberry-blonde curls to ease her concern about her appearance. Her weight has dropped, and her complexion matches the bleached sheets.

Consultation among medical professionals across disciplines and across medical facilities results in the long-awaited diagnosis: anaplasmosis, one of more than a dozen tick-borne diseases caused by the nasty and pervasive parasites. A black-legged deer tick is the guilty party – a tick that had bitten Doris three days before while she worked in the yard. The bite didn't leave the tell-tale bull's eye; most don't, the absence of which leads to a false sense of safety.

In fact, the bite was so inconsequential – the tick didn't even burrow in – that no one mentioned it to hospital personnel during intake.

An intravenous mega-dose of Doxycycline (Doxy) helps get Doris back on her feet after a few days. When she returns home, I offer her over-the-counter probiotics to combat the depletion of good stomach bacteria stemming from antibiotic treatment. Doris checks with her doctor who then prescribes them for her, although prior to her inquiry, he'd failed to offer them. They help her tolerate the cure.

Ticks had discovered Dolly early last spring. And Dolly discovered them right back in an overgrown berm between my property and the next. Beautiful wildflowers grow there, enjoyed by butterflies, bees, wasps, beetles...and ticks. Although she was expressly forbidden to wander into this wilderness, she expressly chose to ignore the roaming parameters I fruitlessly set.

Not yet familiar with this particular parasite, I didn't initially recognize them. When I'd pluck tiny round poppy seeds off Dolly's furry head, they'd cling to my fingers, eager to dig into a host. I started lightheartedly calling her "My Little Buggy Girl," ignorant of how life-threatening ticks can be.

I soon learn that most of my neighbors and their dogs have contracted some form of a tick-related disease. Lyme disease has been called *The Great Imposter* because it can masquerade as many other conditions, from Alzheimer's to Parkinson's. One neighbor went to five specialists before being accurately diagnosed; they'd been treating her for rheumatoid arthritis. There's also a new case of Parkinson's on my lane.

Because I go where Dolly goes (to retrieve my retriever), I periodically get tested for Lyme. Thus far, I've tested negative. But false negatives are not uncommon with the Western blot test; currently, no clinically-accurate test has been developed.

Rain and warm weather create the perfect breeding

ground for ticks in the spring and fall. Summer's heat and winter's frost make them subside to a certain degree, although they're highly adaptable to adverse conditions and rapidly mutate. Plus, due to climate change, they're moving further north. Mice and other small critters get ticks from deer and provide transit everywhere. Cats do as well although they don't contract tick-borne diseases.

Contrary to popular belief, ticks don't jump. But they're clever enough to move to the highest vegetation to have a better chance of latching onto any mammal that brushes against them. They *quest* by holding onto leaves with their third and fourth pair of legs while outstretching their first pair of legs to grab onto a host.

Ingenious. Diabolical.

It's hard to detect a nymph with the naked eye. That's why they're often not detected until they engorge from sucking blood because their bite anesthetizes, leaving the host unaware that they've latched on.

Ticks are gross. And scary. They could star in a horror movie. Spiders? A welcome alternative. Snakes on an airplane? I'm good. But ticks? Worse than Biblical locusts.

Doris and I attend an all-day conference on tick-borne diseases sponsored by the Lyme Action Network and are dismayed to learn the medical community is divided on how seriously to take the problem and how best to treat it. Ticks are the leading carriers of disease in the United States, yet there's no comprehensive public health plan or funding to deal with them; the 850 known species (not all of which cause Lyme) are breeding faster than our resolve to stop them. It's also possible to get more than one disease (co-infections) from a single bite, including Powassan virus, which causes swelling around the brain and is untreatable.

The Center for Disease Control (CDC) reports more than 7,000 new cases each week, A naturopath tells me we'll all eventually end up with a tick-related disease and advises her patients to build up their immunity through diet, exercise, stress management, sleep, and supplementation in order to combat the bad effects.

For dogs, some of the unintended consequences of ticks come from preventative treatment options. The popular products *Frontline* and *Advantix* are applied at the base of the dog's neck to repel and kill fleas and ticks. Upon application, these pesticides are stored in the oil glands of the dog's skin. They then self-distribute through the dog's hair follicles for one month. Both products work by attacking the parasites' nervous system after they bite the dog. But the chemicals can also impair a dog's nervous system because spot-on treatments and collars infuse deadly chemicals into the pet's blood stream.

Poisoning our pets to poison what hurts our pets.

Warning labels caution to not let young children get too close to the dog for a while after application. More than one website associates the pesticides in these products with serious problems like rashes and burns, organ damage, cancer, and infertility. Pet-parents, groomers, and vets provide substantive anecdotal evidence. My local pet store owner, who stocks these popular treatments, refuses to use them on his own dogs.

So do I.

After Rusty was anesthetized at four years of age because of a large tumor between his shoulder blades, I met with the vet to discuss what could have gone wrong. "Might there be a correlation between the site of Rusty's tumor and the application of a spot-on treatment we'd applied every month in that same location?" I asked, adding, "That's also where you've injected most of his vaccinations."

The young vet looked me in the eyes and ruefully responded, "I can't tell you that caused the problem. And I can't tell you it didn't. We're just starting to suspect there may be a link."

Like suspecting a link between Alzheimer's and aluminum?

That was more than a dozen years ago; they're still just suspecting. And still weighing the costs and benefits of contracting Lyme versus contracting a treatment-related disease. It's even possible to get both; friends who use spot-on treatments report they still find ticks latched onto their dogs.

There aren't a lot of good alternatives. I bought a deshedding tool and a fine-tooth comb and spend ten minutes combing and brushing Dolly each time she comes in the house. (I scream each time I collect a little bastard on her comb.) Tick bodies are so hard that I drown them in the sink to make sure they're no longer a threat to (wo)man or beast. I also had her vaccinated against the disease, including the subsequent booster. So I was surprised when a routine blood test last summer revealed that Dolly was Lyme-positive. And scared because the bacteria can cause nephritis (inflammation of the kidneys) in certain breeds, including goldens.

Dolly was put on a month-long course of Doxy, which upset her already-sensitive stomach. I called Nature's Farmacy to get advice: Water-soluble probiotics were recommended. She also had to drink a lot of water right after swallowing the antibiotic so it didn't burn her esophagus by coming back up.

I could lead her to water but couldn't make her drink. To entice her, I added a little canned dog food. From that moment on, she'd never again drink plain water without it being spiked with something tasty.

Her blood work was sent to Cornell University to determine why the vaccine failed. The lab found no trace of any related antibodies in her system, as if she never received the vaccine. (The vaccine's ineffectiveness is why the human version was taken off the market.) No good explanation was provided, so the manufacturer offered to pay her medical bills for up to two rounds of Doxy, after making me sign a release that if she dies, they're not responsible.

If she dies, they're not responsible.... Then who would be? They manufactured the ineffective vaccine that I trusted.

Not yet knowing what a long-term and debilitating

disease Lyme can be, I signed the waiver. I also signed off because my pet insurance refused to pay for Dolly's Lyme disease treatments, declaring it a pre-existing condition. That made no sense: There were no symptoms or diagnosis when I signed onto the plan when she was a pup. But her medical records prior to enrollment noted a tick bite on her face. The insurance representative hinted that maybe I hadn't been a responsible owner because I didn't apply spot-on treatments to Dolly's skin, the poison that can cause cancer in dogs. It didn't matter to them that I'd had Dolly vaccinated, and she still contracted it.

I contested the insurance company's denial in writing numerous times, pointing out that not all tick bites lead to Lyme disease, any more than sex always leads to pregnancy. There are variables, such as type of tick and length of attachment. (The brown dog tick, for instance, doesn't cause Lyme disease.) I provided them with a database of research on the damage spot-on treatments can cause, reminding them that since goldens are prone to cancer, I was trying to improve her chances.

Denied.

Denied.

Denied.

Published in a subsequent issue of that insurance carrier's pet journal was an article outlining the dangers of the very same stuff I refused to apply. But after three denied appeals, I surrendered. Isn't that how the powers-that-be usually win? By outlasting us. By wearing us down. The business model for pet and human health insurance depends on finding ways to say *NO*. Clauses excluding pre-existing conditions from health coverage can be manipulated using convoluted logic to deny treatment. Covering pre-existing conditions must be a non-negotiable component of any health care package offered to pets and humans.

The tail shouldn't wag the dog, so to speak.

I recalled the day a notice from my parents' health insurance carrier arrived, denying payment for my mother's brain biopsy and radiation treatments because my parents had been living "out of network" for longer than six months.

They'd been living out of network because they'd become terminally ill and couldn't return home. They had to live near me as their caregiver.

The insurance company still denied over $100,000 of medical bills.

HOW CAN YOU DO THIS? I wanted to scream. *THIS ISN'T THEIR FAULT! THEY DIDN'T INTENTIONALLY GET SICK. THEY WOULD LOVE NOTHING MORE THAN TO BE "IN NETWORK" AGAIN.*

My brother-in-law, an attorney, filed a successful appeal to get the claims paid. I then had to find another health insurance carrier that would take a terminal brain tumor patient. A challenging task, to say the least. United Health accepted her application for coverage and served us well.

I end up incurring thousands of dollars of out-of-pocket medical expenses to test and treat Dolly for Lyme. She continues to test positive, even after completing several antibiotic, acupuncture, and Chinese herb regimens. I'm assured that's because of ramped-up antibodies. In response, I launch a crusade against the parasitic beasts to protect Dolly and myself. Especially after Doris' experience.

To make it easier to find ticks on Dolly as we head into tick-friendly temperatures, I take her to the groomer. "Make her look like a Labrador retriever," I instruct.

"Are you sure? Her undercoat will be lighter than her red fur."

I'm certain. A bad tick season is predicted. I want to be able to spot them immediately. It will also make grooming easier.

When Dolly emerges, her deep red fur is gone. She's been stripped down to her undercoat, her baby soft undercoat. All but her head is shaved; all but her head is light blonde. Her starkly-red head makes her look like a woodpecker. Her once-fancy tail is long and thin, causing her to look like the average pound puppy. She looks much smaller too, causing

Kevin to ask, "Is Dolly sick?"

She hangs her head. From experience, I know some dogs can be sensitive as to their appearance and don't like to be laughed at. She seems to know she's no longer a head-turner. She's still "My Beauty Queen" yet may now be first runner-up.

I hug her tight and kiss her soft head. "I'm sorry, Dolly. I'm sorry."

It's going to take a while for her fur to grow back; I worry she'll be cold heading into winter. Trying not to dwell on it, I remind myself I did it for her own good. And soon she seems no worse for wear. Same old Dolly: solemn, playful, sleepy, eager to ingest non-food items. But I miss my fancy red dog with tufted ears and fancy feathers on her legs and tail.

I spray her with an all-natural repellent consisting of cedarwood, citronella, lavender, lemongrass, orange, and thyme essential oils. She sneezes upon application and smells like a spiced ham. Kevin tells her she smells "like a hussy" and playfully advises Murphy to stay clear of her.

She wears an Anibio Tic-Clip on her collar, which supposedly harnesses the power of the bioenergetic field around her to create a barrier that repels insect-pests for two years. According to their marketing, this energetic charge adapts to the dog's unique bioenergy frequency. It was created in Germany, meeting with success throughout Europe. I want to believe it's working.

I'm ashamed to admit that, after becoming psycho when I find a tick in my bed, I resort to spraying the perimeter of my yard with Triazicide, which boasts of killing over one hundred different insects. Even as I'm in the act, I say to myself, *No one should spray poison. It's just not right.* I watch as moths and other benign insects – the kind birds eat – flutter to the ground. I know what I'm doing is wrong; I know I'm poisoning the ecosystem.

The proverbial rock and a hard place: *Kill or be killed.* But it's for my Dolly that I spray these trees. Ticks that threaten her life live in them, and I must do all I can to ensure she's not re-infected. But I will not poison her directly to do that. Instead, I'll poison her surroundings. Our surroundings. Mother Earth.

Am I an imposter? Espousing the responsibility to be a good steward of God's green Earth yet applying poison for my personal benefit? How situational is my morality?

There's clearly danger to Dolly in this approach also, as well as to the broader community. What a mess it would be if we all just worried about taking care of our own! If we all just worried about our own survival without concern for the common good and overall quality of life for all.

Maybe that's already the problem. My holistic vet tells me dogs live longer if their lawns are not treated with chemicals; at least two types of canine cancers are linked to such treatments. Almost every lawn I see has little warning flags on them signaling recent application. At least 15 major diseases, including cancer, are attributed to the use of Monsanto's weed-killer *Roundup*. Lawsuits proving direct causality abound.

A friend points out a blog in the local newspaper written by a local veterinarian specializing in canine Lyme disease. I place a call, being fortunate enough to get the author on the line.

Interrupting my tale of woe, she brusquely asks, "What do you feed her?"

When I tell her kibble and canned food, she tells me I must switch to a raw food diet, consisting of raw meat, bone, organs, and vegetables. She relays disturbing stories about how kibble is made; at least two of the byproducts are known carcinogens. Makes me wonder if kibble contributed to our losing three prior goldens to cancer.

Similar to what the naturopath told me, she declares, "The only way you're going to beat this is to build up her immune system. The way to do that is to feed her what her ancestors ate. A dog's genetic makeup is more than a 99% match with the wolf, so dogs should eat the way wolves eat."

She starts to tell me how to prepare and feed Dolly raw

meals. This time, I interrupt her.

"I can't do that. I'd be too afraid to feed her raw eggs, to let her chew on chicken bones. What about salmonella? I just can't. What else could I do?"

"Let me ask you this, then: Do you love your dog?"

A rhetorical question that I defensively answer anyway. "Of course, I love my dog! Would I be calling you if I didn't?"

"Then this is what you have to do."

Two weeks later, I'm sitting in a raw food seminar as they explain away the danger of salmonella in dogs: *Pets' digestive tracts have higher levels of acid than humans, which kill most bacteria. Their tracts are also shorter than humans', giving surviving bacteria little time to multiply. Cooked bones are too brittle for dogs; raw bones are not.*

I watch puppies lap up raw eggs and chew raw chicken wings.

"I can't do this," I admit again. They provide me with names of companies that sell pre-packaged raw meals, complete with ground-up bones.

Dolly's transition from civilized canned food and kibble to chunks of bloody meat and raw eggs is surprisingly easy. She gobbles it down, licking the bowl, while I, a would-be vegetarian, try not to gag at the thought of her eating raw flesh. I wash the blood from my hands, from my counter, and from my sink because there's a danger to humans if raw food-handling practices are not strictly adhered to.

There's another upside: Dolly no longer has to fear the ping of kibble. The best? Her stools are perfectly formed!

Now that Dolly's returning to her lupine genus, she seems friskier, pulling a little harder and growling a little deeper when we play tug. Before too long, her coat is shinier, and she's more muscular. Her blood work reveals a significant decrease in the marker that denotes the presence of Lyme-induced bacteria.

My dog has gone wild. And I've gone rogue, becoming cynical of the pushing of medications and vaccinations. I may be turning into one of those much-reviled parents whose kids aren't allowed in school because she refuses to vaccinate. I begin to wonder if Dolly could have contracted Lyme via the vaccine. I ask three vets if it's possible that injecting her with the bacterium made her sick. All readily assure me it's not; even the holistic vet thinks me foolish.

I respect the progress western medicine has made in eradicating numerous communicable conditions; the benefits far outweigh the risks. It's the frequency of administration that is of primary concern because the duration of immunity is typically much longer than indicated by the vaccination schedule – for humans and pets. When Dolly was a puppy, I made sure she got every required vaccine. Against the vet's advice, I even requested two at a time, not wanting this pup to take up more of my precious time than necessary. I didn't know that could compromise her immune system. I didn't know about life-threatening vaccinosis or vaccine-associated sarcomas, which may have caused Rusty's untimely death.

When my holistic vet informs me I can instead request a titer to determine if there's sufficient concentration of an antibody to preclude the necessity of a repeat vaccine, I begin to substitute these simple-yet-expensive blood tests for scheduled vaccinations. At four years of age, Dolly's recent titer results indicate she has sufficient antibodies to sustain her immunity for several years – perhaps for the rest of her life. No more vaccines for parvovirus or distemper may be necessary.

The titer alternative to the rabies vaccine is not approved unless there's a compromised immune system. Dolly's a few weeks overdue, so the western vet wants to administer it this visit even though he's just injected another vaccine for leptospirosis.

I already feel guilty for allowing Dolly to get injected with this new lepto vaccine. Her western vet recommended it because lepto incidences are on the rise, it's waterborne, and transmitted by the urine of squirrels and racoons. Since we live in a wooded area on a lake much of the year, I meekly consented. I cringed when he put the needle in her neck, realizing I acquiesced after being told lepto is one of the few diseases people can get from their dogs.

Although Dolly's health records are filled with my declinations of various treatments (as are my own), I asked no questions. *Did I give my dog an additional vaccine to keep myself safe?*

The vet interrupts my silent self-flagellation. "She's not covered against rabies right now. She could be in danger. So could you."

Dolly in danger? My heart races.

"If I'm a responsible pet owner, I'll do this, right?" I ask to justify going against my better judgment.

"It's not up to me to judge pet owners' decisions," he wisely responds. "Rabies is fatal – if a dog gets it, she dies."

He goes on to explain: Either we do it now or wait two weeks so one vaccine doesn't counteract the other. Yet together they'd drive her immunity down. He proceeds to describe symptoms of vaccine intolerance. It isn't pretty, but I consent to give Dolly the rabies vaccine anyway.

As he approaches with a needle, I cry out, "Wait! This doesn't feel right. Let's do it in two weeks."

He silently retreats.

When I leave his office, my decisions feel heavy. I regret the lepto vaccine. And now, will there be an unintended consequence for delaying the rabies vaccine? Can hurting masquerade as helping? My gut told me not to give her both vaccines at the same time, based on what I've read and believe. And in my own best interest too: I want Dolly around for a very long time.

I call the holistic vet to confess; she tells me she'd have recommended against the lepto because there are many strains, and the vaccine only safeguards against a few. Furthermore, the disease is still relatively rare where we live. She tells me to forgive myself, though, because worrying about Dolly compromises my own immune system. "Let it go; you're doing the best you can."

That night, I hold Dolly as she sleeps. I tell her I'm sorry.

Two weeks later, she receives the rabies vaccine as scheduled. I'll later find out the duration of immunity for the rabies vaccine may be as high as seven years, in contrast to the three-year mandated booster.

Whenever I come up against the medical community, heavily-incentivized by drug companies, I doubt my own instincts and wisdom. The experts recite manufacturer-provided research and data, leading us toward a course of action. The little examining room, for pets or humans, feels like a pressure-cooker; decisions are expected on the spot. Every educational poster on the walls is sponsored by a drug company. Our small voices get drowned out; we lose our power. One study reports that the average patient gets eleven seconds to state symptoms before being cut off – time is of the essence to overworked medical professionals. Meanwhile, our innate sense of what's best based on our connectedness to our physical bodies begins to feel inadequate or wrong. Like a vortex that sucks us in and, as we spin, we warp out of our own orbit, our own consciousness.

The ultra-rapid recitations of potential side-effects at the end of drug commercials say it all: *Should we really risk death to tamp down our psoriasis? It'll kill you or cure you* is not a trite expression.

Locusts AND pestilence.

* * *

I know what every square inch of Dolly's body feels like. So when I feel a small bump on the back of her head as I mindlessly pet her, warning bells go off.

Is it a tick? A tick that can re-infect her with Lyme disease?

I grab a magnifying glass and a flashlight. Upon further inspection, I'm relieved it isn't a tick. *So then, what is it?*

On the Internet, I research all the dastardly conditions it could be. And then decide to ignore it, choosing hope instead of fear. It could, after all, be just an infected hair follicle. And no matter what it is, I have the potential to heal her if need be.

Don't I?

I apply alcohol with a Q-tip; I provide Reiki and apply essential oils. But a few days later, the bump starts to scare me. It's unchanged but still there.

It's a small lump – but so was Punkin's.

She seems fine – but so did Dryphuss.

She's young – but so was Rusty.

All died from seemingly innocuous lumps and bumps. Small. Round. Soft. Deadly. Bumps.

Cancer – the pestilence of our time.

WORRY! PANIC! I can't ignore it. I want medical reassurance. Because a few months ago, my former-husband's golden retriever, Buddy, started limping for no apparent reason and, after several veterinary examinations, a small mast cell tumor was discovered on his foot, resulting in a toe amputation. Hopefully, it was caught before spreading despite a delayed diagnosis.

Since learning of this, I've been praying for Buddy's and Peter's highest good. I'd prefer to pray for a specific outcome, like Buddy-be-free-of-cancer. But what if the highest good for Peter at this time is to lose Buddy, to learn the lessons embedded in that loss? Who am I to try to steer the course, to tell the Universe what I want or believe to be best for others?

I've settled on believing prayer isn't an either-or proposition; it's a process of asking, listening, and expressing gratitude. My compromise is to ask for a specific intervention while adding this caveat: "… if it be for the highest good," in addition to Williamson's, "All this and more."

I'll be taking Dolly to the veterinarian this afternoon to check on this bump.

When I conclude my energy routine, trying to stay centered, Dolly places herself below my hands as I push the qi down to my base chakra. "All is well. All is well. All manner of things is well," I intone.

She sits, seemingly absorbing the affirmation and looking up at me. She's in the cross-hairs of the energetic field, and

I believe she's sending me back a confirming message: *All IS well.*

On the way to the vet's, I return a call from my cousin in New Mexico. When prompted for news about my life, I tell her we're on our way to get a bump checked out. Of all the things going on in my life, I'm not sure why I choose that update.

"Want me to tell you what my vet said when my dog got bumps and lumps?" she asks.

I don't want her to tell me. I'm sure it's about the danger of mast cell tumors.

"Sure, go ahead." I can't possibly become more worried than I already am.

"He told me my dog has lumps because my husband has lumps. He said dogs are so empathic that they can pick up conditions of their owners. Especially if there's a lot of focus on the human ailment, psychologically or medically."

Marianne is quite avante garde, so I had to probe. "A *real* vet said this? A medical vet? Not a shaman or anything like that?"

"Yes, a DVM. Do you have bumps?"

For decades, my fibrocystic breasts have had much diagnostic attention...and caused much angst. Rick has sebaceous cysts, which have also been the subject of medical intervention.

Likely not a coincidence I'm chatting with her en route to the vet. That I'd bring it up. That she had experience with it. That I have lumps and bumps too.

Dolly is compliant in the vet's office as she's poked and prodded, her head buried under the vet's arm. He extracts cells with a needle, to be examined under a microscope.

"We always have to worry about mast cell," he says gravely. "Cancerous tumors can appear anywhere, so all growths should be checked."

He leaves with his cell sample, and I begin to pray: "Please not yet. Please, God, no. No. No. No. Not Dolly. Not yet."

Praying for what I don't want rather than what I do want.

The Universe must be shaking its proverbial head. I weigh how much I would put her through. How many surgeries? How many days of painful recovery?

When the vet re-enters, I'm laser-focused on his face. He has a slight smile and immediately pronounces, "All is well," just like I recited during my morning practice. It's a sebaceous cyst; nothing to be done. He gives me high praise for being vigilant enough to notice the small bump.

I thank him. And thank God I have Dolly to bring me to my knees in prayer.

That reminder of how quickly it can all fall apart clings to me like bad perfume. While awaiting the test results, I lost ten minutes of my life. You don't soon forget a visit to hell, no matter how brief it was.

Why do I readily abandon my practice? I only half-heartedly tried to heal Dolly. Yet just yesterday, I met a woman who told me amazing stories about healing she'd done on her father. Stories I know from experience to be possible. So why do I rush off to a doctor or vet for reassurance when I know another way?

Perhaps I don't rely on my healing practice because the stakes are so high. That's also why it makes sense to use an integrated approach: western and holistic. Both are powerful in different ways. Western medicine is needed for more conventional diagnoses, prescriptions, and treatments – something I don't readily accept but recognize that the marvels of modern medicine cannot be denied. Holistic medicine works with the body's own energy systems and innate healing potential to systemically prevent future occurrences. Why not consider it all?

To complicate matters, veterinary science is inexact – with neither the research nor equipment to best aid diagnosis. Pet owners with limited means must often decide to end a life if a large expense would be incurred to treat. A friend left the equine veterinary profession for that very reason: *They shoot horses, don't they?* I'm fortunate that a long career in public service and pet insurance have provided the means to seek the best care for Dolly.

My Western vet doesn't seem interested in getting to the root cause of Dolly's cysts. But I am. And my holistic vet is loaded with theories related to the yin-yang balance.

The Universe has opened another window through which to explore its mystical ways. And continues to provide opportunities for me to practice my healing modalities and to test my faith.

Come Hell or High Water

If there is magic on this planet, it is contained in water.

- Loren Eiseley

Water captivates me. I grew up near the shores of Lake Ontario, chose my college primarily based on its location near the same Great Lake. My home on this Adirondack lake is my refuge, my sanctuary where I escape the regimented life. I named it *Healing Waters* following Dolly's revival in its fluid molecules after her fall from the deck.

I marvel that something that feels as soft and smooth as water can be so strong. It wears away rocks, it deteriorates wood, it erodes shorelines, it crashes through dams. Isak Dinesen wrote that the cure for anything is salt water: sweat, tears, or the sea. I believe all water is curative in nature; it's always felt so for me.

It helped heal Dolly.

Biblical stories are filled with water imagery: The Red Sea parted; water destroyed all but the ark. Jesus was baptized in water, calmed the water, walked on water, changed water into wine. There are many forms of hydrotherapy dating back to ancient Greece and Rome, and it was prescribed by medical doctors as early as the 1800s. Franklin Roosevelt sought healing for his polio in mineral baths both in Saratoga Springs, New York and Warm Springs, Georgia. Research suggests prayer and intention can change the composition and shape of water molecules. This has implications for healing since, on average, sixty percent of the adult human body is water. Same for dogs.

As a preschool teacher, water play was my go-to to soothe a troubled, anxious child. My answer to the recently-posed question, "When do you feel most alive?" was, "When I'm swimming in a lake." Maybe that's because I was born under the zodiac sign of Aquarius, represented by the water carrier, the mystical healer who bears and bestows spiritual knowledge, in the form of water, upon the land.

Dolly might give the same answer.

For a waterfowl sporting dog like Dolly to have a lake at her disposal is a dream-come-true. Especially when the weather is hot and humid. But Dolly could also join the Polar Bear Club, diving into the lake way before and after the human swimming season. She, too, is drawn to water to drink, to swim, sometimes merely to stand in. In my dreams, she's often swimming – frequently in peril, leaving me to figure out how to rescue her. Hasn't that been my role to date?

This summer, her amphibious ways bring Dolly both pleasure and pain, like in the Bible where water both destroys and renews. Yin and yang.

In an unusual move, Dolly stops romping with a visiting neighbor dog to bolt to her potty area and squat. She moves a few feet away and squats again. And again. I run over to see what's going on and realize nothing is coming out.

Just last week, I'd thought again about how much easier my life would be without Dolly. *I'd have much more freedom, no time constraints,* I fantasized. Then felt guilty for suggesting to the Universe that I'd like to be without Dolly. Without my precious Dolly.

Strike that thought, I'd immediately messaged. *I do NOT wish Dolly gone.* Now I'm reminded once again of the power of thought and how the Universe drives it home in a not-so-subtle fashion: *Be careful what you wish for.*

Negative thoughts aren't considered as potent as positive thoughts, per the Law of Attraction. With mindfulness, we can expunge them from our minds quickly before they stick, before they attract negative consequences. We can say "Cancel" or replace them with imaginings of pleasant outcomes.

I head down to the shore to contemplate a reasonable explanation for Dolly's condition. As I gaze out at the shifting waves, I recall kneeling in the water with my puppy after her fall from the deck five years ago, dousing her with water, baptizing her. Our lives have become so intertwined since then that *when something is wrong with my baby, something is wrong with me*, as the co-dependent lyric goes.

It's Sunday afternoon, so a medical consult must wait until tomorrow. I can make a choice right now to be anxious about this all night or remain hopeful until I can get answers from Dolly's veterinarian tomorrow. I refuse to surrender my confidence, my faith. My power. But despite my resolve, Dolly experiences physical and psychological discomfort, compelled to urinate with little output. As soon as I bring her into the house, she whines to be let out again where she squats and squats and squats, rendering mere dribbles.

I'm grateful she waits to be let out each time.

Before we end our long night, I perform Reiki on her. As I lie in my bed with her on the floor next to me, I fall asleep envisioning her in the palm of my hand.

In the middle of the night, my knee aches. I then feel a hand on it – a big strong hand, although I'm alone. But it isn't just a hand; I feel a presence, a God-like presence, spanning Dolly and me – a hand on each of us.

I feel comforted, so cared for. When I wake in the morning, my knee no longer hurts. And Dolly has slept through the night without incident.

Following the veterinary appointment, I call Rick in New Jersey. "There's good news and bad news. The good news is the urine doesn't reveal any major issues; this is likely just a bladder infection. The bad news is that, based on preliminary results, the vet believes more diagnostic testing is in order to determine if her kidneys are involved."

"So right now, there's only good news," he chirps. "Having more tests isn't necessarily bad news. Let's wait to see what the other tests reveal. Maybe there'll be more good news then."

Rick lives in the moment, like a golden retriever. He's not only half-full; he's overflowing. Because his happiness comes from within, his mood isn't affected by external events, allowing him to experience joy no matter what may be looming. It's refreshing and annoying-as-hell at the same time – an interesting counter-balance to my tendency to catastrophize, which makes me more like a chihuahua, yipping and anxious. His philosophy is aligned with the teachings of the Dalai Lama elucidated in *The Book of Joy: Lasting Happiness in a Changing World*: If we tie our emotions to external events and specific outcomes, our emotional well-being is always in flux. Instead, we must be internally grounded, believing *the Universe is unfolding as it should.*

Because we're waiting on more detailed lab work to determine the source of the infectious bacteria, nothing is as yet prescribed, leaving Dolly uncomfortable. I take her out every twenty minutes, becoming zombie-like. After much prodding, I obtain the lab results and the long-awaited antibiotic to treat a simple bladder infection caused by bacteria ascending into her urethra. A consequence of lake swimming if not dried off.

Her kidneys have not been affected. Rick was right: *There's only good news.*

But within fifteen minutes of Dolly taking the long-awaited antibiotic, she dry heaves. For a moment, I approach meltdown until something inside me shifts; I remember to pray for trust and faith. I'm guided to rub Dolly's head, do Reiki on her tummy. I play songs honoring Quan Yin, the Goddess of Compassion, to calm us both.

Dolly kicks in with her own therapy by licking my knee, the one that hurt the other night. It's something I wouldn't normally encourage, but licking is emotionally and physically soothing for dogs. So lick she does, with abandon. I then give her two natural curatives for an upset stomach: pureed pumpkin and probiotics.

Dolly doesn't vomit. I vow to do whatever it takes to help her tolerate this medication, including calling the drug company directly. The customer service representative tells me to give it with food, although the label says to administer on an empty stomach. I don't understand why the prescription label instructions are contrary to what the rep told me. There are over 7,000 wrongful deaths each year in the United States from medication errors, including dispensing the right drug in the wrong way. As advocates for ourselves and others, we're obligated to ask questions. Sometimes the same question more than once.

A urinalysis five days later reveals that the antibiotic did the trick. We both survived.

Remembering the hell I went through with bladder infections in my younger days, I know they can recur. It's also determined that Dolly has a hooded vulva as a result of early spaying. The vet suggests adding powdered cranberry with Vitamin C to her food. I also become her stylist, trimming her "privates" to remove the implicated fur and then blow-drying between her legs after each romp in the water, of which there are several each day. I then apply an anti-bacterial spray to the area.

And I'd thought washing Dolly's feet was a lowly task of servitude.

There are other occupational hazards for a water sporting dog. Acute moist dermatitis can appear suddenly, forming large red lesions (hot spots), which can spread like wildfire once a dog begins to irritate the site, causing pain and infection. Dolly hasn't suffered any of the skin conditions many goldens endure, so when she starts obsessively scratching her neck, I'm surprised to find a four-inch blood-red patch of irritation running from her neck to her shoulder.

Damn.

The vet tech suggests I bring her in. That area will have to be shaved so air can get to it; that's the only way it will heal, she tells me. But we're in the mountains, and the vet is an hour away. I decide instead to use a topical spray to stop the itch, give her a homeopathic allergy pill, and apply Reiki. I pray for her healing so I won't have to shave her lovely red coat, take her to the vet, give more meds, and continue the medical cycle.

Two hours later, the patch returns to white except for a

few small blotches. I spray them and again perform Reiki. Soon all is well.

I tell a friend and can sense she wants to believe I healed Dolly's hot spot, but her tone is incredulous. I understand – it's hard for even me to believe that nasty hot spot disappeared so quickly, yet it's getting easier as I continue to experience the power of natural healing.

I do wish Dolly would help herself more. Her foraging isn't abating as she matures; rather, it continues in earnest. Within weeks, the following scene unfolds, which would be more appropriate in a Stephen King novel.

Approaching the deck after a boat ride, I see Dolly's contorted face peering through the glass door. She doesn't usually wait for me at that door, typically content to lie by the couch when alone. But today, she has good reason to be waiting for – and needing – me.

"Oh, my God! She's leaking," I scream. Partially-deaf Pete, visiting for the weekend, continues to hang up beach towels. His son, Rick, is still down at the shore.

"Pete! Rick! Dolly's leaking! She's all wet – her face!"

Drool is free-flowing out both sides of her mouth. There's a stream of water coming out her eyes, matting the fur on her face. Her nose is running.

I dry her face with my beach towel, but she's leaking faster than I can mop it up. There are puddles of Dolly's bodily fluids in all the places she hangs out.

Although we've only been gone an hour, she's dehydrated. She gulps a full bowl of water, then lies down. I place a towel under her.

We each start to do what we do best: I seek guidance from the vet's office on the phone; Rick tries to reassure me while researching "leaky dogs" on the Internet; Pete changes his clothes, ready to leave for the vet's at a moment's notice; Dolly lies there, leaking.

Rick shouts out information he's gleaning from the Internet, most of it frightening. But the tech's voice on the phone is reassuring. "It's likely an allergic reaction to something Dolly ate – perhaps a mushroom in the yard." After checking with the vet, she advises, "Rinse Dolly's mouth with warm water and give her two Benadryl."

Dolly has been relocated to the deck – a location more appropriate for secretions. I fill the turkey baster with warm water and squirt it into her mouth, causing her to gag and recoil. When I realize I'm waterboarding her, I stop.

I force the two antihistamine tablets down her throat. She lies down immediately, exhausted from all the ministrations. I give her Reiki while she continues to drip from her mouth and both eyes. I place another towel under her.

It doesn't take long before she's leaking from her other end as well.

After a few hours, all leaking stops. As quickly as it started.

I'm worn out from watching her suffer and by the reminder that she's forever toddler-like, needing supervision 24/7. We don't know where or what she'd eaten, so now I must monitor her outdoor activity even more closely. She seems unable to make good decisions, living by the canine code: *If it smells good (i.e. bad), eat it. If it runs, chase it. If it beckons, go to it. If it's yours (or you want it to be), pee on it.* Her propensity to gobble debris – any old debris – is now legendary. She's stealth, like a Venus Flytrap.

Such indiscretion confuses me: Instincts are supposed to protect us. The basic animal instinct is survival – so why/how would this animal override that? If I eat something that makes me sick, like shellfish, I'll remember how lousy I felt and not indulge again. Yet judging by our consumption of booze, tobacco, sugar, and other drugs, we're all able to make repeated bad decisions. I've certainly had more than one hangover. Are they worth it?

Was it worth it, Dolly? Does foraging make you feel most alive?

The biggest danger water poses to any of us is the direct result of the harmful choice we make to abuse our waterways. Eight million pieces of plastic are dumped into oceans every day, poisoning marine life. Factories dump toxic chemicals into streams and rivers, polluting wells and shorelines. And private corporations are buying up water rights, contributing to life-threatening water shortages in vulnerable communities. If we expect water to heal us, we must insist on necessary legislation to protect and heal our water. And change our wasteful habits.

By what metrics do we measure the pros and cons of a potentially harmful choice? How do any of us determine that the pleasure will be worth the pain – come hell or high water?

Walking Each Other Home

To travel in the company of animals is to walk
with angels, guides, guardians, jesters, shadows and
mirrors.

- Suzanne Clothier

I've walked two-plus miles every day for forty years. Until the moment I step outside the door, I dread going, endlessly looking for excuses as to why I can't: *It's too hot/cold/icy/rainy; I don't have time; I'm too tired.* I dread getting suited up and heading out into the weather – any weather. Walking can be boring, and I often feel guilty passing neighbors expending their energy and calories doing physical labor, giving them something to show for their sweaty brows. Then, there are the runners who breeze past me, tricked-out in the latest fitness fashion. Although I walk pretty fast (Dolly and I were once clocked at four miles per hour by a speed trap registering the metal on her collar), I feel like the tortoise as hares sprint past.

Somewhere en route, I become filled with gratitude that my two legs can carry me. That my hips are strong enough for a rapid gait. That I can be outside, bearing witness to the beauty nature has to offer. That my lungs effortlessly take in fresh air and propel me forward like a balloon releasing air. That I have a dog to keep me company; I might not transcend my reluctance to venture out on foot if I didn't.

On many days, Dolly's need for exercise is the only reason I walk. She negates all my excuses.

I always return with a renewed buoyancy, my endorphins, serotonin, and dopamine replenished. A natural high. And wonder why I tie myself up in knots beforehand.

Over the course of their lifetimes, each of my parents had both hips replaced. Before becoming paralyzed from a brain tumor, my mom limped with a worn-out artificial hip and still walked faster than anyone I knew until her legs wasted away in the unforgiving hospital bed. My uber-athletic father, once a physical specimen, was confined to a wheelchair at the end of his life. He clapped with joy the day they let him try to use a walker. Only once.

I've never been so grateful to be able to distance-walk as after recovering from a sprained ankle that had prevented me from doing so. Like my mom, I have osteoporosis, creating some uncertainty about my long-term mobility. Watching a man with arm-brace crutches navigate a treacherous root-covered trail confirmed what I already know and strive to remember: Mobility is sacred...and likely fleeting. I must walk while I still can. The benefits are profound, protecting against heart disease, type 2 diabetes, hypertension, arthritis, depression, and osteoporosis.

On our walk through a grove this morning, I fondly reminisce about the three-legged dog who used to run down his driveway to greet us. He was fast and spunky, undeterred by his disability, but I haven't seen him in a while. I do spot a hefty beagle charging toward us...until his rear legs give out. He skids on his face on the gravel, gets back up to make another run at us, and falls again. Although I'm relieved he was derailed, I read embarrassment on his sagging face.

"Hip problems?" I ask the owner sitting nearby.

"Yes," she replies without elaboration.

"I couldn't do that to you, Bug," I tell Dolly as we walk on. "I'd hate to lose you, but I wouldn't let you lose your dignity like that."

I consider the wheels some owners attach to their dogs' hindquarters and again speak my thoughts out loud to Dolly: "I wouldn't do that to you either. I don't think you'd want me to." (In fact, she'd be terrified – she won't even wear booties in the winter.)

A fellow walker crosses the street to meet Dolly, telling me her daughter rescues goldens, especially those surrendered because of mobility issues. "You know, the ones that might otherwise be euthanized. She helps them get hip surgery or wheels or whatever they need so they can continue to enjoy their remaining days. They still have a lot of love to give even when they're impaired."

Where is this coming from? The serendipity of my remembrance of the three-legged dog, the stumbling dog who tried to give chase, my pledge to Dolly to not put her through heroic measures, ending with a conversation that perhaps turns my pledge on its head. All within five minutes.

I hope to never understand the synchronicity of these incidents. I vow to perform Reiki on Dolly's hips each morning....and on my own.

I've walked many dogs over the years, some easier to manage than others—depending on their size and attitude. Dolly was my first car-chaser. I don't know why or how this chasing impulse developed; her first few months of life were spent in the mountains with little traffic. Yet whenever we walked, she'd lunge at every car that passed, jerking me hard on the other end of our shared leash. Weighing in at all-of-thirty-five pounds, she apparently thought herself a match for a one-ton car.

My little David taking on Goliath.

What would she have done had she caught a car? I'm sure she had no idea – that didn't stop her from her big-game fantasies. Dogs think big; size is irrelevant. My fear was a car catching her should she get loose near a road.

A career in human resources taught me what every parent of an adolescent knows: *Behavior that is not confronted will not change.* While shouting, "No car!" (my commands have always sounded Tarzan-like), I'd hold her close and, if she started to pursue, yanked on her Martingale nylon collar. This behavior modification technique using a consequence (collar pinch) for starting to chase and a reward (treat) for ignoring her would-be prey, worked after one week. But when she's asleep and her furry teddy-bear paws run in place, I know of what she dreams.

Once established, habits are hard to break for two- or four-legged beasts. And new habits are hard to form. Conventional wisdom used to be that humans could assimilate a new behavior by doing it for 21 days. A recent study determined it takes 66 days on average for a new habit to become automatic.

It seems to take Dolly all of one occurrence to form a habit if it's something she wants to do or have. If dogs can seemingly adopt a habit after one occurrence, does that make them superior to humans? Or do dogs simply cling to their desires more stubbornly, not being afraid to risk looking foolish to get what they want?

When we walk in the dog days of summer, a term from Ancient Rome based on the brightness of the Dog Star in July and August, Dolly often pants from overheating. If we're far from our house and her condition seems severe, I let her swim at a few easy-access shorelines – making sure no one is around to catch us trespassing on private property.

Dolly's never forgotten a swimming hole. Ever. Even if we've only stopped once prior, she still halts at that once-upon-a-time location, staring longingly down the path to the water – potentially exposing our bad manners. It's not just her clandestine swims that linger fondly in her memory. Every yard where a dog has ever appeared or where I've stopped to chat with a neighbor seems to be seared onto her canine brain as a wondrous place of possibility. She pauses at each, interrupting our otherwise fast-paced clip, as if to say, *Hey, c'mon! We had fun here once, remember?* A whole year may have passed since she had an adventure there, with numerous attempts to reprogram her – it makes not a lick of difference.

Hope springs eternal in dogs. *Dogged* pursuit often works.

Knowing I walk briskly for exercise, my then-husband used to chastise me, "It's the dog's walk too, ya know. Remember to let him stop so he can experience his surroundings." Today, I admit, "Dolly, you're a better walker than I because you fully engage. I've met many people with you by my side. While I have one purpose in mind, you engage in a multi-sensory adventure. You understand that the walk isn't about a destination but a journey. While I focus on the pavement so I don't trip, you hold your head high into the wind, searching. You cause me to look deep into the woods that border the road because you sense the life force within.

"You notice changes along the way. That red and white bag wasn't on that lawn yesterday, so you want to check it out (YANK). What's with that yellow boot and yellow can of furniture polish side by side? You'd like to reflect on that image a little longer, wouldn't you (YANK)?

"There have been other people and animals here, and they've all left their scents. You're curious about them too (YANK). You want to wait and greet the neighbors when you hear the hum of their garage doors. In fact, you think they're coming out to see you (YANK).

"You want to savor the treats I slip you. You'd like to stop and chew, while I want you to keep moving (YANK). You also want to sample nature's fare along the way, turning the walk into a culinary experience. Are those dandelions yummy (YANK)?

"All along our walk, you hear, 'Hurry up!' as I yank on your collar. You know what it means; you've been hearing it since you were a little pup. But you have an exercise of the heart in mind. And for that, I should slow down. Maybe you should be holding my leash."

I don't know if the neighbor could hear my one-way conversation, but we exchange a cordial greeting before he asks, "Which of you is having the most fun on your walk?"

I stammer a bit; I'm not sure I've ever thought of my daily constitutional as fun. I then respond, "She is. She wants to experience it all!" And then reconsider my answer. Dolly wants to run and be free, stopping and sniffing along the way. But she's restricted by my pace – no slower (*I have to keep my heart rate up*) and no faster (*I'm already maxed out*). I control the walk using the 6-foot leash to telegraph directions to her. It's the price she pays for staying safe while walking along the road. So I may be the one having the most fun on this walk, enjoying the company of my exuberant tour guide.

There's one property at the lake where three dogs ferociously bark and snarl at us. Theoretically, they can't get to us due to the invisible fence, but they sound like they'd rip us apart limb-by-limb if they could, using their strong jaws to sink their teeth into our jugulars. One is a Rottweiler, a breed of German origin, commonly used as guard dogs. The breed is banned in four countries, including Ireland and Poland.

I want this one banned from my neighborhood.

Dolly struts past this overgrown property, not even looking in the dogs' direction. I've trained her to ignore them by providing a treat when she looks away rather than facing them down. Once beyond their yard, she looks up at me for her reward.

"The last thing we want to do," I advised her, "is appear challenging by making eye contact. You're so sweet, you wouldn't know, but mean dogs don't want your pretty little face looking at them! Got it?" (It's hard to assess comprehension in dogs.)

Today, I'm geared up to be the mean dog. I've had it with being subjected to three vicious-sounding dogs when I walk on my own road. The invisible fence isn't much comfort since their thick necks suggest they wouldn't feel the shock when breaking through. And if they did, it would be worth it for them: Dolly and I would make a tasty and defenseless treat.

As they make menacing sounds and stare us down, my rage builds. And judgment. *Shut up! I hate you,* I silently scream at the dogs. *I HATE you! I HATE you!* A reaction hard for a dog lover like me to reconcile. Even Dolly is better mannered, ignoring them as trained.

Do as I say, not as I do.

I feel ashamed of my base instincts. Ashamed that my fear of them has translated into hatred. Making things worse, I've just dumped all that negative energy into an already-tense situation.

Their barks get louder and more rapid. Serves me right.

Instead of hate messages, I should send these dogs loving kindness. Appreciation for being dogs, for doing their job of guarding their homestead, for (hopefully) staying behind the invisible fence, for not attacking us (yet).

When I transition to sending good energy their way, their barks subside.

I watch Dolly – so disciplined in minding her own business, acting like she can't even hear them as we continue on. The anticipation of a treat is motivation enough for her. A wave of peace washes over me; that's my reward.

A few days later, the Rottweiler of the trio again does his thing: barking fiercely, jumping up and down like Pooh's Tigger – a rabid Tigger with distemper. He charges beyond the border of the invisible fence as I've always feared, plummeting into a small gully. (The Law of Attraction in action?) Snarling like a wolverine, he emerges and stops right in front of us, blocking our passage with bared teeth, bristled fur, and a stiff stubby tail. Every muscle in his ultra-muscular body is twitching.

As if in a horror movie, Dolly and I freeze. Each time we try to take a step, he inches closer.

He sniffs Dolly while she shakes, cowering. I've trained my little girl to not be antagonistic, and now a big bully is threatening her. I slacken Dolly's leash so she's not restricted in case her instincts tell her to make a move and so it doesn't inadvertently raise her head, which can be construed as challenging.

I scream for help.

"Help! Help me, please!" I shout repeatedly at the house. Despite three cars in the driveway, no one appears. The other two dogs remain behind the invisible fence, a few feet away, growling with teeth bared. If they escape, we're done for.

Our captor won't let us move in any direction, so we stand on the side of the road with no rescue in sight. Dolly continues to shake, head to tail. So do I, while continuing to shout toward the open windows.

"Help me, somebody! Please! Help me!"

My voice is high. Damsel in distress. Olive Oyl. *HE-ELP! HE-ELP!*

A large lumber truck speeds by, changing lanes to not hit us. This distracts the rottie, so Dolly and I make our move, creeping forward while he remains in the road watching us. Dolly and I both glance back periodically to make sure he's not approaching from the rear.

I begin to cry and start screaming back at the house, "Fuck you! Fuck you and your dogs! FU-UCK YOU!"

I then see a small, bow-legged, white-haired man ambling down the road toward us.

"Did you hear me calling for help?" I shout to him, trying not to care that he likely heard my profanity.

"Was that you? What's wrong?"

I tell him about being held hostage by the dog still standing in the road behind us.

"Oh, that dog won't hurt you," he calmly replies. "He's gentle. But if the small dog gets out, he might kill both of you. He's a real bastard."

The irony that I'd judged their fierceness by their size is not lost on me. And that it wasn't the worst of the pack that terrorized us.

It's not the size of the dog in the fight; it's the size of the fight in the dog.

"Are they your dogs?" I accuse.

"No, I'm just familiar with them."

I thank him for responding to my cries for help, not taking the time to correct his misconception that the Rottweiler isn't dangerous. I just want to get home.

When I turn into our driveway, my tear-streaked face turns upward to the heavens to give thanks for the truck that provided cover for us, for the man who answered my plea for help, and for my red dog who is now safely at play in her own yard.

It takes several months for me to screw up the courage to walk past that house with Dolly again. I want to get over my fear, not letting a past incident take away my right to walk where I choose. There are only two choices, and turning right instead of left out of the driveway is a nicer walk: The view is better, there's more sunlight and more people for Dolly to encounter. Plus, when we walk the other way, there's another Rottweiler tied to a large tree, which he'd probably tear out by the roots should he charge at us. The difference is that his owners are always present, telling Joker to behave. (I tell them Joker doesn't seem to be kidding.)

We turn right at the end of the driveway, and soon encounter the three dogs looking and sounding as vicious as ever, ten feet away from the shoulder of the road. They stay confined, but fear of another escape keeps me vigilant as we pass. Dolly isn't able to ignore them any longer. She keeps turning her head to check on their whereabouts, no longer deterred by the promise of a treat.

One mile later, we turn around and head back, with an anticipatory knot in my stomach. *How can this walk be good for my health?*

Again, the dogs bark and snarl. To my horror, the Rottweiler again charges through the so-called fence. His lips are curled, focused on Dolly's face. Four inches away from her sweet little face. His head twice the size of hers.

I'm filled with fear that he'll try to kill my dog – it wouldn't take much. I speak to him, to calm him down, but he pays no attention. It's Dolly he wants.

I again slacken her leash. No longer the droopy-headed, scaredy-cat dog the rottie terrified last time, Dolly positions herself between him and me, her tail stiff, head erect.

She's afraid of her food bowl but not of this would-be assassin?

Despite the terror I feel, I find myself momentarily filled with pride and gratitude that my little Dolly isn't going to take this dog's crap any longer. I'd like to think she's being protective of me, but I don't know what caused this dramatic change in demeanor.

We're frozen once again in the road, only this time Dolly's ready to rumble. I'd rather he hurt me than her. *Would she run to get help for me?*

There are again three cars in the driveway; the house windows are open. Yet there's no response to my cries for help. A bicyclist stops one house away to shout, "Is there anything I can do?" I yell back not to put herself in danger. She waits on the side of the road and watches.

Like the first time, a car zooming by distracts the Rottweiler, allowing me to slowly inch Dolly away. I thank the bicyclist for stopping, and she expresses fear about having to go past these dogs to get home.

Safely in my house, I tell Rick I'm going to drive back to get the house number so I can call the animal control officer. Rick warns me not to strike up a conversation with the owners if they're outside. I tell him not to worry, I don't intend to engage them.

As I approach, I see a woman on the porch shucking corn into a black trash bag. I pull into the driveway and, speaking to her through my car window, ask if I can talk to her about her dogs. She nods without looking at me.

"Are the dogs inside? I'm afraid to get out of my car if they're not."

She nods again, so I approach the porch. I start to tell the story, which she interrupts. "I'll go get my daughter. They're her dogs. I'm only here because we're going on a picnic."

I'll later find out they are indeed her dogs.

"Please don't let the dogs out when you go inside," I plead. "They scare me."

I stand in the driveway waiting for several minutes. I hear a commotion through the open windows so get back in my car in case they do let the dogs out.

Out they come. All three. Snarling.

A blonde woman with a rottie-build in her late forties follows the dogs, carrying a toddler. She walks over to my car window.

"Yeah?"

"I came to tell you what happened with your Rottweiler today. But I can't get out of my car because, as I told your mother, I'm afraid of your dogs."

She stands there, scowling at me, bouncing the toddler on her hip. The dogs patrol like alligators outside my car door. In as nonjudgmental a tone as I can muster, I relay what happened, sounding like the Tin Man explaining to the Wizard of Oz why they have the audacity to stand before him: *You see, a while back, we were walking down the Yellow Brick Road, and....*

"Hmmm...that's never happened before. My husband was washing the car this morning and forgot to put the shock collars on the dogs. So I guess he got out."

No apology; no remorse. She might as well have shouted, *Silence, whippersnapper!*

She continues to stare at me, not unlike her Rottweiler. I'm beginning to understand where the dogs get their endearing personalities. "Actually, this is the second time it's happened to me," I contradict. "The last time was eight months ago, and I haven't walked past your house since. But this morning, I thought I'd give it another try, only to have it happen again."

"Well, like I said, my husband made a mistake. Maybe you don't make mistakes, like you're not human or somethin'. So you can't understand when someone else makes a mistake. Guess you're perfect."

In truth, I do try.

"Look, I came here with good intentions. As a neighbor, concerned not only with my safety and my dog's but with your dog's as well. He could get hit by a car. I'm just asking you to pay attention to this matter before someone gets hurt."

"You're accusing us of not paying attention to our dogs? I'm insulted! Our dogs are outside 365/7, and you have the nerve to say we don't pay attention?"

It's only half-registering with me that her logic is illogical.

"YOU'RE insulted? My dog and I were threatened in the road by your vicious dog. Twice! And YOU'RE insulted?"

"Well, you said we don't pay attention. That's insulting!"

"If you'd been paying attention, maybe you would've heard me screaming for help right in front of your house a few minutes ago. All your windows were open, and your cars were here. But no one came to my rescue."

She smiles at the toddler. "Must've been vacuuming."

Realizing I'm wasting my time, and that Rick was right, I put my car in reverse and back out of the driveway. I don't feel safe with these dogs or these people.

There's often a correlation.

When I return home, Rick is pacing. "What took so long?"

"I spoke with the owner. It didn't go well."

"Did you think it would? I told you not to engage with them."

"I'd hoped we could've resolved it, that she would apologize and promise it would never happen again. I just want to be able to walk in that direction."

"You can. Carry mace with you."

Perhaps I'd been naïve to believe that positive energy and face-to-face communication could resolve this conflict involving angry dogs and angry people. Or perhaps I didn't believe hard enough.

A few days later, with no forethought or plan, I irrationally decide it's time to reclaim our right to turn right at the end of our driveway. As we approach, the dogs sound more threatening than ever. Dolly starts growling and barking back, further agitating them. My mild-mannered dog has also had enough of being bullied.

I remember the protection that's always with us: angels.

After rejecting the religion of my birth, it took me a long time to get comfortable with the concept of angels again. Yet even secular philosophers, such as Mortimer J. Adler, have acknowledged angels as part of the fabric of the Universe. Angels, as an embodiment of spiritual energy, can help us get unstuck if we ask for their guidance and intervention. They're available to move us beyond our day-to-day challenges, to help us achieve our divine purpose. Fulfill those agreements we made. There's a higher calling for each of us, but we must first transcend the fears and anxieties that keep us stuck. Archangel Michael can bring courage to us in those situations. Guardian angels protect us from harm – if for our highest good.

Not too long ago, Rick's dad and I had a near-miss, potentially-fatal incident when he ran a red light on a rainy night. When we pulled over, shaken and grateful, he told me angels had saved us. I'd sensed their divine presence, too, when one by one the four lanes of cars coming at us from both directions came to a screeching halt. Pete then showed me the blessed medal he wears around his neck as protection. Such faith in a higher power has served him well for many decades.

So I now unleash the angels, praying, *Please keep us safe as we walk past the dogs' yard. Surround us with your grace and protection.*

No mace. Only angels.

The dogs stop barking, and the rottie doesn't escape his confines.

On our return, this Doubting Thomas tells Dolly to walk quietly so they won't hear our footsteps. But the angels already have it under control. There's no sign of the dogs who are "outside 365/7"; it's as if they've disappeared. We walk past without incident.

When back in our yard, I give thanks for that divine energy there for the asking. I just have to remember to ask, which may be the hardest part.

Enlisting divine intervention becomes my only hope when six-year-old Dolly suffers a relapse in car-chasing frenzy, running after friends' cars as they caravan up my long driveway to the road.

Knowing it's useless to try to stop Dolly in flight, I scream to my friends, "STOP! STOP! STOP! PLEASE STOP." I can't run as swiftly up the long gravel drive as I used to or as fast as Dolly who's in hot pursuit. But I can call on angels to protect her.

Please let the drivers see Dolly. Keep her safe.

Kathy's is the first car in line, and she stops before turning onto the road because a car is coming. Marie stops behind her. Making the worst possible decision, Dolly gets in between the two cars, unable to be seen by either. I continue to run and call out their names, hoping one might have her window down; yet I'm barely audible due to being winded. All I can do is continue to storm the gates of Heaven for divine intervention.

Kathy opens her car door and gets out. Dolly gleefully runs over to her, and Kathy has the sense to grab her collar. As if moving through gelatin, I continue to trudge toward them. Kathy says she heard something that sounded like kids playing, so she got out to make sure they weren't in her path.

Do angels sound like children playing? Maybe chubby cherubs interceded.

Dolly is safe because, at the exact moment when Kathy would've turned onto the road, a car came along. Yet when I walk Dolly later that day, we see fewer than five cars in our 30-minute jaunt.

I tell Dolly that God's car saved her. "That doesn't mean you should chase cars to try to thank him. Or her."

* * *

Angels aside, I'm convinced Robert Frost was right: *Good fences make good neighbors.* Because, back at my townhouse, there are other dogs-at-large to contend with – like the chocolate Labrador retriever who resembles a bear on all fours. He frequently barrels down the hill behind us and charges at Dolly, hitting her broadside. Mangy and drooling, he pees and poops indiscriminately in my yard where Dolly's trained to only go in one designated area. So I'm less than enthused when this nameless beast decides to follow us on our walk.

With Dolly on a leash, we head down our lane. The Creature walks parallel to us on the other side of the road, big as a Smart Car. When we get to the street behind mine, I'm sure he'll head home. He doesn't. We continue onto a busier street; he stays with us, semi-running to catch up after he pauses to sniff and pee. Dolly tries to wait for him, so I pull her along (YANK).

The heavier traffic makes it more dangerous for this off-leash dog to follow us. Drivers shout out their windows at me, "Put your dog on a leash!" or "Get your dog out of the road." I just shrug hoping they'll realize MY dog IS on a leash, NOT in the road.

Those who don't yell, slow down to glare at me. Spewing judgment. Giving me the type of dirty look my father was famous for while driving.

One of those glaring drivers pulls over across the street from us. "Is that your dog?" she asks in a thick Long Island accent.

"No. He's just following us."

She gets out of her car, opens her back door, grabs a leash, and orders the dog to "Get in," pointing at the car. To my amazement, he waddles over, she hooks the leash onto his grungy collar, and he meekly climbs into her back seat. All 100 pounds of him.

I watch, incredulous that she's willing to let him in her clean white car, and he's willing to go.

"I do this all the time," she says in response to my gaping jaw. "I can't even tell you how many dogs I've picked up. Stray dogs. I'll get him back to his owner."

Dolly watches him being driven away as I narrate: "Dolly, that could happen to you if you ever run away." A teachable moment, I figure. And then have my own teachable moment when a pang of guilt washes over me that I'd let that dog wander dangerously, judging it rather than helping it find its way home. *Why did someone else have to do that? Why wasn't I the Good Samaritan?*

Maybe that was God's car too.

* * *

Dolly's usually compliant when on her leash these days, sticking close to my left side, rewarded periodically for doing so. But today, she pulls me down an incline to an asphalt path. It's a route we sometimes take, but I'm in a hurry to return home, so I try to redirect her. No dice. She tugs on the leash, aligning all four feet with her preferred direction. Because this behavior is so rare, I acquiesce, believing this will be a short detour once she sniffs whatever scent she's caught. Arriving at the path, she continues to walk straight ahead, fixated on a man coming toward us, then starts to pull with her sights on him like the hunting dog she is.

Choking herself, she lunges toward him.

My hands burn from her pulling the nylon leash. "I'm sorry. She's not usually like this."

"Oh, please, can I pet her?"

The two join as one as she leaps for joy, and he kneels down to rub her all over.

"I really needed this," he continues. "I just put my dog down, and I'm hurting bad. He was a fourteen-year-old German Shepherd, and I miss him so much. I want to get another, but my wife isn't ready. I took this walk today just to grieve."

He continues to hug Dolly. I tell him she seemed called to come down the path, perhaps because of him. We discuss the pros and cons of dog ownership.

"I love having a dog," I tell him. "But the pain of losing one is intense, I can understand not getting another." I've wondered for a while if Dolly will be my last dog; I'd like her to be because I'd like her to live forever.

He takes exception. "The rewards you get every second of having a dog are well-worth the eventual heartache. Think of it as the price you pay for a decade of unconditional love."

I again offer my condolences, and we part. I interrogate Dolly as we head back: "You sure are a self-appointed therapy dog! Is that man the reason you insisted on taking this path today? Did his dog call you to intervene on his behalf?"

She doesn't confirm or deny my suppositions. She doesn't have to.

We have a similar experience weeks later when Dolly uncharacteristically starts barking frenetically at a woman walking toward us. Her tail is wagging like a metronome as the woman coos encouraging words to her.

"You'd better watch out!" she warns me. "I'll take her from you."

"I'll let you." It'd been one of those days.

"No, you won't." The response of someone who's known the love of a dog.

Soon she and Dolly are greeting each other. She asks me questions about Dolly and tells me she recently gave her golden retriever to her 89-year-old father so he wouldn't be alone.

"Wow. Didn't that break your heart?"

"It did. But I see them every couple of weeks. They're both excited to see me. And then when I leave, there are two sad, gray faces watching me."

I'm ashamed to remember that I tried to give Dolly away when first given to me. Knowing what I know now, I couldn't stay away from an elderly parent or my dog for long. How interesting that the woman who so wisely knew I couldn't give my dog away has given her own beloved dog to a father whom she must love more – or at least as much. That would be a lot.

Her dog will be walking her father home.

I sometimes fantasize about going for a walk alone or with another adult – without Dolly. And every once in a while, I take off by myself. It's a different kind of walk, allowing me time to reflect, to look around more, and maintain an even pace. No tugging on a leash, no potty stops. I enjoy the freedom it affords me. Kinda.

Because when I do leave her behind, a phantom dog is by my side. I leave enough space to my left for her to walk on the road's shoulder. I stop to shield her when cars speed by. I think of her when I pass her favorite stops for swimming or toileting. I talk to her, pointing out what she's missing. I reach for treats to give her at certain junctures. I miss her shadow, her ears bouncing as she prances alongside me.

When we're connected by her leash, it feels like home –

like she's an extension of my body. She picks up directional cues, and we move as one. Her tugs and pulls feel natural, part of the rhythm of my walk. Of my life.

When I see that little red head facing into the wind, leading the way, I wonder why I'd even consider going for a walk without her, being without her. And I pray that all four of our hips stay strong for a long time.

The following summer, a fellow walker tells me the attack-rottie died of heat exhaustion when left under the porch in hot, humid weather. "May be just as well," she said. "He bit a delivery man on the arm, and the authorities told his owners to start securing their dogs better."

I thought I'd be relieved that he's gone, but I'm not. I didn't even know the dog's name, but he was a worthy opponent. I'd feared him, wished him gone, but it wasn't his fault. And now I grieve his loss. Florence Scovel Shinn wrote "No one is your friend. No one is your enemy. Everyone is your teacher."

The rottie was one of my teachers. Dolly's too. He reminded us of the power of divine intervention when we need protection.

The next time we walk by his house, Dolly makes huffing sounds, struggling to breathe. I stop to examine her but, once past his house, her breathing returns to normal. It happens again one month later. Was she imbued with his spirit? An involuntary acknowledgement of his suffering? A reconciliation?

"We're all just walking each other home," Ram Dass wrote.

Transformation

Dogs' lives are too short. Their only fault, really.
            – Agnes Sligh Turnbull

Pete hasn't seen Dolly for a few months, so the changes are all-too-obvious to him. "She's not a puppy anymore, is she? She looks like a dog now."

At 92, he's no stranger to the aging process. And is confirming what I already know – Dolly's face has been transformed from puppy to dog. I'd caught a glimpse of it last week and chose to ignore it, not wanting the passage of time to affect her. Wanting us all to be exempt from the ravages of aging.

Little Dolly has grown up.

It's hard to describe the difference. Her features are more defined, her snout more pointed, her cheeks less full. Her eyes more serious, more intense.

At seven, Dolly is well beyond puppyhood. But she'd retained her puppy-like appearance until recently. At times, I can still see it.

It's hard to bear witness to a loved one's aging – and easy to deny the same is happening to you. When I'd visit my elderly parents after a few months' absence, I'd be struck by how much harder physical activity had become for them. It's irrational, but easy, to get angry at someone for aging, for disappointing us with their failings of stamina and memory. As if it's their fault. As if they could help it. When I was a child, I believed everyone was born a certain age and would stay that age; I was just lucky enough to be born young, not one of those old people who could hardly move.

I'd journal as I observed my mother's challenges and have since wondered if she knew I was recording my sadness and fear over her advanced years, her inevitable passing. She never asked what I was chronicling; I never offered. And now, every scrawled entry has outlasted my mother, tucked away in what she used to call my "little book."

Our words can and do survive us. My husband used to say, "You can write the word *shit* on a piece of paper, and it will last longer than you."

SHIT. Good thing I'm a writer.

I regret not talking to my mother about how she felt watching her physical beauty fade – stolen from her. After seeing her in agony at the end, I worried I might someday forget her true essence. I know now I won't.

In this story called *Life*, we age, we watch loved ones age, they die, we die. As the Wicked Witch of the West told Dorothy in a menacing tone when all were trapped in her castle, "The last to go will see the other three go before her." A simple yet haunting line, worthy of a witch. She intended to save the cruelest punishment for Dorothy by having her witness the death of her three friends before her own inevitable demise.

Such is the paradox of life: Those who are "lucky" enough to outlive their loved ones suffer the heartache and pain of losing them one by one.

If I'm lucky, I'll be around to watch Dolly die; Pete wants to die before her. When his best friend dies, he requests a visit from Dolly to help comfort him. That's when he announces, "I want Dolly at my funeral. Right next to my casket. At the mass too."

His tone tells me he's not kidding. This healthy, yet elderly, man wants my dog present at his Roman Catholic funeral mass.

"Yeah, well, what priest would we have to talk to about that?" Rick jokes with his dad.

"I don't know who'll be around, but that's what I want. You can tell them."

"Ya know," Rick continues. "There's a chance Dolly will go first – that you'll bury her."

"I don't want to be around for that," Pete replies, his eyes misting up. "I'd rather go first than lose her." I fully understand.

My first dog, Punkin, attentively watched movies. His entire head would move with the action on the screen. We bought him the *Old Yeller* video but always hit *Stop* before Old Yeller died. The night before Punkin was to be put down, we let him watch the ending. And watch, Punk did. But we couldn't.

Dryphuss and my mother died within six months of each other. As blasphemous as it sounds, they were equally hard to lose, a truism only those who've known the love of a dog could understand. A dog is with you day and night, making every second of their absence noticeable. My mother didn't live with me; she wasn't waiting at the door for me every time I came home. Until the end of her life, she wasn't dependent on me for her well-being.

Dryphuss was. When he was diagnosed with cancer, I wrote this tribute to him:

> *I look at his earnest face*
> *Kind brown eyes*
> *Black nose*
> *Gentle mouth*
> *Soft silken ears*
> *Deep red coat, turning snowy on his face*
>
> *This miracle dog*
> *came into our lives*
> *at the most desperate of times*
> *The most perfect of creatures*
> *loves me more than I love myself*
> *But not more than I love him -*
> *that would be impossible*
>
> *I see God's handiwork in him*
> *A divine being, an old soul*
> *Lord, be gentle with him*
> *when time for him to depart*
> *Be gentle with us*
> *as you rip our hearts away.*

The years go swiftly by for both dog and human. The aging process in canines is more dramatic because it's accelerated. Changes can be detected from one day to the next. The deep, inextricable bond we form seems to arrive at the edge of a cliff in no time – sooner for larger breeds like Dolly. Having lost one dog at four years of age quells any complacency I may have about my remaining time with Dolly. My mom's brain tumor diagnosis crushed my belief that there's always tomorrow.

Dolly's now about 49 in people years, although the calculation is not the straight 1:7 ratio often applied to determine the human to canine age equivalency.

"She's getting white under her chin," Rick casually points out.

I call Dolly over to look for myself. "No, she's not. That's just bleached from the elements. She's not white."

I look away as I did when my mother's aging was too graphically exposed. I don't want to see it; it portends heartache. I've prided myself on having a middle-aged dog who most mistake for a puppy. Her muzzle is still red. The holistic vet said that's a sign of good yin.

In truth, that precious face is sporting white fur on her chin. I'm saddened by it, realizing how the remaining years seem to go faster once a dog starts to show her age. Yet I'm powerless to stop it – except possibly getting her some more good yin, which I'm working on.

"I don't mind getting older. I just don't like seeing my youngest child's hair turning gray," a neighbor's mother told her. I understood it theoretically, intellectually. Now I understand it emotionally.

Rabbi Harold Kushner's child died from that rapid-aging disease, progeria, forcing him to reconcile his notion of a benevolent, intervening God with the possibility that life is random, resulting in his seminal book *When Bad Things Happen to Good People*. He'd dedicated his life to God yet lost faith when forced to watch his young son catapulted into old age and die. Such a deep, rapid loss was transformative for him.

All loss is.

Dolly stole my heart, and I'll have to learn to live without it someday. Just as I initially feared. Exactly why I resisted becoming responsible for her.

But my feelings for Dolly transcend "responsible for." The times she doesn't wake me up at 7am, which she's done nearly every morning for seven years, I panic until I find her asleep elsewhere. I'm reminded to not take her – or anyone – for granted. We're all transient on this Earth.

This is a magical time. A time when I have a healthy, well-trained dog in my home. I'm still young enough to take care of her, to walk and brush her. To play ball and chase her. She's still young enough to want to do it. These days of both of us being young enough won't last forever; this window will close.

It always does.

While shopping for dog supplies (she's taught me we can never have enough squeak toys), I notice a man looking at housebreaking pads. He looks at the rack, walks away, and returns. I remember feeling overwhelmed by how many things puppy-Dolly needed – and how much I had forgotten about puppies. Other shoppers at the time had volunteered information, probably because I was sputtering out loud. I was grateful for their kindness and will now pay it forward to help this man.

"I remember those days," I empathetically offer, nodding at the housebreaking pads he's holding. "Puppies are such a pain, aren't they?"

He looks at me with tear-filled eyes. "Oh, no. We're at the other end of our dog's life. He's 14 and becoming incontinent. We need to protect our floors, but we'll do whatever is needed to keep him with us as long as possible."

My heart aches for him as I reflect on *the incredible journey* we take with dogs. That dog you couldn't control. That dog who made messes, chewed chair legs, and randomly wrecked things. That dog who embarrassed you with her unbridled enthusiasm. That dog who ran so fast with boundless energy. That dog who took you for a walk.

That dog. That dog too soon becomes the dog who slowly ambles through the house. The dog who only follows you with her eyes. The dog who no longer needs a leash. The dog you can't bear to lose. But you will. Willingness to risk loving these fur-babies in the face of inevitable loss is the hallmark of pet-parents.

I tell him I understand how profound his pain is – I've lived it and will again too soon. I tell him my neighbors had put diapers on their dog but often forgot to take them off before he went outside, so I'd see them running out of the house chasing him, never quite in time.

The things we do for love.

My husband and I spent thousands in veterinary bills in Punkin's last year of life, trying to save him from heart disease and cancer. We would have mortgaged our house if that was what it took. Those who live a dog-free existence marvel, and often cringe, at the lengths pet-parents will go for the sake of their fur-babies. It can even startle me as a dog-lover.

Unconditional love is priceless. The registrar doing intake for my routine blood work keenly demonstrates that to me.

"How are the roads?" she asks me.

"Not good. The wind is blowing snow back onto them. The plows can't keep up."

"Well, I hope it gets better. I have to drive into the Adirondacks after work. It's my dog's birthday."

"Is that where you live?"

"No, I used to live there but moved seven years ago. The landlord let me bury Pogo there though – he was such an Adirondack dog. I still pay rent on the property so I can visit his grave whenever I want. It's only $400 a month. Worth it to me."

Without prodding, she continues: "He died on Christmas. Even though I'm Jewish, that's a lousy day to lose your dog."

Any day is a lousy day to lose your dog. But Christmas… damn!

I quickly do the math in my head: So far, this woman has spent close to $34,000 in rent for her dog's gravesite. I want to tell her Pogo's no longer in that expensive grave. His soul has left his body, and his spirit is all around her.

She has her own ideas about where she'll find him. "My religion doesn't believe in Heaven or Hell. But I know he's in Heaven, and I'll see him again when my time comes."

"You'll meet at the Rainbow Bridge," I offer.

She tearfully nods. "Yes, he'll be there waiting for me."

As I rise to walk into the lab, I briefly tell her about Dolly. That her birthday is Mother's Day, and I can't even think about her end date. I wonder what I'll do on Mother's Day when Dolly's gone – her arrival had taken the sting out of that holiday after my mother died.

The pain of losing a dog can cause us to swear them off forever, as I did after my last one passed. Most are unable to keep that pledge, although it can be a relief to be dog-free.

"I won't do this again," my neighbor Kathy declares. "We're not getting another dog." She and her husband both have tears in their eyes as they relive the story but are resolute in their decision. They had rescued Nola after Hurricane Katrina devastated New Orleans. They worked hard to manage the resultant behavioral issues. When she bit someone after six years, they felt they had no choice but to put her down.

They're also clear that they're "done being a dog family." The extra responsibility, doggie messes, dog hair, boarding, and behavioral issues are no longer worth it for them. What was worth it was the greeting at the door, the wagging tail, the companionship, the snuggling, the routines, the bark that kept strangers away. Until she bit one.

Dolly will definitely be my last puppy. In addition to the stamina it takes, I wouldn't want to worry about his fate if he survives me. Having to name a guardian. But I'm not ready to say I'm "done being a dog family" – despite the grass and stick chunks vomited on the rug this morning.

Having a dog comes with a high cost – emotionally and

financially – like any relationship worth having. It's messy, too, like all relationships. But there's no other relationship like it.

I once heard a joke on National Public Radio that if you're not sure whether to give up your dog or your spouse, lock them both in the trunk of your car for an hour and choose the one who's happy to see you when you open it.

A dog makes you feel like you're the most fascinating person in the world. They closely watch you and want to be near you. Their ears perk up when you speak. And when you return from being away from them, they jump up to greet you, to smell your adventure. Even if your absence was a whole five minutes.

To your dog, you matter. You're important; you're interesting.

I know this because Dolly watches me put my socks on as if nothing else matters. So nothing else does.

Be the person your dog thinks you are, the bumper sticker reminds us.

Seven years ago, I lay in bed fantasizing over who might be the worthy recipient of the unwanted gift I'd named Dolly. Never imagined I'd have been transformed by the very nature of her unassuming presence. That I'd wish for her immortality. That my pillowcase would be damp from a nightmare that she's terminally ill.

In my dream, after hearing the diagnosis, I decide to free her, to let her live life the way she wants without constraint. To let her run, to eat whatever she pleases. Animals know how to take care of themselves, I reason. She'll die a natural death rather than being subjected to medical procedures. And I won't have to witness her demise.

I remove her collar, the one she resisted as a wild puppy, and walk her outside. "Go, Dolly!" I command. A command I'd given in disgust too many times.

She reluctantly trots up the driveway as I watch her leave.

Crying, I head back toward the house. Dolly comes running back to me, smiling and wagging.

"Go on, Dolly. Run away! You're free," I tell her again, waving my arms. "It's what you've wanted. Go!"

She runs off again, only to return seconds later. I try one more time without success.

I bring her inside, realizing it's too late to give Dolly her freedom. She doesn't know how to care for herself, would choose human contact over any other experience that might await her. It's my obligation – no, my honor – to guide her on this last leg of her journey, as she's helped guide me on my path.

It's too late for us to be separate, one from another, the dream-me concludes. We are a unit *'til death do us part.*

When Dolly wakes me from this nightmare, her sweet face resting on the mattress near my pillow, I'm delighted to see her bright, eager eyes ready to begin her day. Our day. And she won't leave my side until we do our morning routine... together. A routine that includes my meditation and, today, concludes with this journal entry.

> *Help me to recognize*
> *what's important, I prayed.*
> *I opened my eyes,*
> *and there lay Dolly.*
> *Basking in the sun,*
> *content to feel the warmth of its rays.*

In *Romans* 12:2, the Apostle Paul writes, "Do not be conformed to this world, but be transformed by the renewal of your mind, that by testing you may discern what is the will of God, what is good and acceptable and perfect."

Dolly has been a medium for my renewal and testing. For transformation. Transformation happens over time. It's a process. Sometimes painful. Often painful. There are few *AHA!* moments in real life, unlike fiction or the big screen, because lessons aren't offered or learned in big chunks. Like any good teacher, the Universe doles them out slowly. Transformation occurs when seemingly small, inconsequential occurrences mount to form a critical mass of heightened awareness. Enlightenment comes in baby steps if we pay attention to the higher vibration and call upon divine intervention.

The lessons this once-unwanted gift is teaching me are numerous: to accept what's given; to play, trust, laugh, rest; to embrace others, withhold judgment, risk. To live each moment. I may be the one who's had a career in education, but Dolly's taught me with the pedagogy of a master: modeling; waiting for teachable moments; incorporating incidental learning; repeating lessons when the student is slow on the uptake; making it fun; bringing in other masters when necessary. All without spoken words. She affords me the opportunity to test and apply my healing beliefs and practices on a sentient being who can't skew the results based on her own beliefs or judgments. Perhaps that's been her greatest gift to my spiritual and emotional development. Her accommodating and trusting spirit gives me the perfect motivation and subject for *discerning the will of God, what is good and acceptable and perfect.*

"You're the cutest, Dolly," I tell her. She'd been at her sitter's for four days so seems especially endearing upon my return. Absence does make the heart grow fonder.

"What makes her so cute?" Rick asks.

"She's vulnerable," I begin. "And trusting. She doesn't judge, she's cuddly and loving..."

"She just accepts things as they are," he interjects.

I must be the un-cutest thing in the whole world.

The will of God is made known to us "with all the force of a hint," per Reverend William Sloane Coffin. If we pay attention, we get exposed to new learnings, to new ways of interpreting our experience. These mini-lessons are easy to miss or dismiss until we see the interconnectedness of self with our external reality. And that usually only happens with repeated exposure to the same situation or dynamic. Repetition is the key to "getting it" – repeated exposure to chip away at our internal blocks. We then have a choice

– relive it the same old way or discern why we're having this experience again in order to push beyond it. To be transformed by AFGO: *Another fucking growth opportunity.*

"Why do you still go to AA?" I ask a friend celebrating his 30th year of sobriety who still goes to meetings every day. "You never even seem tempted to drink. You seem way beyond that. Are you showing up to support other people?"

He looks me squarely in the eye: "Why do you think I seem like I don't need AA?"

"Uh, because you go to AA?" I sheepishly mumble.

Transformation happens through repetition leading to heightened awareness.

I ask myself why Dolly has been so transformative in my life. After all, she isn't my first dog. Is it because of the agreements we'd both made prior? Because I single-parented her since puppyhood? Because I'd recently suffered several significant losses and was alone? Because she fell and was healed? Because when I was ready for the lesson, this furry teacher appeared?

Perhaps all of the above. I'll never know for certain...in this lifetime. In the end, none of the reasons matter if we remain open to our highest good. I'm grateful she found her way to me.

Dolly has transformed me from a non-believer, following the death of my parents, to a believer in the power of collective consciousness, which I no longer hesitate to call *God.*

Praise God in all manifestations!

Praise dogs in all manifestations!

My God is a loving God, a god who exists in each of us. A golden retriever, tail-wagging type of spirit that loves all creation without judgment or condemnation. *Corinthians* 13:4-8 best describes God and dog kind of love: "Love is patient, love is kind. It does not envy, it does not boast, it is not proud. It does not dishonor others, it is not self-seeking, it is not easily angered, it keeps no record of wrongs. Love does not delight in evil but rejoices with the truth. It always protects, always trusts, always hopes, always perseveres."

Protects. ✓

Trusts. ✓

Hopes. ✓

Perseveres.✓

Corinthians 13 describes my Dolly Lama.

I found God in dog – divinity in a red coat.

Spirit works in magical ways.

In the Broadway musical *Wicked*, Elphaba and Glinda sing a poignant song of reconciliation: *Because I knew you, I have been changed for good.* I've been changed for good by the gift of a puppy who jumped off the deck to catch up with me and, in the process, transformed us both.

I've been trying to catch up with her ever since.

Divine Completeness

Another name for God is surprise.
-Brother David Steindl-Rast

Dolly is a gentle, playful, healthy dog who I now dub "My Angel Dog," a far cry from "Damn-It-Dolly" in her youth. However, she's still high-maintenance. *Floor is still water* as she gingerly navigates uncarpeted flooring. Thunder, loud noises, and the high-pitched sound of a dying smoke detector battery send her scurrying down the basement stairs. She shakes like a leaf while being groomed, although still eagerly runs into veterinary offices.

She no longer tests positive for Lyme. Together, we still walk at least two miles each day; Reiki and chiropractic treatments, glucosamine/chondroitin, and other nutraceuticals help us maintain a fast clip. She eats with gusto, and I savor the sound of her bowls clanging – a joyous noise I'll never take for granted. I give her fresh or frozen organic fruits and vegetables for treats, like blueberries, strawberries, cranberries, carrots, celery, broccoli and cauliflower. Her outdoor foraging continues unabated. She's thriving in her private boarding situation with three cats, although I hate to leave her.

Rick's become an important part of her life, seeking her out rather than running from her. She follows him like Mary's Little Lamb, perhaps because he's more generous with treats than I. He's also a beneficiary of the reciprocal healing Dolly offers, performing Reiki on her as well. I periodically hear him whisper, when he thinks I'm out of earshot, "You've taught me so much, Dolly. Thank you."

I hadn't realized Dolly had other students.

Dolly's deep-red fur is untarnished by tell-tale white, save for that patch under her chin. She's still mistaken at least once per walk for a puppy. When asked how old she is, I deceptively reply, "Nine," delighting in hearing them ask, "Nine months?" Most are incredulous when I clarify.

Nine years old. My puppy is nine years old. Where have the years gone?

The number 9 holds powerful symbolism in divination practices, such as tarot and numerology. Nines hold the energy of attainment and completion, followed by new beginnings and renewal. The Nine of Cups, for instance, is associated with happiness and satisfaction.

Likewise, Biblical scholars believe the number 9 symbolizes divine completeness or finality. For them, 9 also represents the nine fruits of the Holy Spirit, virtues that come from living in accord with the spirit of God: faithfulness, gentleness, goodness, joy, kindness, patience, love, peace, and self-control.

My Dolly embodies all of these attributes...except, of course, that *self-control* thing. I fear I've failed her at times in the *patience* category but perhaps made up for it in *love*.

Although indoctrinated with Trinity theology since childhood, I long ago rejected the concept of "one God in three divine persons." Why three separate "persons" rather than one universal life-giving force? (Actually, the word *trinity* doesn't appear in the Bible.) The symbolism of the Holy Spirit most closely correlates with my adult belief system. The Holy Spirit represents powerful, necessary-for-life energy. It's God's power in action, an active force. In the Bible, the Holy Spirit appears as early as the second verse of *Genesis*, the Hebrew term *ruakh*, meaning wind, breath, or spirit. According to theologians, this spirit empowers individuals for specific tasks; it empowered Jesus at his baptism to heal the human condition.

Spirit continues to heal. And challenge.

My Reiki master, Gina, has been asking for almost three years when I'll finish "the Dolly Lama book." I made excuses, eventually admitting to having trouble discerning when to end the telling. She knowingly responded, "You haven't finished it yet because Dolly's story isn't over yet." She was right. In this, Dolly's ninth year, there are more manifestations of her healing influence warranting inclusion. Some I could do without.

Like when Dolly starts regurgitating daily between 9pm and 6am. A high-pitched howl also emanates from her stomach. I cover the floors with towels at night and bolt upright when I hear the heaving begin. I consult three different vets, all of whom are stumped because it only happens late night or early morning. Her blood work is excellent, she's not tender anywhere, and her stools are fine. However, I'm warned that, despite her good blood work, cancer could be "hiding" in her GI tract, which wouldn't show up on tests conducted thus far.

Her foraging is a primary suspect. I search the Internet for answers, consult other pet-parents, call food manufacturers, and call on higher powers, including Archangel Raphael and....my father who loved dogs. Nothing helps; some treatments (like antacids) make it worse. When Dolly expels again after my prolonged entreaty to Raphael, I begin to doubt my ability to help her. Each time I feed her, I feel I'm poisoning her, energetically making it worse. She's less enthusiastic about eating, has lost weight, is listless, and her coat looks dull.

I'm sleep-deprived after ten-days, so everything sounds like retching: the generator, the refrigerator, the clock, an overhead airplane, television, a car engine.

The next step is x-rays, which show no pathology. (She freaks on the table, however.) We'd ruled out food as the underlying cause for logical reasons, but, trusting my own instincts, I switch her to a bland dog food recipe consisting of boiled sweet potatoes, canned pumpkin, and boiled raw food. It just feels right, and Dolly agrees. She eats enthusiastically and, for the first time in ten days, sleeps through the night without vomiting. I sleep too. Based on one vet's recommendation, I also apply ginger essential oil to her stomach area to aid digestion. One week later, I switch her to a locally-produced brand of raw food without further incident.

Although there'd been no recalls on her food and no

other filed complaints, it clearly was the cause of Dolly's illness. The dog food company reimburses me for all recent purchases and for veterinary expenses. I will continue to feed raw, believing it contributes to Dolly's overall good health, but will proceed with a heightened level of caution based on FDA warnings.

Year Number Nine has more challenges in store for us when, in early fall, a splash of bright red blood stains Dolly's blonde tail feathers. The next morning, I make a vet appointment and contact Marie – the friend I called for reassurance after Dolly's fall – to ask for a reading.

"It's inflammation," Marie reports confidently. "Apply oils to her and call on the angels to help." I'd started doing both already, as well as giving her Reiki treatments.

The vet isn't as reassuring, concerned about "suspicious" cells on Dolly's vaginal culture, which must be sent to cytology to examine. For three days, I try to reconcile that, despite my taking precautions to safeguard Dolly's health, I might still lose her at a relatively young age. My anticipatory grief goes deep: *Isn't this the dog I didn't want? Now, I feel I'll die without her.*

Rick shares my concern for Dolly, and I don't want to exacerbate that by falling apart in front of him. I admit to a friend that I've been going into the garage to cry when he's here so as not to appear weak. "Crying is not weak," Nancy declares. "To show your vulnerability to someone is a sign of strength. Don't be afraid to reveal yourself."

Her perspective makes me view my behavior differently. Good friends do that for us; they invest in our stories. I realize I cry in the garage to protect my image as a competent, capable woman. It's not about protecting Rick; it's about my not wanting to appear vulnerable.

"Do you think Dolly's condition is bringing up unresolved issues for you?" Rick astutely asks. I don't hesitate: "Yes, every time I came to a crossroad with my mom's illness, it went the wrong way. There was nothing I could do. I'm afraid to hope because I can't take the disappointment."

I hadn't realized I was still enmeshed in those caregiving memories, fourteen years later. Long-term caregiving can result in unresolved trauma being carried in our bodies. In our DNA. Hell, I wrote a book about losing parents, and I'm still not purged.

Dolly clearly had a job to finish.

True-to-form, Rick reminds me to stay in the moment, not to project. I often equate his homeostasis with not getting it, with not caring, which isn't fair. He loves Dolly as much as I do and, when the time comes, will grieve her deeply. For him, that time is not now, so he'll remain hopeful until there's reason not to be.

Experts agree: Worrying isn't good for us. It's a waste of time and energy, distracting us from enjoying the moment. I don't agree that it's always futile, however – worry motivates me to look ahead, to contingency plan, to take action to reduce the likelihood of a fear becoming reality. Yet it's exhausting and, to paraphrase Mark Twain, most of what I worry about never happens. Even worse, according to the Law of Attraction, worry can attract the outcome we fear. Is being prepared for something that *might* happen worth the time spent worrying? (In this manuscript alone, I've used the word *worry* 28 times.) Hard to calculate the payoff. I just know it feels logical and necessary to look ahead because I believe I can influence outcomes – tangibly or energetically. I'm still trying to accept that there are different ways to take action – sometimes it's simply a matter of turning it over to a higher power.

Grant me the wisdom to know the difference...

Poor Dolly – I'm such a slow learner.

Trying to manage my angst over Dolly's health issue, I turn to Doreen Virtue's *Healing with Angels* oracle cards, drawing *Surrender and Release*:

When you hold on tightly to something that's not working, it has no room to heal. But if you open your hands and free the situation, it will either be washed

*away and replaced by something better or it will heal
in a miraculous way. The angels ask you to try not to
control the outcome. Let go, and let God help you.*

When I heed the advice (offered through various media) to surrender, my head clears, and I get a spirit message that Dolly's vagina is irritated, but it isn't cancer. Marie had labeled it "inflammation." I must stop imagining the worst and instead send healthy, positive energy forward.

Life goes on, I tell myself. *Life goes on…until it doesn't.*

In the middle of this, I get a text from my friend Darlene: "Do you do Reiki on dogs?"

Her golden retriever, Maizie, is nine years old. Like Dolly, her birthday is on Mother's Day. Darlene tells me the devastating news: Maizie has cancer in her liver and spleen. Darlene's hoping to buy some time. We always do. *Please not yet,* we pray.

Since diagnosis, Darlene's been pursuing advanced holistic remedies and cures. It's what we do when western medicine fails us. The vet's prognosis was three months; Darlene's hoping for a year. "We're going to beat this, Maizie," she tells her beloved dog. Positive thinking. An attitude like that can make that goal a reality.

I easily get in touch with Darlene's despair. I harken back to the deep grief of losing my prior goldens – grief that lingers in my DNA. Grief that's so close to the surface, I can conjure up the moment of impact. And with a nine-year-old dog, I'm queued up once again to have my heart ripped away.

Darlene struggles with the questions we all confront at the end. "I can't help but wonder about all the interventions we did – vaccines, medications, chemicals, toxins, x-rays. We fed her grain-free kibble, but we recently consulted a holistic vet who told us to start feeding raw to build her immunity. Next time, I'll do things differently."

We know modern medicine can cause disease as well as cure it. A friend beat brain cancer only to develop throat cancer because the chemo suppressed his immune system, enabling a new site to grow. What level of risk is posed by beaming radiation into squashed tender breast tissue during annual mammograms? According to a recent report by the U.S. Preventive Services Task Force, no study to date has shown that mammograms reduce overall mortality for women of any age. In fact, false alarms in 50% of women are known to cause significant psychological distress. What about routine dental x-rays so near our brains and throats?

There are no guarantees – we have to do our own due diligence and trust our guts as we ask for intervention for our highest good.

I'm gratified to hear resilience in Darlene words "next time," but I have few words of consolation to offer this devoted pet-parent who pampers Maizie as much as I pamper Dolly. "Maybe this is just Maizie's path," I feebly say.

"Maybe it's my path too," she adds. Darlene gets it; our journeys are all interconnected.

I send Reiki to Maizie. A big, happy golden's face appears, surrounded by yellow light. "Help her on her healing journey," I invoke. "For her highest good, no matter where that takes her."

Early the next morning, I take Dolly for a walk, during which she's quite frisky. As she tugs on the leash in her mouth, I hear a male voice say, "She's beautiful." But no one's around.

"In the truck," the voice says. I turn to see a man sitting in a pickup in a vacant house's driveway. "She's a puppy, right?"

"No, she's nine years old," I say flatly. Sobered by a pending diagnosis, I don't exude the same hubris regarding her age.

"Wow, she's in great shape."

Tears fill my eyes as he continues. "We just put one down. It was awful. Goldens are prone to cancer." I tell him we're awaiting pathology results and ask, "How do you get over the loss?" Although I've been through it three times, I no longer remember.

I don't want to remember.

"My wife's having a hard time, even though it's been over

two months." He gets out of the truck and holds Dolly's head between his rough hands. "She's beautiful," he repeats.

"Yes, she is."

That's what the aides in the hospital said about my mom right up until the end. I don't take comfort in it today. The stranger wishes me well, and I head home to do my energy work during which I receive a telepathic message from a long-time friend. In his characteristically deep froggy voice, I hear, *Stop worrying. We don't want your bratty little girl over here anyway. You can keep her.*

Classic Tim, comforting me by being a wise guy. Despite his brash ex-military exterior, he excelled at consoling his numerous female friends. Knowing my Reiki master, Gina, had treated him during his illness, I text her to say I heard from him. She responds that she had as well, just the day before – on his birthday – for the first time since his death one year prior.

I ask Gina to send Reiki to Dolly. She not only does so, she engages a group of distance healers, none of whom know the specifics or me. No serious issues are detected, and the messages received are powerful: *Dolly is a sweet soul...she's connected to a loving female companion...she's surrounded by love...she's trying to heal herself...she misses being with other dogs.*

I laugh at the last one. Dolly hasn't seen her buddy Murphy in quite a while; I'm sure she misses him. And "Uncle Kevin."

I cup Dolly's head and speak to her of my love. I tell her she's been "my dog." Although not my first, she's the one I've treasured the most – treasured her essence, her peculiarities. Yet possibly every dog we have is our most treasured...at the time.

My furry teacher stoically sits, Buddha-like, indulging my pathos.

When the vet calls to say Dolly has three co-infections, including staph, in her reproductive tract, she expresses surprise that the bleeding has stopped before treatment. I'm not. Complementary treatment *had* begun: Many people had sent her Reiki. Plus, she was "trying to heal herself." A high-potency antibiotic regimen is prescribed for a month – the goal to stop the infections from reaching her organs, which would be more serious. One Reiki sender had foreseen stomach issues, so, in addition to the probiotics, I bless the bottle of Zeniquin tablets, saying, "I bless the Divine within you. We offer Dolly this gift of healing energy with love..." I draw Reiki symbols, a cross, and hearts on the prescription label. I place the container in her bed overnight so an energetic bond is formed. With each dose, I thank western medicine for the diagnosis and cure. Her holistic vet suggests I also work to energetically draw the infection out of her system.

Marie's otherworldly diagnosis of "inflammation" had not been far off.

Dolly suffers no side effects, and her culture is clear of all infection after just 21 days. I shout a big *YAHOO!* and get down on my knees to give thanks. To thank all the friends and professionals who supported us through the ordeal. To thank Dolly for being part of the healing process. To thank the Universe for yet another lesson.

Since there is no clear answer as to how she may have contracted these infections, I now wipe her butt after each bowel movement, grateful every time I get to do it. Of course, antibiotics also contribute to vaginitis. A cure can sometimes cause another ailment.

Thanks to her loving family, Maizie ends up staying longer than predicted. She now waits for them at the Rainbow Bridge.

The lessons resume.

On a routine walk on a cold winter day, a 100-plus pound shepherd-mix barrels into Dolly, pins her down, and grips her neck in his jaws. She gives a wounded cry and lies motionless. Standing paralyzed, I scream, "NO! Stop! Stop!" alerting the dog's owner who comes running with fear in his eyes, which only increases my terror. He grabs his dog by the collar, pulling him off his immobilized prey just as the dog starts to shake Dolly by the neck. The man's hands drip blood as the dog stands on his hind legs in resistance, taller than his owner. I run to Dolly who slowly begins to move and then stands, dazed but seemingly unharmed. The attacker is put in a truck, where he bounces off the windows, rocking the truck sideways, continuing to snarl.

The man apologizes profusely, explaining that his dog is a trained guard dog in a nearby city and was off-leash because he'd been told no one lives at the lake in the winter. Just then, two other neighbors appear in response to the commotion, proving that assumption wrong.

Dolly and I had come up for a weekend retreat. A fateful decision, it would turn out.

The owner assures me his dog is current with vaccinations and offers to pay any veterinary bills. Together, we examine every inch of Dolly. There's no blood, no broken skin. (The blood on the owner's hands came from his dog biting him.) Shaking and unsteady, I walk Dolly home. She seems unaffected, eager to chase a ball when we arrive. Shame washes over me that I'd done nothing to protect her. I didn't block her attacker as he charged at us. I didn't kick him in the head. I'd left Dolly vulnerable; I'd let her down. I'd let myself down.

"We don't know the ways of the animal kingdom," my friend Peggy consoles. "What you might have done could have made it worse."

"Dolly *was* protected," Marie intuits. "There was a force that saved her from the dangerous attack."

Upon examination, the western vet assures me Dolly suffered no serious injuries other than soft tissue damage, informing me "a dog's neck is tough to puncture." He, too, uses the word *protected* but in a different context: "Dolly was protected by her instinct. The attack dog simply wanted dominance; he didn't want to kill her because if he did, he easily could have. She knew enough to be submissive, playing dead so he got what he wanted. If you'd fought him, this could've had a very different ending. For both of you."

There are times it's better to surrender.

Dogs know everything they need to know. Perhaps instinct comes from a higher source. Perhaps my instinct guided my inertia.

I think back to the days of Dolly playing possum in my driveway, protesting the newly-attached leash. Her defense was to lay there until I backed off. It worked for her then and now.

I stop second-guessing myself but see evidence we're both suffering from PTSD. Dolly seems less trusting of other dogs (as am I) and more prone to pre-emptive barking sprees (as am I) when we walk past dogs in their yards. Her bunny-chasing dreams occasionally give way to nightmares, evidenced by low growls in her throat and a thrashing torso. Her holistic vet warns that trauma can permanently alter a dog's gentle disposition. She prescribes Chinese herbs and *Star of Bethlehem* flower essence to cleanse Dolly's DNA of attack memories.

The attack scene flashes into my head periodically, so convinced had I been that I'd just witnessed my dog being savagely killed. So I, too, self-medicate with drops of *Star of Bethlehem*. Since our bodies can't differentiate the effects of real and imagined trauma, I speak with a counselor who tells me, "As horrible as that was, remember you were protected too. The dog's owner was concerned and helpful. Neighbors came to check on you. And your dog is okay. Remember to appreciate the good parts of the story."

I walk the labyrinth, giving thanks to those who protected us on this plane and beyond. And for the power in trusting our instincts. Dolly's latest round of health issues have brought me to an even deeper understanding of how divine intervention works. (More unwanted gifts...) The Universe doesn't swoop down to "fix" things. It works through us, helping us find solutions. I know my quest to help Dolly is aided by higher powers. As I declare, "Praise God," I see curled-up Dolly surrounded by Archangel Raphael's emerald-green glow.

Each experience brings me closer to "getting it" and trusting the universal healing power. I don't welcome the challenges but am grateful for the opportunity to learn. And it doesn't take me as long as it once did to reach a deeper understanding of the divine design. An obvious remaining lesson for me is to steel myself against future loss and trauma so I'm not dependent on others for information, reassurance, and comfort. We're all temporary on this plane, and I'm moving into a time of inevitable loss. How can I fortify my trust, my inner reserves?

We've dodged health scares in the past, but that dreaded day will come when I lay my hands on Dolly's warm, soft body for the last time. I can't hold her earthbound forever. Any regrets won't be founded in negligence or casualness. I've done everything in my power to take care of this furry angel entrusted to me. I had only her to focus on during our early years together. And she had only me to observe, to obey, to please. To bug. To teach. I've been both a hard and a loving master; her watchfulness tells me that is true. But when she's afraid, when she doesn't feel well, it's me she seeks. To lie by my side, inviting soothing words of comfort, my healing hands upon her stomach and back. She's been a mirror, reflecting who I am – not just in relation to her, but who I am in relation to the world.

Dolly's taught me so much about love and healing. What if her final lesson is teaching me how to cope with loss? To cope without my Dolly.

The counterbalance yang to the above yin experiences is that, in late summer of her ninth year of life, Dolly falls in love when she meets JB, a six-year-old black Lab built like a coffee table, a drop-out of *Guide Dog Foundation* training due to ambulatory issues. At first, she's intimidated, his tail alone being strong enough to knock her over. But she apparently goes for the strong, silent type because, before too long, my spayed dog begins approaching JB with seductive front leg moves and a wanton look in her eyes as she humps the air in his general vicinity, redefining *doggie companionship*.

Good-natured and clueless, JB has no interest in my little seductress yet has to tolerate her pining for a week when his pet-parents sit for Dolly, who insists on sharing his bed. She doesn't even seem to mind their bare wooden floors. Friends joke that my love-sick pup should be re-named *Delilah*, saying they'll never look at her the same way.

Isn't love the greatest healer of all?

There are many ways in which we all need to heal and many modalities for doing so. Dolly Lama's innate wisdom was presented to me with *all the force of a hint*, offering guidance I didn't know I needed. I've not yet fully integrated all she's tried to impart, but I'm conscious of the recurring opportunities to learn the lessons. I'm still on the journey and now get there quicker, minor setbacks aside.

Her tutelage of me and others will continue, but this, Dolly's ninth year, feels like the right time to "finish the Dolly Lama book," drawn from the journals I'd kept to try to understand her inconvenient arrival in my life.

My unwanted gift became my gift of grace. My blessing.

Nine: Attainment. Divine completeness. Satisfaction.

There are more stories of our healing bond than shared on these pages. They all speak to this universal truth: Divine energy is within and around us, with the capacity to heal us emotionally and physically. We have only to tap into it and trust that the divine design is perfect. And remember that our most important lessons may come disguised as unwanted gifts that change our lives in unexpected ways.

If you're lucky, yours will come wrapped as a red irascible puppy.

Epilogue

After typing what-was-to-be the last sentence of this manuscript, I walk out to my labyrinth. I tell Dolly to stay in her play area; she's never been allowed near the labyrinth for fear of her considering it her toilet or buffet. She's always honored that command. Until now.

I slowly walk in and sit on the bench in the center. I thank the Universe for giving me the inspiration and courage to authentically relay our story. I pray what I've written about my canine teacher will resonate with others. Pray readers will find their own meaning in my confusion and hard-earned lessons. Pray my truth will find a home. Pray I'll be responsive to divine guidance from the Universe, that I'll recognize the gentle nudges.

As I sit, hands folded in prayer, I hear a crunch. Opening one eye, I see Dolly standing nearby, chomping away on God-knows-what. Rather than reprimanding her for breaking the *stay,* entering the labyrinth, and foraging, I lean over and hug her, thanking her for the reassurance that we indeed have a story worth telling. I express gratitude for this unwanted gift – a subtle prod from the Universe that turned out to be not-so-subtle.

Dolly falls in line behind me as we wend our way out of the labyrinth.

She runs ahead to the garage, seeking refuge from the summer heat. Our eyes lock and, in that moment, I catch a glimpse of that puppy I brought here nine years ago. The puppy who vexed me. The puppy who changed my life. I walk over to her, putting one arm under her belly and the other around her neck. I kiss her soft head as I did the first day we met. Through my tears, I whisper, "I love you so, my Dolly Lama." Tears that make me wish I had it to do all over again.

Back in the house, I meditate while listening to an ancient

Sufi song, whose words and resonances were designed to awaken and release the power of cellular intelligence.

> *I woke*
> *In burst of light*
> *To see Love's perfection*
> *A glimmer of eternity*
> *In you.*

When it ends, I open my eyes to see Dolly in all her perfection. She raises her head, a princess waking from a spell. On her side, legs outstretched, trusting she is safe. In complete repose. *Love's perfection.*

Dolly offers me *a glimmer of eternity* as I know her love transcends. It's time to share the greatest unwanted gift with seekers and readers.

Stay, Dolly. Stay.

Three Years Later...

We agree to help them leave us when their time comes and to feel the inexorable pain when they're no longer by our side – words I penned when Dolly was still a puppy. They weren't theoretical; I remembered the pain from past canine losses. But I'd forgotten how much it hurts. Or perhaps Dolly was my "heart dog," the one who captures your heart like no other before or since, so the pain goes even deeper. If that's possible.

After Dolly passed, she offered one more lesson. It's the lesson David Kessler explores in his book *Finding Meaning: The Sixth Stage of Grief:* Learning to remember those who have died with more love than pain and moving forward in a way that honors them. Dolly showed me a way to honor her. And all beloved pets.

When I stopped to pay the last bill, the vet and I lamented that so many pets die of cancer and other painful diseases. I knew the lessons in this book could help, but was there more we could do to postpone the tragic loss we eventually must experience as pet parents? Upon returning home,

I contacted the Morris Animal Foundation, a nonprofit organization studying how pets could live healthier and longer lives; I decided to raise money for them in Dolly's name. I excerpted a verse from this manuscript, coupled it with a photo Rick had taken of Dolly, and my friend Kurt designed a card to commemorate the adoption, celebration, or loss of a pet. Within 24 hours of initial conception, Dolly's Card Project was born.

Feeling some peace after a torturous two weeks of grieving, I attended a virtual healing session that evening with my Reiki master. At the end of the session, Gina announced to all who'd participated, "There's been a dog here with me, sitting quietly to my left through the entire session. Her name is Dolly, and she's in Heaven now. She wants everyone to know she is happy to be helping other dogs and to help humans understand what dogs need."

Where did that come from? Neither Gina nor any of my friends knew about the *Healing with Dolly Lama Card Project* yet – it had all come together so quickly. In fact, I hadn't discussed Dolly's passing with Gina at all. There is no explanation other than Dolly Lama is continuing to heal others by raising awareness of and funds for the Morris Animal Foundation's longitudinal study on canine health.

The Dolly cards and this book are in fulfillment of the promise made to the Universe that Dolly would "do something good in this world," her gifts to those seeking a higher purpose and consciousness.

Dolly couldn't *stay,* but she is helping to heal my broken heart by helping me find meaning in her absence – an absence I feel every minute of every day. Readers can visit the *Healing with Dolly Lama Card Project* at https://morrisanimalfoundation.rallybound.org/golden-retriever-lifetime-study-fundraisers/DollyLama. If you'd like to assist with this mission, email us at hwdollylama@gmail.com.

Thank you, Dolly Lama. *Because I knew you, I have been changed for good.*

About the Author

Besides being Dolly Lama's student for almost twelve years, Patricia A. Nugent has written/edited three books, all with the theme of *They Live On*. Whether it be her infirm parents, trailblazing foremothers, or her dog, her work gives voice to those who might otherwise be silenced. She's also been published in trade and literary journals as well as in anthologies. Following a career in public and higher education, she now volunteers to teach writing to adult learners and writes personal essays on social justice issues, which can be found on her blog at www.journalartspress.com.

She is grateful to the many who supported this project, as well as those who helped raise Dolly Lama to become the amazing dog she was – after a rough start. This includes friends and family, as well as veterinarians (appearing as composite characters), healers, trainers, and editors, who took precious time to answer her endless questions. Over twenty readers from diverse disciplines reviewed the manuscript, and their input made all the difference in a book that started out as journal musings about an unwanted, spirited puppy – ultimately, the most cherished of gifts.

Other Books by this Author:

• *They Live On: Saying Goodbye to Mom and Dad*

• *Before They Were Our Mothers: Voices of Women Born Before Rosie Started Riveting*

Glossary of Healing Modalities Referenced

- Acupuncture: Pricking the skin or tissues with small needles along meridians to alleviate pain and treat physical and emotional conditions.

- Angel Medicine: Health guidance received from angels to support an individual's emotional, spiritual, and physical well-being.

- Applied kinesiology: Evaluating structural, chemical, and mental aspects of health using manual muscle testing combined with other standard methods of diagnosis.

- Archangels: Referenced in Christian, Jewish, and Islamic texts, archangels are considered divine messengers of the highest order, each known for a specific role/purpose.

- Aromatherapy: Inhalation or application of essential oils for therapeutic purposes that can cause a chemical reaction in the brain to trigger healing.

- Ascended masters: Spiritually-enlightened beings who were ordinary humans in past incarnations and have undergone spiritual transformations.

- Attunement: Process by which recipients become vessels of healing energy for themselves and others.

- Blessing: Infusing with benefits such as wellness, spiritual redemption, mercy, protection, divine will, hope, and/or approval.

- Chakras: Considered the loci of life energy, these centers of spiritual power vitalize the physical body to address physical and emotional conditions.

- Channeling: Serving as a medium through which spirits can communicate with living beings.

- Crystals: Transmit healing or spiritual energy through their high vibrations and frequencies; specific types are used to address certain conditions.

- Divining Tools: Instruments and devices used to receive wisdom and knowledge from higher sources regarding innermost questions; examples include oracle cards, spirit/ouija boards, crystal balls, pendulums, and dowsing rods.

- Earthing/grounding: Maintaining direct contact with electrons on the Earth's surface by walking barefoot or lying outside, enabling the transfer of energy from the ground to the body.

- Essential Oils: Highly-concentrated oils extracted from flowers, leaves, roots, and other parts of plants that may be ingested, inhaled, or applied; considered helpful for cleansing, purifying, soothing, and healing.

- Healing Touch: Hands-on stimulation of a body's life force energy (qi) to encourage the body's own natural healing ability.

- Holistic Care: Seeks to restore health by taking into account the mind, body, and spirit of the patient.

- Homeopathy: Stimulates the body's own healing mechanisms by mimicking the disease state, thereby rousing the body to correct the underlying imbalance that caused the symptoms.

- Hypnosis: Induction of a state of consciousness in which a person is highly responsive to suggestion or direction; often used to recover repressed memories or to facilitate behavioral changes.

- Imaging/Visioning: Using mental images to influence bodily processes, reverse disease, ease pain, or succeed in an endeavor.

- Intention: A mental state that represents the ability and commitment to make a desired outcome happen.

- Karma: The sum of a person's actions in this and previous states of existence, which may determine their future fate.

- Law of Attraction: The belief that positive thoughts are magnets for positive life experiences, and negative thoughts attract negative experiences.

- Magnetic Therapy: Using energy fields from negative poles of magnets to relieve pain and heal disease; magnets of varying shapes and sizes are placed on/near the body.

- Massage: Manipulation of soft tissue by rubbing, kneading, or tapping with the hands to stimulate circulation, promote health, and relieve tension or pain.

- Meditation: A technique for focusing the mind on a particular object, thought, or activity to achieve a mentally clear and emotionally calm state.

- Meridians: A set of pathways in the body along which vital energy (qi) flows; there are fourteen such major pathways in the human body associated with specific organs.

- Mindfulness: A mental state achieved by focusing one's awareness on the present moment while calmly acknowledging and accepting one's feelings, thoughts, and bodily sensations.

- Naturopath: A health care professional who emphasizes prevention and treatment using therapeutic methods and substances that encourage individuals' inherent self-healing. abilities.

- Prayer: An invocation or appeal seeking to affect an outcome through a higher power or to express gratitude.

- Qi (pronounced *chee*): The circulating life force in every living being, the balancing of which promotes healing and health.

- Quan Yin: One of the most popular deities in Buddhism known as the Goddess of Compassion and Mercy; the Buddhist "Mary."

- Reiki (pronounced ray-kee): A Japanese healing modality, meaning *spiritually-guided energy*, through which a practitioner becomes a channel for healing, connecting vibrationally with the recipients own energy system, activating their natural ability to heal body, mind, and spirit.

- Reiki Symbols: Sanskrit-derived Japanese forms essential to the Reiki practice, each with its own vibration and purpose; when drawn, they connect with the recipient's energy.

- Smudging: Native American practice of using the smoke from burning sacred herbs to purify the air and remove negative energy, creating a more positive atmosphere and mood.

- Sound Healing: Using sounds, rhythms, and vibrations at healing frequencies attuned to chakras to restore physical, emotional, and spiritual well-being.

- Spirit Circle: A place to connect with higher knowledge, spiritual wisdom, or spirit entities in order to transcend limitations of the physical world.

- Traditional Chinese Medicine (TCM): Used for centuries in China to address unhealthy energy patterns that manifest in a variety of symptoms, helping the patient regain balance and strengthen resistance to disease.

- Universal Laws: Fundamental, unchanging rules governing our Universe deriving from the wisdom of ancient cultures.

- Visualization (see *Imaging*)

- Western/Allopathic/Modern Medicine: A treatment system in which medical doctors and other healthcare professionals treat symptoms and diseases using medication, radiation, and/or surgery.

- Yoga: A physical, mental, and spiritual practice originating in ancient India that aims to join the mind, body and spirit. Twelve basic postures promote healing and alignment.

Bibliography/Resources Cited

Adler, Mortimer J. *The Angels and Us,* 1993

Agency for Toxic Substances and Disease Registry. www.atsdr.cdc.gov

American Cancer Society. www.cancer.org

American Kennel Club. www.akc.org

American Psychiatric Association www.psychiatry.org

Angel, Lizi. www.caninemind.co.uk/

Arnst, William et al. *What the Bleep Do We Know?* (movie), 2004

Aslan, Resa. *Zealot: The Life and Times of Jesus of Nazareth,* 2013

Byrne, Emma. *Swearing is Good for You: The Amazing Science of Bad Language,* 2017

Byrne, Rhonda. *The Secret,* 2006

Cash, Rosanne. *Black Cadillac* (CD), 2006

Center for Disease Control. www.cdc.gov/

Chopra, Deepak. *Why is God Laughing? The Path to Joy and Spiritual Optimism,* 2008

Clothier, Suzanne. *Bones Would Rain from the Sky,* 2005

Coger, Laurie, DVM. www.healthydogworkshop.com

Collins, Mabel. *Light on the Path,* 1885

Coren, Stanley, Ph.D. "Florence Nightingale: The Dog and the Dream," *Psychology Today,* 2010

Cousins, Norman. *Anatomy of an Illness,* 1979

The Dalai Lama. *My Spiritual Journey,* 2009

The Dalai Lama and Desmond Tutu. *The Book of Joy: Lasting Happiness in a Changing World,* 2016

Davis, Adelle. *Let's Eat Right to Get Fit,* 1954

Davis, Adelle. *Let's Get Well,* 1965

Dog Food Adviser. www.dogfoodadvisor.com

Ehrmann, Max. *Desiderata,* 1927

Eiseley, Loren. *The Immense Journey,* 1957

Environmental Health Perspectives. https://ehp.niehs.nih.gov/

Environmental Protection Agency. *Review of Enhanced*

Reporting, March 12, 2010

Environmental Working Group. https://www.ewg.org/

Feinstein, David and Donna Eden. *Energy Medicine: How to Use Your Body's Energies for Optimum Health and Vitality,* 1998

Family Caregiver Alliance. www.caregiver.org/about-fca

Faulds, Danna. *Go In and In: Poems from the Heart of Yoga,* 2002

Frankl, Victor. *Man's Search for Meaning,* 1946

Frost, Robert. *The Poetry of Robert Frost,* 1962

Hanh, Thich Nhat. *Anger: Wisdom for Cooling the Flames,* 2002

Hare, Brian and Woods, Vanessa. *The Genius of Dogs; How Dogs are Smarter than You Think,* 2013

Hirschfield, Jane. *The Lives of the Heart,* 1997

Houston, Pam, Jon Katz, Michael J. Rosen, et al. *Dog Is My Co-Pilot: Great Writers on the World's Oldest Friendship,* 2004

The Holy Bible, New International Version

International Lyme and Associated Diseases Society. www.ilads.org/

Jong, Erica. "A Woman's Best Friend," 2000

Kessler, David. *Finding Meaning: The Sixth Stage of Grief,* 2020

Kerasote, Ted. *Merle's Door: Lessons from a Freethinking Dog,* 2008

Kerasote, Ted. *Pukka's Promise,* 2014

Korngold, Efrem and Harriet Beinfield. *Between Heaven and Earth: A Guide to Chinese Medicine,* 1991

Kushner, Harold. *When Bad Things Happen to Good People,* 1981

Ladinsky, Daniel. *Love Poems from God: Twelve Sacred Voices from the East and West,* 2002

Life Science Product and Publishing. *Essential Oils Pocket Reference,* 2016

Lyme Action Network. www.lymeactionnetwork.org/

MacLaine, Shirley. *Out on a Limb,* 1983

Miller, James E. *The Rewarding Practice of Journal Writing: A Guide for Starting and Keeping Your Personal Journal*, 1998

National Center for Biotechnology Information. www.ncbi.nlm.nih.gov/

Nature's Farmacy. www.naturesfarmacy.com

Ober, Sinatra, and Zucker. *Earthing*, 2014

Peale, Norman Vincent. *The Power of Positive Thinking*, 1952

Putnam, Robert. *Bowling Alone*, 2000

Ruiz, don Miguel. *The Four Agreements: A Personal Guide to Freedom*, 1997

Scerba, Pamela, DVM. www.holisticpetcaretoday.com

Schinto, Jeanne (ed). *The Literary Dog: Great Contemporary Dog Stories*, 1994

Shinn, Florence Scovel. *The Wisdom of Florence Scovel Shinn*, 1989

Siegel, Bernie, MD. *Love, Medicine and Miracles*, 1984

Siegel, Bernie, MD. *Peace, Love and Healing*, 1989

University of Virginia. https://med.virginia.edu/perceptual-studies/our-research/

U.S. Preventative Services Task Force. www.uspreventiveservicestaskforce.org

Virtue, Dr. Doreen. *Angel Medicine: How to Heal the Body and Mind with the Help of the Angels*, 2004

Weil, Andrew, MD. *Sound Body, Sound Mind: Music for Healing*, 2005

Williamson, Marianne. *Illuminata: Return to Prayer*, 1995